WAGES OF REBELLION

ALSO BY CHRIS HEDGES

War Is a Force That Gives Us Meaning

What Every Person Should Know About War

Losing Moses on the Freeway

American Fascists

I Don't Believe in Atheists

Collateral Damage

Empire of Illusion

Death of the Liberal Class

The World As It Is

Days of Destruction, Days of Revolt
(with Joe Sacco)

WAGES OF REBELLION

CHRIS HEDGES

NATION
BOOKS
New York

Published by

Nation Books, A Member of the Perseus Books Group

116 East 16th Street, 8th Floor

New York, NY 10003

Nation Books is a co-publishing venture of the Nation Institute and the Perseus Books Group.

Books published by Nation Books are available at special discounts for bulk purchases in the United States by corporations, institutions, and other organizations. For more information, please contact the Special Markets Department at the Perseus Books Group, 2300 Chestnut Street, Suite 200, Philadelphia, PA 19103, or call (800) 810-4145, ext. 5000, or e-mail special.markets@perseusbooks.com.

Set in 11 point Minion Pro

Library of Congress Cataloging-in-Publication Data

Hedges, Chris.
    Wages of rebellion / Chris Hedges.
        pages   cm
    Includes bibliographical references and index.
    ISBN 978-1-56858-966-4 (hardback) — ISBN 978-1-56858-490-4
(e-book) 1. Revolutions—Social aspects. 2. Social movements.
3. Protest movements. I. Title.
HM876.H43 2015
303.48'4—dc23   2014044940

10 9 8 7 6 5 4 3 2 1

For Eunice,
y en cuanto a mí no olvides que si despierto y lloro
es porque en sueños sólo soy un niño perdido
que busca entre las hojas de la noche tus manos

Contents

The tolerance which is the life element, the token of a free society, will never be the gift of the Powers That Be; it can, under the prevailing conditions of tyranny by the majority, only be won in the sustained effort of radical minorities, willing to break this tyranny and to work for the emergence of a free and sovereign majority— minorities intolerant, militantly intolerant and disobedient to the rules of behavior which tolerate destruction and suppression.[1]

—HERBERT MARCUSE, "REPRESSIVE TOLERANCE"

The pious say that faith can do great things, and, as the gospel tells us, even move mountains. The reason is that faith breeds obstinacy. To have faith means simply to believe firmly—to deem almost a certainty—things that are not reasonable; or, if they are reasonable, to believe them more firmly than reason warrants. A man [or woman] of faith is stubborn in his [or her] beliefs; he [or she] goes his [or her] way, undaunted and resolute, disdaining hardship and danger, ready to suffer any extremity.

Now, since the affairs of the world are subject to chance and to a thousand and one different accidents, there are many ways in which the passage of time may bring unexpected help to those who preserve in their obstinacy. And since this obstinacy is the product of faith, it is then said that faith can do great things.[2]

—FRANCESCO GUICCIARDINI, *RICORDI*

The civilization and justice of bourgeois order comes out in its lurid light whenever the slaves and drudges of that order rise against their masters. Then this civilization and justice stand forth as undisguised savagery and lawless revenge . . . the infernal deeds of the soldiery reflect the innate spirit of that civilization of which they are the mercenary vindicators. . . . The bourgeoisie of the whole world, which looks complacently upon the wholesale massacre after the battle, is convulsed by horror at the desecration of brick and mortar.[3]

—KARL MARX, *THE CIVIL WAR IN FRANCE*

Introduction

We live in a revolutionary moment. The disastrous economic and political experiment that attempted to organize human behavior around the dictates of the global marketplace has failed. The promised prosperity that was to have raised the living standards of workers through trickle-down economics has been exposed as a lie. A tiny global oligarchy has amassed obscene wealth, while the engine of unfettered corporate capitalism plunders resources; exploits cheap, unorganized labor; and creates pliable, corrupt governments that abandon the common good to serve corporate profit. The relentless drive by the fossil fuel industry for profits is destroying the ecosystem, threatening the viability of the human species. And no mechanisms to institute genuine reform or halt the corporate assault are left within the structures of power, which have surrendered to corporate control. The citizen has become irrelevant. He or she can participate in heavily choreographed elections, but the demands of corporations and banks are paramount.

History has amply demonstrated that the seizure of power by a tiny cabal, whether a political party or a clique of oligarchs, leads to despotism. Governments that cater exclusively to a narrow interest group and redirect the machinery of state to furthering the interests of that interest group are no longer capable of responding rationally in times of crisis. Blindly serving their masters, they acquiesce to the looting of state treasuries to bail out corrupt financial houses and banks while ignoring chronic unemployment and underemployment, along with stagnant or declining wages, crippling debt peonage, a collapsing infrastructure, and the millions left destitute and often homeless by deceptive mortgages and foreclosures.

A bankrupt liberal class, holding up values it does nothing to defend, discredits itself as well as the purported liberal values of a civil democracy as it is swept aside, along with those values. In this moment, a political, economic, or natural disaster—in short a crisis—will ignite unrest, lead to instability, and see the state carry out draconian forms of repression to maintain "order." This is what lies ahead.

The historian Crane Brinton, in his 1965 book *The Anatomy of Revolution*, explores the preconditions for revolution in the English, French, American, and Russian Revolutions. He cites a discontent that affects nearly all social classes, including "economic grievances . . . not in the form of economic distress, but rather a feeling on the part of some of the chief enterprising groups that their opportunities for getting on in this world are unduly limited by political arrangements."[4] A sense of entrapment and despair combine with unfulfilled expectations to fuel the crisis. Brinton argues that a decaying power elite in a prerevolutionary society exploits not only the populace but also its own natural allies. Louis XIV, for example, frequently revoked his patents to new nobility and resold them.[5] Corporations, in a modern twist on the same exploitation of those most inclined to support them, defraud shareholders and investors, especially the small investors in the middle class who make up the bulwark of a capitalist democracy.

Brinton lists other preconditions for revolution, including a unified solidarity in opposition to a tiny, discredited power elite; a refusal by the press, scholars, and intellectuals to continue to defend the actions of the ruling class; an inability of government to respond to the most basic needs of citizens; and a steady loss of will within the power elite to rule. The denial of opportunities to the sons and daughters of the professional class and the middle class galvanizes resistance. A crippling isolation soon leaves the power elite with neither allies nor outside support. Finally, the state is convulsed by a crisis—usually triggered by economic instability and often accompanied by military defeat, as was the case in Czarist Russia, or a long and futile conflict, as is the case with our own wars in Afghanistan and Iraq. It is at the moment of crisis that revolution begins.

It is never the poor, however, who make revolutions, as understood by Karl Marx and Friedrich Engels, who disdained the revolutionary potential of the *Lumpenproletariat*. Marx and Engels correctly saw the

Lumpenproletariat as providing the primary fodder for the goons, militias, and thugs employed by a discredited regime to hold on to power through violence. "The 'dangerous class,' the social scum (*Lumpenproletariat*), that passively rotting mass thrown off by the lowest layers of old society, may, here and there, be swept into the movement by a proletarian revolution; its conditions of life, however, prepare it more for the part of a bribed tool of reactionary intrigue."[6]

This is a key factor in understanding the precursors for revolt. "The idea that the very oppressed and poor are important as initiating and maintaining revolutions is a bourgeois one," Brinton writes.[7] He adds another important caveat:

> No government has ever fallen before attackers until it has lost control over its armed forces or lost the ability to use them effectively—or, of course, lost such control of force because of interference by a more powerful foreign force, as in Hungary in 1849 or in 1956, and conversely that no revolutionists have ever succeeded until they have got a predominance of effective armed force on their side. This holds true from spears and arrows to machine guns and gas, from Hippias to Castro.[8]

While violence and terrorism are often part of revolutions, the fundamental tool of any successful revolt is the nonviolent conversion of the forces deployed to restore order to the side of the rebels. Most successful revolutions are, for this reason, fundamentally nonviolent. The Russian Revolution was victorious once the Cossacks refused to fire on the protesters in Petrograd in 1917 and joined the crowds. The clerics who overthrew the Shah of Iran in 1979 won once the Shah's military abandoned the collapsing regime. And the harsh Communist regimes in Eastern Europe were doomed in 1989 when the security forces no longer defended them. The superior force of despotic regimes is disarmed not through violence but through conversion.

James Davies, in his essay "Toward a Theory of Revolution," names the "intolerable gap between what people want and what they get" as the most important component of revolt. "The rapidly widening gap between expectations and gratifications portends revolution," writes

Davies. "The most common case for this widening gap of individual dis-satisfactions is economic or social dislocation that makes the affected individual generally tense, generally frustrated. That is, the greatest portion of people who join a revolution are preoccupied with tensions related to the failure to gratify the physical (economic) needs and the needs of stable interpersonal (social) relationships."[9]

However, like Marx, Engels, and Brinton, Davies adds that "socio-economically deprived poor people are unlikely to make a successful rebellion, a revolution, by themselves." It is rather a disenfranchised middle class and alienated members of the ruling class who orchestrate and lead a revolt. "Without the support of disaffected bourgeoisie, disaffected nobles, and disaffected intellectuals, the French Revolution might have been some kind of grand, episodic upheaval," he notes.

> But it would not likely have amounted to the successful assault on the political power structure that a revolution amounts to. The same can be said for the American Revolution. Those who signed the Declaration of Independence and/or became rulers of the new nation were gentle-man farmers like Washington and Jefferson rather than callous-handed yeomen, who became the rank and file of the Continental Army. The Russian Revolution, particularly in its 1905 phase, depended on the dis-affection not solely of factory workers and peasants but also of urban bourgeoisie and—almost incredibly it seemed at first glance—of sub-stantial numbers of the landed nobility.[10]

Brinton and Davies argue that expectations have usually been most frustrated—especially when coupled with economic depression and in-creased repression—immediately after periods when the standard of living rose and the political space opened. This is what took place in Russia, for example, in the latter half of the nineteenth century. Alex-ander II emancipated the serfs in 1861, began the process of industrial-ization, and created a state-administered legal system that attempted to wrest absolute authority from the noblemen and landowners, who had been imposing jail terms and punishment by fiat. The urban popula-tion nearly doubled between 1878 and 1897. Strikes, union organizing, workers' associations, and emergent political groups, along with a dissident press, gave hope for the future. Wages rose. The estimated annual net income at the end of the nineteenth century for a peasant family of five was 82 rubles. A factory worker could make 168 rubles.[11] The process of reform ended when Alexander II was assassinated on March 13, 1881.

Alexander III and his successor, Nicholas II, attempted to return the country to a rigid autocracy. Repression mounted, and the opening provided to a free press ended, especially in 1907 with the reinstatement of censorship and the banning of publications. Executions for offending the Czar mounted: there were 26 death sentences during the thirteen years of Alexander III's reign (1881–1894) and 4,449 between 1905 and 1910—just six years of the reign of his grandson Nicholas II.[12] "This fifty-six year period [from the freeing of the serfs in 1861 to the Russian Revolution in 1917] appears to constitute a single long phase in which popular gratification at the termination of one institution (serfdom) rather quickly was replaced with rising expectations which resulted from intensified industrialization and which were incompatible with the continuation of the inequitable and capricious power structure of Tsarist society," Davies notes.[13]

The expectations for political and economic improvement were further stymied when the country entered World War I. The poorly equipped Russian army suffered catastrophic defeats and massive loss of life. The economy broke down. By 1916, inflation had made food difficult to afford, and famine gripped parts of the country. But more than deprivation itself, Davies and Brinton highlight, it was the cycle of heightened expectations, economic improvement, and then frustrated hopes that led to revolt. "In reality the mere existence of privations is not enough to cause an insurrection; if it were, the masses would always be in revolt," Leon Trotsky noted.[14]

Today this key component of revolution—the gap between what people want, and indeed expect, and what they get—is being played out in the United States and many states in Europe during a new age of mounting scarcity, declining wages, joblessness, government-imposed "austerity" measures, and assaults on civil liberties. The rising living standards experienced by the American working class in the 1950s have been in precipitous decline since the 1970s. The real earnings of the median male have declined by 19 percent since 1970, and the median male with only a high school diploma saw his real earnings fall by 41 percent from 1970 to 2010.[15] Moreover, the memory of the postwar moment of prosperity and the belief that prosperity should still be possible—along with the revocation of protections under the Constitution that most Americans want restored—have left Americans increasingly alienated, frustrated, and angry. They have experienced the diminished expectations highlighted by Davies and Brinton. They have set those expectations against the bleakness of the present.

Politicians, a moribund labor movement, and the mass media—either cowed or in the service of corporate power—assure the population that the old prosperity is still attainable, but via a different route. Prosperity will no longer come from expanding the manufacturing base, which characterized the very real prosperity of working men and women immediately after World War II. The neoliberal version of the promise of rising living standards is based on the fallacy of economic deregulation and financialization. Let us be rich, the elites say, and you will share in the spoils. All you have to do is work hard, obey the rules, and believe in yourself. This myth is disseminated across the political spectrum. It is the essential message peddled by everyone from Oprah and the entertainment industry to the Christian Right and positive psychologists. But this promise, as the masses of underemployed and unemployed are discovering, is a fiction.[16]

In this discovery, this understanding that workers will never have what they expect, lies revolutionary fodder. Today's economic stagnation, accompanied by a steady stripping away of civil liberties and the creation of a monstrous security and surveillance system of internal control, has followed the kind of roller-coaster pattern of rising and then declining hopes that presages revolt, according to Brinton and Davis.

The revolutionary ideal, the vision of a better world, the belief that resistance is a moral act to protect the weak and the poor—in short, an ideology—fuses with the sense of loss and betrayal engendered by a system that can no longer meet expectations. The revolts and revolutions that have convulsed the Arab world and the unrest in Greece and Spain share these vital characteristics. The primacy of corporate profit in a globalized economy has become universal. So have its consequences.

Professor Rami Zurayk, who teaches agriculture and food sciences at the American University of Beirut, pointed out in *The Guardian* in 2011 "that when international grain prices spiked in 2007 and 2008 Egypt's bread prices rose by 37 percent." Fifty percent of the calories Egyptians consume, he wrote, come from outside the country. Moreover, Egypt, as the world's largest wheat importer, is hostage to world commodity prices, and he notes that only three corporations—Cargill, Archers Daniel Midland Company, and Bunge (all American)—control 90 percent of the global grain trade.[17] Zurayk argues that the rising price of food (especially bread)—which puts a family's ability to feed itself in jeopardy, as happened during the French and Russian Revolutions—was one of the major causes of the uprisings across the Arab world in 2010 and 2011. "Should the global markets be unable to provide a country's need, or if there are not enough funds available to finance purchases and to offer price support, then the food of the poor will become inaccessible to them," Zurayk writes, adding:

> Already, in Egypt and Yemen, more than 40 percent of the population live below the poverty line and suffer from some form of malnutrition. Most of the poor in these countries have no access to social safety nets. Images of bread became central to the Egyptian protests, from young boys selling *kaik*, a breakfast bread, to one protester's improvised helmet made from bread loaves taped to his head. Although the Arab revolutions were united under the slogan "the people want to bring down the regime" not "the people want more bread," food was a catalyst.[18]

The contraction of the Greek economy by 20 percent in the last five years resulted in an unemployment rate of more than 27 percent. An estimated 10 percent of Greek children arrive at school underfed, hungry, or malnourished. Dr. Athena Linos, a professor at the University of Athens Medical School who also heads a food assistance program at

Prolepsis, a nongovernmental public health group, told the *New York Times:* "When it comes to food insecurity, Greece has now fallen to the level of some African countries."[19]

The poor population in the United States—15 percent of the total population and a disturbing 21.8 percent for children under the age of eighteen—is expanding. The 46.5 million people living in poverty in 2012 was the largest number of poor counted during the fifty-four years in which the decennial census has calculated poverty rates. The weighted average poverty threshold for a household of four was an annual income of $23,492.[20] That is well below what many economists believe constitutes a realistic poverty rate.[21] And among those classified as poor, 20.4 million people lived in what was categorized as "deep" poverty, meaning that their incomes were 50 percent below the official poverty line. One-quarter of the nation's Hispanic population, 13.6 million people, and 27.2 percent of African Americans, 10.9 million people, lived in poverty.[22] There are 73.7 million children in the United States, and they represent 23.7 percent of the total population. Yet in 2012 they made up 34.6 percent of Americans living in poverty and 35 percent of those living in deep poverty.[23]

Climate change will only exacerbate these conditions. As pointed out by the United Nations Intergovernmental Panel on Climate Change (IPCC), climate change will cause a decline in crop production and food prices will soar.[24] Poverty and hunger have already begun to expand in the developing world and parts of the industrialized world.

The realization that our expectations for a better future have been obliterated, not only for ourselves but more importantly for our children, starts the chain reaction. There is a loss of faith in established systems of power. There is a weakening among the elites of the will to rule. Government becomes despised. Rage looks for outlets. The nation goes into crisis. Vladimir Lenin identified the components that come together to foster a successful revolt:

The fundamental law of revolution, which has been confirmed by all revolutions, and particularly by all three Russian revolutions in the twentieth century, is as follows: it is not enough for revolution that the exploited and oppressed masses should understand the impossibility of living in the old way and demand changes, what is required for revolution is that the exploiters should not be able to live and rule in the old way. Only when the *"lower classes" do not want* the old way, and when the "upper classes" *cannot carry on in the old way*—only then can revolution win.[25]

I have covered, as a foreign correspondent, revolts, insurgencies, and revolutions, including the guerrilla conflicts in the 1980s in Central America; the civil wars in Algeria, the Sudan, and Yemen; the two Palestinian uprisings (or intifadas); the revolutions in East Germany, Czechoslovakia, and Romania; and the war in the former Yugoslavia. I have seen that despotic regimes in the final stages collapse internally. Once the foot soldiers of the elite—the police, the courts, the civil servants, the press, the intellectual class, and finally the army—no longer have the will to defend the regime, the regime is finished. When these state organs are ordered to carry out acts of repression—such as clearing people from parks and arresting or even shooting demonstrators—and refuse their orders, the old regime crumbles. The veneer of power appears untouched before a revolution, but the internal rot, unseen by the outside world, steadily hollows out the edifice state. And when dying regimes collapse, they do so with dizzying speed.

When the aging East German dictator Erich Honecker, who had been in power for thirteen years, was unable to get paratroopers to fire on protesting crowds in Leipzig in the fall of 1989, the regime was finished. He lasted another week in power. The same refusal to employ violence doomed the Communist governments in Prague and Bucharest. In Romania the army general on whom the dictator Nicolae Ceaușescu had depended to crush protests was the general who condemned him to death in a hasty show trial on Christmas Day. Tunisia's Ben Ali and Egypt's Hosni Mubarak also lost power once they could no longer count on the security forces and the military to fire into crowds.

Historians and political philosophers have often described these episodic revolutionary moments in human history, which are not confined by national borders, as waves.[26] Walter Benjamin, in his essay about Goethe's novel *Elective Affinities,* makes the same point. The novel is about the decay of institutions—in this case marriage—and the forces that are unleashed when institutions, and most importantly the ideas and rituals that sustain them, lose their hold over the imagination. In these moments, Benjamin argues, the mythic and the ideas of the visionary cause people to abandon established mores and traditions to revolt.[27]

Benjamin noted that the role of the critic, like that of the rebel, is to steer the reader, or the population, toward the mysterious forces embodied in great art, or in revolutionary visions. Language restricts both art and the possibilities of re-creating human society. In these moments, it matters more what is felt, Benjamin understood, than what is said. Immanuel Kant made much the same distinction between transcendental and critical forces in human existence. Once the transcendental is liberated through the decay of institutions, it harnesses a mythic power, or vision, that can inspire people to tear down the decayed structures that confine them.[28] Revolt by the populace in one nation, inspired by these transcendental forces, inspires revolt in another nation. The important point that Benjamin and Kant make is that revolutions, whether in art or in society, are about emotion. These moments engender not simply new ideas but new feelings about established power and human possibilities.

———————

The past few years, particularly since 2011, have witnessed popular uprisings exploding in waves around the world. In the Arab world, protests overthrew in quick succession the governments in Tunisia and Egypt and convulsed Morocco, Yemen, and Bahrain. Massive street protests have rattled Turkey, Greece, Portugal, Spain, the Ukraine, Georgia, and the United States. Movements feed off of other movements. The uprisings of the Arab Spring and the Portuguese and Spanish Indignants in the Iberian Peninsula morphed into Occupy encampments in the United States.

Revolutionary movements, nourished by radical new ideas and the collapse of bankrupt ruling ideologies, have throughout history spread in waves like these across the globe. The American Revolution of 1776 was an inspiration to the French Revolution in 1789. The French Revolution inspired the Haitian Revolution in 1791—the only successful slave revolt in human history—as well as a series of revolts in Europe, from the Batavian Revolution in 1795 to the 1798 uprising in Ireland. The wave of revolt also swept over Latin America in the wars for independence from 1810 to 1826, led by revolutionaries such as José de San Martín and Simón Bolívar.

In 1848 there was another outbreak of revolutionary fever. It first spiked in the Sicilian capital of Palermo before raging throughout Italy and Europe. The uprisings in Paris in February 1848 ended the Orléans monarchy and led to the creation of the French Second Republic. Civil war broke out in Germany, Denmark—which saw the end to its absolute monarchy—Austria, and Hungary, which abolished serfdom. The 1848 revolt in Hungary led to the resignation of Klemens von Metternich, the Austrian prince and foreign minister, and forced Emperor Ferdinand to grant Hungary a constitution, an elected parliament, and the end of censorship. Polish rebels, although unsuccessful, rose up against their Prussian masters. Ireland also saw a failed uprising. Chartism, a working-class movement that from 1838 to 1858 organized millions of laborers to demand political reform and suffrage, arose as a powerful force in Britain and influenced Engels, although it was not a socialist or communist movement.[29]

Revolutionists who took part in uprisings in one part of the globe would often migrate to take part in uprisings in another. Francisco de Miranda, the Venezuelan radical who launched his country's wars of liberation from Spain, went to the United States to meet with revolutionaries such as Thomas Paine, and he participated in the French Revolution. Paine fomented revolt in the United States, England, and revolutionary France, where he was initially embraced as a hero. Giuseppe Garibaldi fought in Brazil and Uruguay before he returned to Italy in 1848 to play a central role in uprisings in Milan and Rome and a few years later in the Risorgimento.

The great European theorists of revolution, including Karl Marx and Friedrich Engels, who published *The Communist Manifesto* in 1848, participated in the revolutionary wave. With his radical views, Marx was denied an academic career despite his brilliance as a scholar. He began writing for the radical journal *Rheinische Zeitung* and soon became the journal's editor. The journal was shut down in 1843 by the Prussian authorities. Marx moved to Paris, the epicenter of nineteenth-century radicalism. France had spawned Henri de Saint-Simon and Charles Fourier, the fathers of modern socialism, who argued that the state and industry should be subjugated to the common good.

Between 1843 and 1850, against the backdrop of worldwide political and economic upheaval and his personal experiences with state persecution, Marx formulated his most important ideas on communism. He returned to Germany with Engels for the uprising of 1848 and started another radical newspaper—*Neue Rheinische Zeitung.* During the year he spent in Germany, Marx functioned as a revolutionist attempting to organize an insurrection in Germany modeled on the French Revolution. His paper was eventually banned, and he was expelled from Prussia. He fled to Paris, but was forced by the Cavaignac government to leave that city in 1849. Moving on to London, Marx found his famous refuge in the reading room of the British Museum.

The anarchist Mikhail Bakunin, who, like Marx, was in Germany during the revolution of 1848, was what the historian Adam Ulam calls "a visiting revolutionary." "There was no insurrection, actual or planned—Prague in 1848, Dresden in 1849, Poland in 1863, the numerous attempted revolts in France and Italy—in which he was not ready to fight, lend his assistance as a drafter of manifestoes, theorist of revolutionary dictatorship, and the like," Ulam writes. Bakunin, as Ulam points out, "never worked out a systematic philosophy of revolution or of socialism. His socialism was mostly of a visceral type: the revolt against any kind of oppression and injustice, rejection of any palliatives or halfway measures."[30]

But Bakunin, however inchoate his own ideas were about the new society, was at the same time remarkably prescient about Marxism. He warned that it would lead to a centralized and oppressive state. He foresaw what would happen to workers once their self-identified representatives in the revolutionary vanguard took power. "Those previous workers having just become rulers or representatives of the people will cease being workers; they will look at the workers from their heights, they will represent not the people but themselves. . . . He who doubts it does not know human nature."[31] Bakunin grew to hate Marx and Marxism. But he never offered much in the way of a concrete vision to replace the capitalist state he sought to destroy.

The Russian anarchist Alexander Herzen, although he did not embrace Bakunin's lusty calls for action, violence, and sometimes terrorism, also detested Marx. But Herzen, like Bakunin, offered little more than hazy notions of volunteerism and autonomous collectives and communes to replace the state. The anarchists proved more adept at understanding autocratic power and challenging it than at constructing a governing system to replace it.

The remarkable French revolutionary Louis Auguste Blanqui, like Bakunin, took part in a series of French revolts, including an attempted armed insurrection in France in May 1839, the 1848 uprising, and the Paris Commune—a socialist uprising that seized control of France's capital from March 18 until May 28 in 1871. Workers in cities such as Marseilles and Lyon attempted to organize similar communes before the Paris Commune was militarily crushed.

Blanqui is an important, if neglected, nineteenth-century theorist, for unlike nearly all of his contemporaries, he dismissed the naive belief, central to Marx, that human history is a linear progression toward equality and greater morality. He warned that this absurd positivism is the lie perpetrated by oppressors: "All atrocities of the victor, the long series of his attacks are coldly transformed into constant, inevitable evolution, like that of nature. . . . But the sequence of human things is not inevitable like that of the universe. It can be changed at any moment."[32] He also foresaw that scientific and technological advancement, rather than a harbinger of progress, could be "a terrible weapon in the hands of Capital against Work and Thought."[33] He even decried the despoiling of the natural world. "The axe fells, nobody replants. There is no concern for the future's ill health."[34] "Humanity," he wrote, "is never stationary. It advances or goes backwards. Its progressive march leads it to equality. Its regressive march goes back through every stage of privilege to human slavery, the final word of the right to property." Further, "I am not amongst those who claim that progress can be taken for granted, that humanity cannot go backwards."[35] His understanding that history can usher in long periods of repression as well as freedom and liberty is worth remembering.

It was Blanqui who first used the phrase "dictatorship of the proletariat."[36] Blanqui's call for a small, conspiratorial group to seize power in the name of the working class was a tactic that would be successfully employed by Lenin, who then set out to dismantle the autonomous soviets and workers' committees. Lenin, with a handful of subordinates, carried out what became, in essence, a right-wing counterrevolution that introduced a system of repressive, centralized state capitalism and state terror.

Marx never embraced Blanqui's or Lenin's call for a small group of disciplined revolutionaries to seize power. Marx hoped that a broad-based mass movement of industrial workers like the Chartists would organize to overthrow the capitalist order and usher in communism. The question of how to carry out a successful revolution, which occupied much of Lenin's thought, brings with it the question of whether the ruthless tactics and a small, disciplined class of professional revolutionaries that make a revolution possible make an open society impossible. Any revolution, once begun, carries the potential for fanaticism. Revolutionaries in power can erect, in the name of a glorious utopian ideal, a system of state terror, as demonstrated by the Leninists and Stalinists, the ideological heirs of the French Jacobins.

The next great revolutionary wave swept Russia in 1905 with its humiliating defeat by Japan. The defeat triggered the abortive uprising against the Czar—the dress rehearsal for the 1917 Russian Revolution—and ignited another round of revolutionary upheavals around the world. The Argentine Revolution of 1905 was followed by the Persian Constitutional Revolution, which took place between 1905 and 1907 and overthrew the monarchy, establishing a free press, competing political parties, and a parliament. The Young Turk Revolution in 1908 reversed the 1878 suspension of the Ottoman parliament, the General Assembly, by Sultan Abdul Hamid II and inaugurated the Second Constitutional Era. These uprisings were followed in 1910 by revolutions in

Portugal and Mexico and by the 1911 Chinese Xinhai Revolution, which overthrew the Qing Dynasty and established the Republic of China. The February Russian Revolution in 1917 forced the Czar to abdicate and, after an armed putsch led by Lenin in October, brought the Bolsheviks to power.

The Russian Revolution inspired socialist uprisings in Germany, Italy, and Hungary—indeed, in most of Europe—and fueled the imagination of radical movements in the United States as well as the Indian independence movement led by Mohandas Karamchand Gandhi. It was the Russian Revolution's catalyzing of the radical wing of the trade union movement that led to the formation of the first communist party in the United States and triggered the "Red Scare" hysteria, which allowed the state to carry out a preemptive war against radical and populist movements. Unions such as the Industrial Workers of the World, or the "Wobblies," were destroyed. Publications such as *The Masses* and *Appeal to Reason* were banned. The socialist leader Eugene V. Debs was imprisoned in 1918. Emma Goldman, along with more than 200 other "radical aliens," was stripped of her passport and deported in 1919 to Russia.[37] Nicola Sacco and Bartolomeo Vanzetti were executed in 1927. By the 1920s, a once powerful and radical labor movement in the United States had been broken. Although it was revived with the breakdown of capitalism in the 1930s, it would be crushed again by World War II and the anticommunist hysteria that followed.

The establishment of what would become the Federal Bureau of Investigation in 1908—led from 1924 until 1972 by J. Edgar Hoover—was a direct response to the revolutionary wave that gripped the American working class. FBI agents, often little more than state-employed goons and thugs, ruthlessly hunted down those on the left. The FBI spied on and infiltrated labor unions, political parties, radical groups—especially those led by African Americans—antiwar groups, and later the civil rights movement in order to discredit anyone, including politicians such as Henry Wallace, who questioned the power of the state and big business. Agents burglarized homes and offices. They illegally opened mail and planted unlawful wiretaps, created blacklists, and demanded loyalty oaths. They destroyed careers and sometimes lives.

By the time they were done, America's progressive and radical movements, which had given the country the middle class and opened up our political system, did not exist. It was upon the corpses of these radical movements, which had fought for the working class, that the corporate state was erected in the late twentieth century.

The great wave of revolution that took place in 1989 with the collapse of the Soviet Union was the last revolutionary wave before the Arab uprisings in 2010. Fourteen Soviet republics in 1989 broke away to form independent states. Albania, Czechoslovakia, Romania, Poland, Bulgaria, East Germany, Yugoslavia, Cambodia, Ethiopia, Somalia, the Congo-Brazzaville, Angola, Mozambique, Benin, Mongolia, and South Yemen all replaced their Communist governments. As a foreign correspondent, I witnessed the swift disintegration of the Communist regimes in East Germany, Czechoslovakia, and Romania.

In all of these countries, a significant portion of the population had abandoned their faith in the ideological constructs of power, just as previous generations had abandoned the belief in the divine right of kings. These populations turned against a corrupt ruling elite. They lost hope for a better future unless those in power were replaced. And they seized in a revolutionary moment upon an ideal—one that was often more emotional than intellectual—that allowed them to defy established power. This revolutionary sentiment, as much a mood as an idea, is again on the march.

————

In a 2011 *New York Times* article titled "As Scorn for Vote Grows, Protests Surge Around the Globe," Nicholas Kulish made this point:

Their complaints range from corruption to lack of affordable housing and joblessness, common grievances the world over. But from South Asia to the heartland of Europe and now even to Wall Street, these protesters share something else: wariness, even contempt, toward traditional politicians and the democratic political process they preside over.

They are taking to the streets, in part, because they have little faith in the ballot box.[38]

Whether an uprising will come in time to save us from the effects of climate change—which some experts say has already passed a point of no return—or whether it will be crushed by internal systems of security is unknown. It is worth remembering Blanqui's warnings that human history can be a march to totalitarianism as well as to liberty. Since the uprisings in Tahrir Square in 2011, the Egyptian military has instituted a brutal counterrevolution. The Occupy encampments in the United States were cleared by force in cities across the country. The pervasive security and surveillance state, which makes us the most watched, spied and eavesdropped upon, monitored, photographed, and controlled population in human history, is being employed against all who rebel.

In three previous books, *Empire of Illusion: The End of Literacy and the Triumph of Spectacle*, *Death of the Liberal Class*, and *Days of Destruction, Days of Revolt*, I examined a cultural, political, and economic system in terminal decline. I chronicled the rise of totalitarian corporate power, or what the political philosopher Sheldon Wolin in *Democracy Incorporated* calls "inverted totalitarianism." Inverted totalitarianism, which does not find its expression through a demagogue or charismatic leader, represents "the *political* coming of age of corporate power and the *political* demobilization of the citizenry," he writes.[39] It is a dispersed, faceless power—"the rule of Nobody," as Hannah Arendt wrote—that is expressed in the blank, terrifying anonymity of the corporate state.[40]

Unlike classical totalitarian movements, the corporate forces behind inverted totalitarianism do not boast of replacing decaying structures with a new, revolutionary structure. They purport to honor electoral politics, freedom of speech, the right to assembly, and the Constitution. But they so corrupt and manipulate the levers of power internally that democracy is extinguished. The Constitution remains in place but has been so radically reinterpreted by the courts and by the executive and legislative branches of government, all serving corporate power, as to be essentially nullified. Inverted totalitarianism, Wolin writes, is not "expressly conceptualized as an ideology or objectified in public policy. Typically it is furthered by power-holders and citizens who often seem unaware of the deeper consequences of their actions or inactions."[41] But inverted totalitarianism is as dangerous as classical forms of totalitarianism. Corporate totalitarianism, for me, is interchangeable with inverted totalitarianism, as Wolin uses that term throughout his book.

I argued in my previous three books that change will only come from mass movements and large-scale acts of civil disobedience. *Wages of Rebellion* examines another aspect of revolt. Exploring the forces and personalities that foster rebellion, it looks at the personal cost of rebellion—what it takes emotionally, psychologically, and physically to defy absolute power.

Rebels share much in common with religious mystics. They hold fast to a vision that often they alone can see. They view rebellion as a moral imperative, even as they concede that the hope of success is slim and at times impossible. Rebels, a number of whom I interviewed for this book, are men and women endowed with a peculiar obstinacy. Willing to accept deprivation and self-sacrifice, they are not overly concerned with defeat. They endure through a fierce independence and courage. Many, maybe most, have difficult and eccentric personalities. The best of them are driven by a profound empathy, even love, for the vulnerable, the persecuted, and the weak.

Revolutions take time. They are often begun by one generation and completed by the next. "Those who give the first check to a state are the first overwhelmed in its ruin," Michel de Montaigne wrote in 1580. "The fruits of public commotion are seldom enjoyed by him who was the first mover; he only beats the water for another's net."[42] Revolutions can be crushed by force—as amply demonstrated by history—or hijacked by individuals, such as Lenin, Trotsky, and later Joseph Stalin, or movements that betray the populace.

Revolutions can even be *faux* revolutions when, through the careful manipulation of counterrevolutionary forces, they demand not reform but the restoration of retrograde power elites. The Central Intelligence Agency has long been a master of this technique. It organized street demonstrations and protests in Iran in 1953 to overthrow Prime Minister Mohammad Mosaddegh and his cabinet. It funded and stoked protests again in 1973 in Chile to prompt the Chilean military to overthrow President Salvador Allende. Seumas Milne raises this point in an article about the 2014 protests in Venezuela featuring the subhead: "Street action is now regularly used with western backing to target elected governments in the interests of elites." Milne writes: "The upsurge in global protest in the past couple of years has driven home the lesson that mass demonstrations can have entirely different social and political meanings. Just because they wear bandannas and build barricades—and have genuine grievances—doesn't automatically mean protestors are fighting for democracy or social justice."[43]

The closer one gets to the street during a revolution the messier it becomes. Movements within the revolutionary body frequently compete for power, fight over arcane bits of doctrine, dispute tactics, form counterproductive schisms, misread power, and engage in self-defeating power struggles. The state uses its resources to infiltrate, monitor, vilify, and arrest or assassinate the movement leaders—and all uprisings, even supposedly leaderless ones, have leaders.

When they are authentic, these movements express a fundamental truth about societies in decay that even those who cannot articulate it are often able to feel. This is the secret of their power. They offer new possibilities, a new language and vocabulary, to those who are being abused by failed systems of governance. Once this truth is unleashed, once it can be expressed, it is very hard to silence.

The Zapatista leader Subcomandante Insurgente Marcos, in an interview with Gabriel García Márquez in *The Nation* magazine, made this point. He pointed out that revolutions entail a new way of communicating. "In my family, words had a very special value," Marcos told the Colombian novelist.

The way we went out into the world was through language. We didn't learn to read in school but by reading newspapers. My mother and father made us read books that rapidly permitted us to approach new things. Some way or another, we acquired a consciousness of language not as a way of communicating with each other but as a way of building something. As if it were more of a pleasure than a duty or assignment. When the age of catacombs arrives, the word is not highly valued for the intellectual bourgeoisie. It is relegated to a secondary level. It's when we are in the indigenous communities that language is like a catapult. You realize that words fail to express certain things, and this obliges you to work on your language skills, to go over and over words to arm and disarm them.[44]

There is nothing rational about rebellion. To rebel against insurmountable odds is an act of faith, without which the rebel is doomed. This faith is intrinsic to the rebel the way caution and prudence are intrinsic to those who seek to fit into existing power structures. The rebel, possessed by inner demons and angels, is driven by a vision. I do not know if the new revolutionary wave and the rebels produced by it will succeed. But I do know that without these rebels, we are doomed.

I / Doomed Voyages

So it came about that multitudes of people acted out with fierce energy a shared phantasy which though delusional yet brought them such intense emotional relief that they could live only through it and were perfectly willing to die for it. It is a phenomenon which was to recur many times between the eleventh century and the sixteenth century, now in one area, now in another, and which, despite the obvious differences in cultural context and in scale, is not irrelevant of the growth of totalitarian movements, with their messianic leaders, their millennial mirages and their demon-scapegoats, in the present century.[1]

—NORMAN COHN, *THE PURSUIT OF THE MILLENNIUM*

Seventy-six-year-old Avgi Tzenis stood in the hall of her small brick row house on Bragg Street in Sheepshead Bay, Brooklyn. Gray-haired and stocky, she was dressed in a bathrobe and open-toed sandals. The hall was dark and cold. It had been dark and cold since Hurricane Sandy slammed into the East Coast a month earlier. Three feet of water and raw sewage had flooded and wrecked her home.

"We never had this problem before," she said. "We never had water from the sea come down like this."

For the poor of the Eastern Seaboard, Hurricane Sandy in October 2012 was the Katrina of the North. It once again exposed the nation's fragile, dilapidated, and shoddy infrastructure, one that crumbles under minimal stress. The storm highlighted the inability of utility companies as well as state and federal agencies to cope with the looming environmental disasters that the climate crisis will cause to grow in intensity and frequency. But most important, Sandy illustrated the depraved mentality of an oligarchic and corporate elite that, as conditions worsen, retreats into self-contained gated communities, guts basic services, and abandons the wider population.

Sheepshead Bay, along with Coney Island, the Rockaways, parts of Staten Island, and long stretches of the New Jersey coast, were obliterated by the 2012 hurricane. In the aftermath, stores a block away, their merchandise destroyed by the water, sat boarded up and closed. Rows of derelict cars, with the tires and license plates removed and the windows smashed, hugged the sidewalks, looking like the skeletal remains of large metal fish. Food distribution centers, most of them set up by volunteers from Occupy Sandy Relief, hastily closed before dark because of looters and thieves. And storm victims who remained in their damaged homes, often without heat, electricity, or running water, told me they clutched knives at night to protect themselves from the gangs that prowled through the wreckage.

Increasingly freakish weather patterns ensure that storms like Sandy—which resulted in some $42 billion in property and infrastructure damage, as well as 147 direct deaths—will become routine.[2] Sandy was the second-costliest hurricane to hit the United States since 1900.[3] Only Hurricane Katrina in 2005, which resulted in $108 billion in damage, was more severe.[4] Many of the 305,000 houses in New York destroyed by Sandy have never been rebuilt.[5] New York City estimated that it would have to spend $800 million just to repair its roads.[6] And that is only the start. Hurricanes will descend on the Eastern Seaboard and other coastal areas with even greater destructive fury. A couple of more disasters like this one and sections of the Eastern Seaboard will become uninhabitable.

This is the new America. It is an America where economic and environmental catastrophes will converge to trigger systems breakdown and collapse. It is an America that, as things unravel, will increasingly sacrifice the weak, the poor, and the destitute.

The emotional cost of the storm for the victims was often as devastating as the physical cost. Tzenis, who was born in Cyprus and immigrated to the United States with her husband in 1956, listed for me her mounting bills. Since the storm, the septuagenarian had paid a plumber $2,000, but that did not cover all the plumbing work that needed to be done. A contractor gave her an estimate of $40,000 to $50,000 for repairs, which included ripping out the walls and floors. Tzenis had received a $5,000 check from an insurance company, Allstate, and a $1,000 check from FEMA. But $6,000 would not begin to cover the cost of repairing her house.

"The insurance company told me I didn't have the water insurance," she said. "The contractor said he has to break all the walls and floors to get the mold out. I don't know how I am going to pay for this."

As she spoke, Josh Ehrenberg, twenty-one, an aspiring filmmaker, and Dave Woolner, a thirty-one-year-old electrician with Local 52, both volunteers with Occupy Sandy, hauled waterlogged and ruined items out of her garage. They put them in green plastic garbage bags.

"My husband had dementia," she told me softly. "I took care of him for six years with these two hands. For a few months the insurance gave me help. Certain medications they pay after six years. They told me once he couldn't swallow no more there was nothing we could do. . . . He died at home last year."

She began to sob.

She muttered, "Oye, oye, oye."

"I was going to hang myself in the closet," she said in a hoarse whisper, gesturing to the hall closet behind me. "I can't take life anymore. My husband. Now this. I don't sleep good. I jump up every hour watching the clock. I've been through a lot in my life. Every little thing scares me. I'm on different pills. I've come to the age where I ask why doesn't God take me. I pray a lot. I don't want to give my soul to the devil because they would not put me in a church to bury me. But you get to an age where you are only able to take so much."

She fell silent. She told me about the bombing of Cyprus during World War II. She said that as a girl she watched a British military airport go up in flames after German and Italian bombs hit it. She talked about the 1950s struggle for Cypriot independence that took place between the British and the underground National Organization of Cypriot Fighters, Ethniki Organosis Kyprion Agoniston, known as EOKA.

She said she wished there was another strong populist leader such as the Cypriot Archbishop Makarios III, who openly defied British authorities in the island's campaign for independence.

"People were hung by the British soldiers," she said. "Women were raped. People had their fingernails pulled out. They were tortured and beaten. My cousin was beaten so badly in jail he was bleeding from his bottom."

The horrors of the past had merged with the horrors of the present.

"They say [hurricanes like] this will happen again because the snow is melting off all the mountains," she said. "It never flooded here before. No matter how hard it rained, not a drop came through the door. But now it has changed. If it happens again, I don't want to be around."

I left her and walked down the street, where I found Rene Merida, twenty-seven, standing on the corner. His house on Emmons Avenue, like all the houses in the neighborhood, did not have electricity, running water, or heat. He and his pregnant wife and two children, ages seven and four, huddled inside the ruined home at night. They fled periodically to live for a few days with relatives. Merida, who had recently lost his job as an ironworker, managed to reach his landlord once on the phone. That had been three weeks earlier. It was the only time the landlord, despite Merida's persistent calls, answered.

"He told me it [the repair] will get done when it gets done," Merida said. "The temperature inside my house is fifteen degrees. I got a thermometer to check."

The state provided little in the immediate aftermath of the hurricane to those affected by the storm. Volunteers hastily collected food in church basements and drove it out to the devastated communities. I made my way to the 123-year-old St. Jacobi Evangelical Lutheran Church; founded by German immigrants, it served as one of the Brooklyn distribution centers. Lauren Ferebee, originally from Dallas, with short auburn hair and black frame glasses, sat behind a table in the chilly basement of the church. On large pieces of cardboard hanging from the ceiling were the words OCCUPY SANDY RELIEF. The basement was filled with stacks of donated supplies, including pet food, diapers, infant formula, canned goods, cereal, and pasta. The church was converted two days after the storm into a food bank and distribution center. Hundreds of people were converging daily on the church to work in the relief effort, and volunteers with cars or vans were delivering supplies to parts of New York and in New Jersey.

Ferebee, a playwright, and hundreds of other volunteers had instantly resurrected the Occupy movement when the tragedy hit to build structures of support and community. As we descend into a world where we can depend less and less on those who hold power, movements like Occupy will become vital. These movements might not be called Occupy, and they might not look like Occupy. But whatever the names and forms of the self-help we create, we will have to find ways to fend for ourselves. And we will fend for ourselves only by building communitarian organizations.

"We have a kitchen about fifty blocks from here where we cook and deliver hot food," Ferebee said. "We take food along with supplies out to distribution hubs. There is a distribution hub about every thirty or forty blocks. When I first went out, I was giving water to people who had not had water for six days."

She sat in front of a pile of paper sheets headed "Occupy Sandy Dispatch." Various sites were listed on the sheets, including Canarsie, Coney Island, Red Hook, the Rockaways, Sheepshead Bay, Staten Island, and New Jersey. As we spoke, Roman Torres, forty-five, came up to the table. We began to speak in Spanish. He told me he sang on weekends in a band that played Mexican folk music. He had pulled his van up in front of the church, and he told Ferebee he was ready to make deliveries. Torres had been coming two days a week to transport supplies.

"Can you go anywhere?" Ferebee asked Torres.

"Yes," he answered.

"Can you do a couple of drop-offs at the Rockaways?" she inquired.

"Yes, if someone comes with me," he said.

Torres fixed himself a cup of coffee in the church kitchen while volunteers carried boxes from the basement outside into the rain. They loaded the boxes into the back of his van.

"We can't ever get enough electric heaters, cleaning supplies, tools, and baby supplies," Ferebee lamented.

I walked up the stairs to the communications and dispatch room. I ran into Juan Carlos Ruiz, a former Roman Catholic priest who was born in Mexico. He took me to his small apartment, and we had a coffee at a small wooden table. Ruiz was the church's community organizer. It was his decision once the storm hit to open the doors of the church as a relief center. He did not know what to expect.

"It was Tuesday night," he said. "We got three bags of groceries and two jars of water. It was the next morning that volunteers began to appear. By the first weekend, we had over 1,300. It was organized chaos. There was all this creative energy and youth. There was an instant infrastructure and solidarity. It is mutual aid that is the most important response to the disasters we are living through. This is how we will retain our humanity. Some members of the church asked me why these [volunteers] did not come to the church service. I told them the work they were doing was church. The commitment I saw was like a conversion experience. It was transformative. It restores your faith in humanity."

———

The consequences of worsening climate change, along with stagnant and declining economies, will trigger mass migration, widespread famine, the spread of deadly infectious diseases, and levels of human mortality that will dwarf those of the Black Death, which between the fourteenth and seventeenth centuries ravaged Asia and Europe. In the fourteenth century alone, the Black Death is estimated to have taken 200 million lives. Scientists now fear that changing climate patterns could lead to its reemergence. Black rats, the bacterium's hosts, have already reappeared in Great Britain.[7]

Rising sea levels and soaring temperatures will make parts of the planet uninhabitable. More than 100 million people will die and global economic growth will be cut by 3.2 percent of gross domestic product (GDP) by 2030 if we continue to refuse to respond to climate change, estimates a report commissioned by the Climate Vulnerable Forum, a partnership of twenty developing countries threatened by climate change. The thawing of the ice sheets in Greenland and Antarctica will see the steady rising of sea levels by an estimated 2.3 meters (7 feet, 6 inches) in the next 2,000 years, assuming temperatures stay at current levels. The rising sea levels will create chaos across the globe as coastal cities and island states are flooded.[8]

As poorer societies around the globe unravel—many of them no longer able to impose the order of organized states—and as our own depressed communities are wrecked, shoddily patched back together, and then wrecked again, the same inchoate hatreds and bloodlusts for vengeance and retribution that I witnessed in disintegrating states such as the former Yugoslavia will be unleashed. Crisis cults, those bizarre messianic movements defined by a belief in magic and mystical religious fervor, will arise, as they did in medieval and Reformation Europe and among the Sioux at the end of the Indian wars. The armed thugs and gangs of warlords— which were common in the war in Bosnia—will storm through blighted landscapes looting, pillaging, and killing. This is already a reality to those affected by the severe droughts in Africa. Recent migrants, religious and ethnic minority groups, undocumented workers, foreign nationals, and homosexuals, indeed all who do not conform to the idealized image of the nation, buttressed by a mythical narrative about a lost golden age, will become the enemy and, for many, the cause of our distress.

Hunger and constant drought, especially in the poorer parts of the globe, will force populations to carry out armed raids and internecine wars to survive and lead many others to flee for more temperate zones. An estimated 200 million climate refugees, most from the equatorial regions of the globe, will descend by the middle of this century on Europe and other industrialized countries, according to figures cited in a study from Columbia University's Center for International Earth Science Information Network.[9] The industrialized states, anxious to preserve dwindling resources and avoid being overrun by destitute hordes, will become ringed fortresses. Democratic rights and constitutional protections will most likely be obliterated. This may be the best we can hope for. The worst will be the complete collapse of our ecosystem and the extinction of the human species. Neither scenario is pleasant.

No act of rebellion can be effective, much less moral, unless it first takes into account reality, no matter how bleak that reality. As our lives become increasingly fragile, we will have to make hard decisions about how to ensure our own survival and yet remain moral beings. We will be called upon to fight battles, some of which we will have no hope of winning, if only to keep alive the possibility of compassion and justice. We will depend on others to survive. This is not the world most of us desire, but it is the world that will probably exist. The greatest existential crisis we face is to at once accept what lies before us—for the effects of climate change and financial instability are now inevitable—and yet find the resilience to fight back.

Civilizations have followed a familiar pattern of disintegration from Sumer to Easter Island. The difference this time is that there will be no new lands to conquer, no new people to subjugate, and no new resources to plunder. When the unraveling begins, it will be global. At first, parts of the globe will be safer and more amenable to life. But any sanctuary will be temporary.

One of the most prescient portraits of our ultimate fate as a species is found in Herman Melville's novel about a doomed whaling voyage, *Moby-Dick*. Melville paints our murderous obsessions, our hubris, our violent impulses, moral weakness, and inevitable self-destruction in his chronicle of the quest by a demented captain, Ahab, for the white whale. Melville, as William Shakespeare was for Elizabethan England and Fyodor Dostoyevsky for Czarist Russia, is America's foremost oracle.

Melville's radical book was poorly received when it appeared in 1851, and two years after publication, the unsold copies were lost in a fire in the publisher's warehouse. Although more copies were printed, the novel never did sell out its first edition of 3,000 copies in Melville's lifetime. Melville, unable to survive as a writer, took a job working with the US Custom Service in Manhattan.[10]

It would be some seventy years before the author and critic Carl Van Doren resurrected Melville, praising the originality and importance of *Moby-Dick* in his 1921 book *The American Novel*.[11] D. H. Lawrence in *Studies in Classic American Literature* concurred with Van Doren.[12]

E. M. Forster called *Moby-Dick* a "prophetic song," and the critic Lewis Mumford helped enshrine the book in the Western canon.[13] William Faulkner, who had a framed print of Rockwell Kent's *Captain Ahab* in his living room, said *Moby-Dick* was the one book he wished he had written.[14] Edward Said drew parallels between Ahab's quest and the folly of empire.[15] C.L.R. James wrote a brilliant study of empire, class, commercialism, and *Moby-Dick,* entitled *Mariners, Renegades, and Castaways: The Story of Herman Melville and the World We Live In.*[16] Contemporary social critics, such as Greg Grandin in *The Empire of Necessity* and Morris Berman in *Why America Failed,* have also turned to Melville to buttress their bleak vision of the voyage we have undertaken as a species.[17] In his book *Why Read* Moby-Dick? Nathaniel Philbrick writes, "Contained in the pages of *Moby-Dick* is nothing less than the genetic code of America."[18]

In the book, Melville gives shape to the United States in the form of the whaling ship the *Pequod,* named after the Indian tribe that was nearly exterminated in 1638 by the Puritans and their Native American allies. The ship's thirty-man crew—there were thirty states in the Union when Melville wrote the novel—is a mixture of races and creeds. The object of the hunt is a massive white whale, Moby-Dick, which in a previous encounter dismembered one of Ahab's legs.

Moby-Dick is narrated in 1850 by Ishmael, a footloose sailor who signs on for a voyage on the *Pequod* with his new friend Queequeg, a tattooed harpooner from an island in the South Pacific. Queequeg, a self-professed cannibal who consults a small idol named Yojo, exhibits throughout the book a generosity and courage that Ishmael admires. The *Pequod* leaves Nantucket on a blustery, gray Christmas Day. Ahab, who remains hidden in his cabin until after the *Pequod* embarks, finally makes his appearance on deck after several days at sea, with his false ivory leg, carved from a sperm whale's jaw. He incites the crew to hunt down and kill the enormous white whale.

When whales are first sighted near the southern tip of Africa, Ahab's private and secret whaleboat crew, led by the mysterious Fedallah, suddenly appears from below the hold to take part in the hunt. As the *Pequod* rounds Africa and enters the Indian Ocean, the crew kill and butcher the whales, then boil down the oil and blubber in a bloody process that Melville describes in detail. Meanwhile, Ahab remains obsessed with finding Moby-Dick and questions passing ships about the white whale. When the *Pequod* encounters the *Jeroboam,* a crazed prophet who calls himself Gabriel warns of destruction to all who hunt Moby-Dick.

Fedallah, who Ahab believes has the power of prophecy, predicts that Ahab will see two hearses before he dies. Mortal hands, Fedallah says, will not have made the first hearse. The second hearse will be made only from American wood. Fedallah predicts that Ahab will be killed by hemp, which Ahab interprets to mean he will die on land on the gallows.

As the ship approaches the equator Moby-Dick is sighted, and Ahab launches his whaleboat in pursuit. Moby-Dick smashes the boat. When the hunt resumes the next day, the whale is harpooned. The wounded whale again attacks Ahab's whaleboat, and Fedallah is pulled into the sea and drowned. On the third day of the hunt, the crew sees Fedallah's corpse, tangled in the harpoon line, lashed to the whale's back. The white whale then rams the *Pequod,* and the ship sinks. The doomed ship and the white whale become the hearses—one made of American wood and the other not by mortal hands—foretold by Fedallah. The hemp harpoon line attached to Moby-Dick whips out of the boat and garrotes Ahab. The other whaleboats, along with the remaining ship's crew, are sucked into the swirling vortex created by the shattered *Pequod.* Ishmael alone survives.

Ahab's grievances in the novel are real. But his self-destructive fury ensures the *Pequod*'s fate. And those on the ship, on some level, know they are doomed—just as many of us know that a consumer culture based on corporate profit, limitless exploitation of the earth, and the continued extraction of fossil fuels is doomed.

We too see the danger signs. The ecosystem is visibly disintegrating. Scientists from the International Programme on the State of the Ocean (IPSO) issued a report in 2013 warning that the oceans are changing even faster than anticipated and increasingly becoming inhospitable to life. The oceans have absorbed much of the excess carbon dioxide and heat from the atmosphere, and this absorption is rapidly warming and acidifying ocean waters. This process is compounded, the report notes, by increased levels of deoxygenation from nutrient run-offs due to farming and climate change. The IPSO scientists call these effects—acidification, warming, and deoxygenation—a "deadly trio" that is causing changes in the seas unprecedented in the planet's history. The scientists write that each of the earth's previous five known mass extinctions was preceded by at least one part of the "deadly trio."[19] The sixth mass extinction of species has already begun, the first in some 66 million years.[20]

Speculators, meanwhile, have seized control of the global economy and the levers of political power. They have weakened and emasculated governments to serve their lust for profit. They have turned the press into courtiers, corrupted the courts, and hollowed out public institutions, including universities. They peddle spurious ideologies—neoliberal economics and globalization—to justify their rapacious looting and greed. They create grotesque financial mechanisms, from usurious interest rates on loans to legalized accounting fraud, to plunge citizens into crippling forms of debt peonage. And they have been stealing staggering sums of public funds, such as the $65 billion of mortgage-backed securities and bonds, many of them toxic, that have been unloaded each month on the Federal Reserve in return for cash.[21] They feed like parasites off of the state and the resources of the planet.

Speculators at megabanks and investment firms such as Goldman Sachs are not, in a strict sense, capitalists. They do not make money from the means of production. Rather, they ignore or rewrite the law—ostensibly put in place to protect the weak from the powerful—to steal from everyone, including their own shareholders. They produce nothing. They make nothing. They only manipulate money. They are no different from the detested speculators who were hanged in the seventeenth century, when speculation was a capital offense.

The obscenity of their wealth is matched by their utter lack of concern for the growing numbers of the destitute. In early 2014, the world's 200 richest people made $13.9 billion, in one day, according to Bloomberg's billionaires index.[22] This hoarding of money by the elites, according to the ruling economic model, is supposed to make us all better off, but in fact the opposite happens when wealth is concentrated in the hands of a few individuals and corporations, as economist Thomas Piketty documents in his book *Capital in the Twenty-First Century*.[23] The rest of us have little or no influence over how we are governed, and our wages stagnate or decline. Underemployment and unemployment become chronic. Social services, from welfare to Social Security, are slashed in the name of austerity. Government, in the hands of speculators, is a protection racket for corporations and a small group of oligarchs. And the longer we play by their rules the more impoverished and oppressed we become.

Yet, like Ahab and his crew, we rationalize our collective madness. All calls for revolt, for halting the march toward economic, political, and environmental catastrophe, are ignored or ridiculed. Even with the flashing red lights before us, even with huge swaths of the country living in Depression-like conditions, we bow slavishly before the enticing illusion provided to us by our masters of limitless power, wealth, and technological prowess. The system, although it is killing us, is our religion.

Clive Hamilton, in his *Requiem for a Species: Why We Resist the Truth About Climate Change,* describes the dark relief that comes from accepting that "catastrophic climate change is now virtually certain."[24] This obliteration of our "false hopes" requires not only intellectual knowledge but emotional knowledge. Intellectual knowledge is more easily attained. Emotional knowledge, which requires us to accept that those we love, including our children, are almost certainly doomed to insecurity, misery, and suffering within a few decades, if not a few years, is much harder to acquire. To emotionally accept the impending disaster, to attain the visceral understanding that the power elite will not respond rationally to the devastation of the ecosystem, is as difficult to accept as our own mortality.

The crisis before us is the culmination of a 500-year global rampage of conquering, plundering, exploiting, and polluting the earth—as well as killing by Europeans and Euro-Americans of the indigenous communities that stood in their way. The technical and scientific forces that created unparalleled luxury and unrivaled military and economic power for a small, global elite are the forces that now doom us. Ceaseless economic expansion and exploitation has become a death sentence. But even as our economic and environmental systems unravel—thirteen of the fourteen warmest years since weather record-keeping began over a century ago have occurred in the opening years of the twenty-first century—we lack the emotional and intellectual creativity to shut down the engine of global capitalism.[25]

Anthropologists, including Joseph Tainter in *The Collapse of Complex Societies,* Charles Redman in *Human Impact on Ancient Environments,* and Ronald Wright in *A Short History of Progress,* have laid out the familiar patterns that lead to the breakdown of complex societies, which usually collapse not long after they reach their period of greatest magnificence and prosperity.[26] "One of the most pathetic aspects of human history is that every civilization expresses itself most pretentiously, compounds its partial and universal values most convincingly, and claims immortality for its finite existence at the very moment when the decay which leads to death has already begun," Reinhold Niebuhr wrote.[27]

The last days of any civilization, when populations are averting their eyes from the unpleasant realities before them, become carnivals of hedonism and folly. Rome went down like this. So did the Ottoman and Austro-Hungarian Empires. Men and women of stunning mediocrity and depravity assume political control. Today charlatans and hucksters hold forth on the airwaves, and intellectuals are ridiculed. Force and militarism, with their hypermasculine ethic, are celebrated. And the mania for hope requires the silencing of any truth that is not childishly optimistic.

The road to oblivion becomes, in the end, a narcotic reverie. The sexual, the tawdry, and the inane preoccupy public discourse. "At times when the page is turning," Louis-Ferdinand Céline writes in *Castle to Castle,* " . . . when History brings all the nuts together, opens its Epic Dance Halls! hats and heads in the whirlwind! panties overboard!"[28]

Our major preoccupation is pleasure. Margaret Atwood, in her dystopian novel *Oryx and Crake,* observes that as a species "we're doomed by hope."[29] The mantra is to be positive, to be happy. This mania for optimism—for happiness—leads to fantasy being mistaken for reality. Reality is dismissed when it is unpleasant.

"We hardly dare face our bewilderment, because our ambiguous experience is so pleasantly iridescent, and the solace of belief in contrived reality is so thoroughly real," Daniel Boorstin writes in *The Image: A Guide to Pseudo-Events in America.* "We have become eager accessories in the great hoaxes of the age. These are the hoaxes we play on ourselves."[30]

Culture and literacy, in the final stage of decline, are replaced with noisy diversions, elaborate public spectacle, and empty clichés. The Roman statesman Cicero inveighed against the ancient equivalent of this degeneration and, for his honesty, was hunted down and murdered. His severed head and right hand, which had written the Philippics, were nailed onto the speaker's platform in the Forum. Fulvia, the wife of Mark Antony, reportedly spat on the severed head, placed it on her knees, opened its mouth, and pierced the tongue with hairpins.[31] The crowd roared its approval. Cicero, the crowd was assured, would never speak or write again.

Mikhail Bulgakov's *The Master and Margarita,* a bitter satire of Soviet life at the height of Stalin's purges, captured the surreal experience of living in the embrace of totalitarianism. Lies are considered true. Truth is considered seditious. Existence is a dark carnival of opportunism, unchecked state power, hedonism, and terror. Omnipotent secret police, wholesale spying and surveillance, show trials, censorship, mass arrests, summary executions, and disappearances, along with famines, gulags, and a state system of propaganda unplugged from daily reality, give to all totalitarian systems a dreamlike quality. Reality is monstrous. But the portrayal of reality in the state-controlled press and popular entertainment is harmonious and pleasant. Justice, in the narratives approved for public consumption, is always served. Goodness always triumphs. Goals are always attained. This dichotomy, although not on the level of Stalin's Soviet Union or Hitler's Nazi Germany, is nevertheless present in American culture and getting worse. The gap between who we are and who we think we are is steadily expanding.

The Master and Margarita is built around Woland, or Satan, who is a traveling magician; a hog-sized, vodka-swilling, chess-playing black cat named Behemoth; a witch named Hella; a poet named Ivan Homeless;

and a writer known as The Master, who has been placed in an insane asylum following the suppression of his book. Other characters include The Master's lover Margarita, Pontius Pilate, Yeshua (or Jesus Christ), and Pilate's dog Banga—the only creature that loves Pilate.

Moral decency has been banished. The amoral is celebrated. Satan holds a ball where Margarita, as queen, plays hostess to "kings, dukes, cavaliers, suicides, poisoners, gallowsbirds and procuresses, jailers, cardsharps, executioners, informers, traitors, madmen, detectives and corrupters of youth."[32] All these guests leap from coffins that fall out of the fireplace. The men wear tailcoats, and the women, who are naked, differ from each other only "by their shoes and the color of the feathers on their heads."[33] As Johann Strauss leads the orchestra, the revelers mingle in a cool ballroom set in a tropical forest.

In this world of total control, you flourish only if the state decides you are worthy to exist—"No documents, no person."[34] When Behemoth and his companion, Korovyov, an ex-choirmaster, attempt to enter the restaurant at the headquarters of the state-sanctioned literary trade union—filled with careerists, propagandists, profiteers, and state bureaucrats, along with their wives and mistresses—they are accosted at the entrance.

"A pale bored citizeness in white socks and a white beret with a tassel was sitting on a bentwood chair at the corner entrance to the veranda, where an opening had been created in the greenery of the trellis," writes Bulgakov.

> In front of her on a plain kitchen table lay a thick, office-style register in which, for reasons unknown, she was writing down the names of those entering the restaurant. It was this citizeness who stopped Korovyov and Behemoth.
>
> "Your ID cards?" she asked. . . .
>
> "I beg a thousand pardons, but what ID cards?" asked a surprised Korovyov.
>
> "Are you writers?" asked the woman in turn.
>
> "Of course we are," replied Korovyov with dignity.
>
> "May I see your IDs?" repeated the woman.

"My charming creature . . . " began Korovyov, tenderly.

"I am not a charming creature," interrupted the woman.

"Oh, what a pity," said Korovyov with disappointment, and continued, "Well, then, if you do not care to be a charming creature, which would have been quite nice, you don't have to be. But, here's my point, in order to ascertain that Dostoevsky is a writer, do you really need to ask him for an ID? Just look at any five pages of any of his novels, and you will surely know, even without an ID, that you're dealing with a writer. Besides, I don't suppose that he ever had any ID! What do you think?"

Korovyov turned to Behemoth.

"I'll bet he didn't," replied the latter. . . .

"You're not Dostoevsky," said the citizeness. . . .

"Well, but how do you know, how do you know?" replied [Korovyov].

"Dostoevsky is dead," said the citizeness, but not very confidently.

"I protest!" exclaimed Behemoth hotly. "Dostoevsky is immortal!"

"Your IDs, citizens," said the citizeness.[35]

Although *The Master and Margarita,* whose working title was "Satan in Moscow," was completed in 1940, it did not appear in print in uncensored form until the 1970s.

When societies break down, their words, or at least the words used in everyday discourse, no longer make sense. What is real cannot be spoken about. What is not real is used to define the legal, moral, and linguistic foundations of society.

"The power structure is symbolized by its anonymity and omnipresence, by its mysterious nature, by its total knowledge against which there is no defense, by its ability to penetrate every space, by putting in an appearance at any hour of the day or night," Karl Schlögel wrote in his book *Moscow, 1937* in speaking of the organs of state security during Stalin's purges. "Investigating officials have no names; they are simply 'they.' The word 'arrest' is replaced by the sentence 'We need to sort something out' or 'We need your signature here.' . . . The authorities are spoken of only indirectly and as if talking about an anonymous body. 'This can be discovered soon enough,' 'They have found out all there is to know,' 'Everything has been deciphered,' 'All of this will be explained, very quickly in fact.' Everyone seems to know of the existence of this organization and they all suffer from its ubiquitous presence. People are afraid and go pale whenever it makes its appearance. It takes people away, confiscates manuscripts and seals up apartments."[36]

Joseph Roth, in his 1924 novel *Hotel Savoy*, peels back the facade of power to expose the same decadence and mendacity explored by Bulgakov. In Roth's novel, Gabriel Dan, an Austrian soldier released from a Serbian prisoner-of-war camp after World War I, finds sanctuary in a hotel that

> holds out the promise of water, soap, English lavatories, a lift, chambermaids in white caps, a chamberpot gleaming like some precious surprise in the little brown-panelled night cupboard; electric lamps blooming in shades of green and rose, like flowers from their clayx; bells which ring at the push of a button; and beds plump with eiderdowns, cheerful and waiting to receive one's body.[37]

In the grand ballrooms of the hotel, the rich, the war profiteers, and the powerful gorge themselves in gluttonous revelry, as they did during the war. But on the upper floors, Dan discovers desperate, impoverished debtors, bankrupt gamblers, failed revolutionaries, chorus girls, clowns, dancers, the terminally ill, and idealistic dreamers. Once those in the upper garrets are fleeced of their money and possessions by the hotel management, they are tossed into the street. Roth's protagonist said:

> The people from the upper storeys also came to me, and there was no end to this. I saw that none of them lived at the Hotel Savoy of his own free will. Each of them was gripped by some misfortune, and the Hotel Savoy was the misfortune and they were no longer capable of choosing between this and that. Every piece of bad luck came to them through this hotel and they believed that Savoy was the name of their misfortune.[38]

Bulgakov and Roth understood that there is no real political ideology among decayed ruling elites. Political debate and ideological constructs for these elites are just so much absurdist theater, a cynical species of public spectacle and mass entertainment. These systems, like our own, are organized kleptocracies.

Not long before the invasion of France, a friend asked Roth, who had fled Nazi Germany for Paris, "Why are you drinking so much?" Roth answered: "Do you think you are going to escape? You too are going to be wiped out."[39]

Melville, who had been a sailor on clipper ships and whalers, was as keenly aware as Roth was that the wealth of industrialized societies was violently wrested by Europeans and Euro-Americans from the wretched of the earth. As Marx and Adam Smith had pointed out, it was Atahualpa's gold that made possible the Industrial Revolution.

All the authority figures on the *Pequod* are white men—Ahab, Starbuck, Flask, and Stubb. The hard, dirty work on the ship—from harpooning to gutting the carcasses of the whales and "pitch[ing] hissing masses of blubber into the scalding pots, or stir[ing] up the fires beneath, till the snaky flames darted, curling, out of the doors to catch them by the feet"[40]—is the task of the poor, mostly men of color. And since a whaler's pay was based on his "*lay*," or share of the catch, and since numerous articles he needed for the voyage were deducted in advance from his *lay*, he could return after a two- or three-year trip and receive little money or find himself in debt to the ship's owners. The streets of whaling ports such as New Bedford, Massachusetts, were lined with the opulent mansions of whaling merchants and crowded with bands of destitute sailors. The sailors were little more than sharecroppers on ships.

Ahab appears on the quarterdeck after secreting himself in his cabin for the first few days of the voyage and holds up a doubloon, an extravagant gold coin, and promises it to the crew member who first spots the white whale. He knows that "the permanent constitutional condition of the manufactured man . . . is sordidness," and he plays to this sordidness.[41] The whale becomes, like everything in the capitalist world, a commodity, a source of personal profit. A murderous greed grips the crew. Ahab's obsession infects the ship, though Starbuck, the first mate, protests, "Madness! To be enraged with a dumb thing, Captain Ahab, seems blasphemous."[42]

Ahab conducts a dark Mass, a Eucharist worship of violence and death, on the deck with the crew. He makes them drink from a flagon that is passed from man to man, filled with draughts "hot as Satan's hoof." Ahab tells the harpooners to cross their lances before him. The captain grasps the harpoons and anoints the ship's harpooners— Queequeg, Tashtego, and Daggoo—his "three pagan kinsmen." He orders them to detach the iron sections of their harpoons, and he fills the upturned sockets "with the fiery waters from the pewter." "Drink, ye harpooners! Drink and swear, ye men that man the deathful whale-boat's bow—Death to Moby-Dick! God hunt us all, if we do not hunt Moby-Dick to his death!"[43]

Later in the novel, Ahab invokes Satan as he tempers his newly forged harpoon—forged specifically to deal death to the white whale— with the freely given blood of his pagan harpooners: "Ego non baptizo te in nomine patris, sed in nomine diaboli" ("I do not baptize you in the name of the father, but in the name of the devil"). And with the crew bonded to him in his infernal quest, he knows that Starbuck cannot "stand up amid the general hurricane." "Starbuck now is mine," Ahab says to himself. The first mate "cannot oppose me now, without rebellion."[44] "Starbuck paled, and turned, and shivered."[45]

The *Pequod* was black. "She was a thing of trophies. A cannibal of a craft, tricking herself forth in the chased bones of her enemies." The ship, Melville writes, was festooned "like any barbaric Ethiopian emperor, his neck heavy with pendants of polished ivory," with the huge teeth and bones of sperm whales.[46]

"Whales were described," writes Nathaniel Philbrick in *In the Heart of the Sea,* his book about the real-life incident that inspired Melville's novel,

> by the amount of oil they would produce (as in a fifty-barrel whale), and
> although the whalemen took careful note of the mammal's habits, they
> made no attempt to regard it as anything more than a commodity whose

constituent parts (head, blubber, ambergris, etc.) were of value to them. The rest of it—the tons of meat, bone, and guts—was simply thrown away, creating festering rafts of offal that attracted birds, fish, and, of course, sharks. Just as the skinned corpses of buffaloes would soon dot the prairies of the American West, so did the headless gray remains of sperm whales litter the Pacific Ocean in the early nineteenth century.[47]

The fierce and massive fires used to melt the whale blubber at night turned the *Pequod* into a "red hell."[48] Philbrick quotes a green hand (a sailor with no previous sailing experience) from Kentucky: "A trying-out scene [in which the blubber is boiled down aboard a whale ship] has something wild and savage in it, a kind of indescribable uncouthness, which renders it difficult to describe with anything like accuracy. There is a murderous appearance about the blood-stained decks, and the huge masses of flesh and blubber lying here and there, and a ferocity in the looks of the men, heightened by the red, fierce glare of the fires."[49]

Our own raging fires, leaping up from our oil refineries and the explosions of our ordnance across the Middle East, bespeak our Stygian heart. And in our mad pursuit, we too ignore the suffering of others, just as Ahab does when he refuses to halt his quest for forty-eight hours to help the frantic captain of a passing ship find his twelve-year-old son, who is adrift in a missing whaleboat.

And yet Ahab is no simple tyrant. Melville toward the end of the novel gives us two glimpses into Ahab's internal battle between his maniacal hubris and his humanity. Ahab, like most of us, yearns for love. He harbors regrets over his deformed life. The black cabin boy Pip—who fell overboard during one hunt and subsequently went insane—is the only crew member who evokes any tenderness in the captain. Ahab is aware of this tenderness and fears its power. Pip functions as the Fool does in Shakespeare's *King Lear,* a play Melville knew intimately. Ahab warns Pip away from Ahab, away from himself. "Lad, lad," says Ahab,

I tell thee thou must not follow Ahab now. The hour is coming when Ahab would not scare thee from him, yet would not have thee by him. There is that in thee, poor lad, which I feel too curing to my malady.

Like cures like; and for this hunt, my malady becomes my most desired health. . . . If thou speakest thus to me much more, Ahab's purpose keels up in him. I tell thee no; it cannot be.[50]

This moment of weakness in Ahab says something fundamental about us. Ahab is nearly diverted from his obsessive quest by the thought of a child, by the power of paternal love. King Lear is transformed by this love once he is stripped of power and authority and able to see. Lear, at the end, embraces his role as a father, and a man, whose most important duty is to care for his child, for all children. It is not accidental that it is love for a child that nearly transforms Ahab and does in the end transform Lear. It is only when the care of another, especially a child, becomes our primary concern that we can finally see and understand why we were created.

For those of us who have spent years in wars, it is the suffering of children that most haunts us. If, as a society, we see that our principal task is the care of children, of the next generation, then the madness of the moment can be dispelled. But idols have a power over human imagination, as they do over Ahab, that defies reason, love, and finally sanity.

One can be brave on a whaling ship or a battlefield, yet a coward when called on to stand up to human evil. The crew of the ship is "morally enfeebled . . . by the incompetence of mere unaided virtue or right-mindedness in Starbuck, the invulnerable jollity of indifference and recklessness in Stubb, and the pervading mediocrity of in Flask."[51]

Starbuck especially elucidates this peculiar division between physical and moral courage. The first mate, "while generally abiding firm in the conflict with seas, or winds, or whales, or any of the ordinary irrational horrors of the world, yet cannot withstand those more terrific, because spiritual terrors, which sometimes menace you from the concentrating brow of an enraged and mighty man."[52] Starbuck is tormented by his complicity in what he foresees as Ahab's "impious end, but feel that I must help him to it." "But he drilled deep down," Starbuck exclaims, "and blasted all my reason out of me!"[53] Moral cowardice like Starbuck's turns us into hostages. Mutiny is the only salvation for the *Pequod*'s crew. And mutiny is our only salvation.

Moby-Dick rams and sinks the *Pequod*. The whirlpool formed by the ship's descent swallows up all who followed Ahab—except one— "and the great shroud of the sea rolled on as it rolled five thousand years ago."[54]

———

Our corporate hustlers are direct descendants of the whalers and sealers, of butchers such as George Armstrong Custer, of the gold speculators and railroad magnates who seized Indian land, killed off its inhabitants, and wiped out the buffalo herds, of the oil and mineral companies that went abroad to exploit—under the protection of the American military—the resources of others. These hustlers carry on their demented wars and plundering throughout the Middle East, polluting the seas and water systems, fouling the air and soil, and gambling with commodity futures while the poor starve. The Book of Revelation defines this single-minded drive for profit as service to the "beast."

Technological advancement and wealth are conflated in capitalism with human progress. All aspects of human existence that cannot be measured or quantified—beauty, truth, love, grief, the search for meaning, and the struggle with our own mortality—are ignored and ridiculed.

Walter Benjamin argues that capitalism is not only a formation "conditioned by religion" but an "essentially religious phenomenon," albeit one that no longer seeks to connect humans with the mystery of life.[55] And it is the religion of capitalism, the maniacal quest for wealth at the expense of others, that turns human beings into beasts of prey.

"A Religion may be discerned in capitalism," Benjamin writes, "that is to say, capitalism serves essentially to allay the same anxieties, torments, and disturbances to which the so-called religions offered answers."[56] Capitalism, Benjamin notes, has called on human societies to embark on a ceaseless and ultimately futile quest to find fulfillment in the endless amassing of money and power. This quest creates a culture that is dominated by guilt, a sense of inadequacy, and self-loathing and that enslaves nearly all its adherents through wages.

Benjamin calls capitalism "a purely cultic religion, perhaps the most extreme that ever existed." In this system, "things have a meaning only in their relationship to the cult." Capitalism, he notes, has no specific dogma or theology. Rather, "utilitarianism acquires its religious overtones." It "is the celebration of the cult sans rêve et sans merci [without dream or mercy]." There are no weekdays. Every day is a feast day filled with consumption. With every acquisition the starting point for new desires, capitalism leaves human beings with a sense of never being able to achieve equilibrium. "Capitalism is probably the first instance of a cult that creates guilt, not atonement," Benjamin writes. The system, he continues, "is entirely without precedent, in that it is a religion which offers not the reform of existence but its complete destruction. It is the expansion of despair, until despair becomes a religious state of the world in the hope that this will lead to salvation. God's transcendence is at an end."[57]

The barbarism of our new Dark Age will hold out Faustian pacts at the expense of others; first the poor in the developing world will be sacrificed, and then the poor at home. Communities and communal organizations that manage to break free from the dominant culture will find a correlation between the amount of freedom they enjoy and the amount of independence they attain in a world where access to land, food, and water has become paramount. Such communities that share the burdens of a disintegrating society, such as the ad hoc one formed in the wake of Hurricane Sandy, are our best hope for sustaining the intellectual and artistic traditions that define the heights of human culture and permit the common good. As those who build these communitarian structures discard the religion of capitalism, their acts of charity and resistance will merge—and they will be condemned by the corporate state.

II / The Post-Constitutional Era

Black milk of daybreak we drink it at dusk
we drink it at noon and at dawn we drink it
at night we drink it and drink it
we are digging a grave in the air [1]

—PAUL CELAN, "DEATH FUGUE"

Lynne Stewart, with short, cropped gray hair and a dark, zippered fleece jacket, sat with her hands folded in front of her at her son's dining room table in Brooklyn, New York. She had been released from a Texas prison thirty-seven days earlier because she had stage 4 cancer and had been given six months to live. She had served four years of a ten-year sentence.

As an attorney, Stewart stood up to state power for more than three decades. She defended the poor, the persecuted, and the marginalized. She wept in court when one of her clients, Omar Abdel-Rahman, was barred from presenting a credible defense. But at the end of her life she was on trial herself, disbarred and imprisoned. Her career coincided with the collapse of the American court system and the rise of the post-constitutional era, in which the courts are used to revoke the constitutional rights of citizens by judicial fiat.

"Can't even work in a law office," the seventy-four-year-old Stewart said when we spoke. "I miss it so terribly. I liked it. I liked the work."

When she started practicing law in the 1970s, she said it was a "golden era" in which a series of legal decisions—including rulings that affected police lineups and the information and evidence that the government had to turn over to defendants on trial—created a chance for

45

a fair defense. But these legal advances were steadily reversed, she said, in a string of court decisions that, especially after 9/11, made the state omnipotent. As citizens were stripped of power, she said, the bar experienced "a death of the spirit." Lawyers gave up. They no longer saw defending people accused of crime as "a calling, something that you did because you were answering a higher voice."

Stewart, working with former US attorney general Ramsey Clark and lawyer Abdeen Jabara in 1995, was the lead trial counsel for Omar Abdel-Rahman, an Egyptian Muslim, known as "the Blind Sheikh," who was convicted for alleged involvement in an aborted bombing campaign in New York City. He received life in prison plus sixty-five years in 1996 for seditious conspiracy, a sentence Stewart called "outlandish." She said that Abdel-Rahman was put on trial, not for any crimes he committed, but because both Washington and the Egyptian government of Hosni Mubarak were frightened by his influence over the Egyptian population. The United States, along with Egypt, wanted to "take him off the scene" and "get him put away where he would no longer exert the influence he had." The cleric, seventy-six and in poor health, is imprisoned in the medical wing of the Butner Federal Correctional Complex in North Carolina.[2]

The proceedings at the Abdel-Rahman trial were a harbinger of the judicial assaults against Muslims in the United States after the events of September 11, 2001. I was based in Egypt as the Middle East bureau chief for the *New York Times* when Abdel-Rahman was arrested. I was stunned at the repeated mendacity of the government prosecutors, who blamed Abdel-Rahman for terrorist attacks he had publicly denounced. The prosecutors, for example, accused him of orchestrating the killing of seventy people in 1997 in Luxor, Egypt, although the sheikh at the time condemned the attack and had no known connection with the Egyptian group that carried out the massacre.[3] When the guilty verdict was read, Stewart burst into tears, "the only time I ever cried in the courtroom."

Stewart continued to visit the sheikh after the sentencing. Three years after the trial, the government severely curtailed his ability to communicate with the outside world, even through his lawyers, under "special administrative measures" (SAMs).

Abdel-Rahman asked Stewart during a prison visit in 2000 to release a statement from him to the press concerning a negotiated ceasefire between the Egyptian government and militants. The Clinton administration did not prosecute Stewart for conveying the press release, although she was admonished and prohibited from seeing her client for several months.

The Bush administration, however, in April 2002, with the country baying for blood after the attacks of 9/11, decided to prosecute her for the two-year-old press release.

Minutes before her arrest on April 9, 2002, her husband, Ralph Poynter, who later would organize the successful fight to win her a compassionate release from prison after she was diagnosed with breast cancer, was outside on the stoop of their house, which in New York, she said, "is where you go sit on the steps in the summertime when you can't afford to go to East Hampton." She heard him in a heated conversation.

"I go to the door, and I hear him saying, 'I don't see any badge, I don't see any warrant, what are you doing here anyway?'" she said.

Assuming Ralph was being arrested, she told him to take it easy, she would have him home by lunchtime.

"I come around the door and the guy looks and says—and he was clearly a cop, you know, the cheap shoes—and he says, 'We're not here for you. We're here for her,' pointing to me," she said. "I was flabbergasted."

The FBI agents arrested her. She was released later on a $500,000 bond.

US Attorney General John Ashcroft came to New York in April 2002 to announce the arrest and appear on *The Late Show with David Letterman*. He told the television audience that the Justice Department had indicted Stewart, along with a paralegal and an interpreter, on grounds of materially aiding a terrorist organization.

The government demanded that Stewart be given a staggering thirty-year sentence. During the trial, the government lawyers spewed endless myths about Islamic terrorism. The prosecutors displayed on a ten-by-twelve-foot screen a photo of Osama bin Laden found in a codefendant's basement. The US District Judge John Koeltl repeatedly told the jury that the photo of Bin Laden wasn't evidence of the truth of the charges.[4] Stewart was sentenced, to most people's astonishment, to twenty-eight months.

After the sentencing, Stewart publicly declared that passing along the information from Abdel-Rahman had been "based on my understanding of what the client needed, what a lawyer was expected to do." It had been "necessary," she said, adding that, in the same circumstances, she would "do it again." A federal appeals court under the Barack Obama administration demanded that the district judge reconsider Stewart's sentence and make further fact-findings. She was given a new sentence by Koeltl—ten years.

The federal government's heavy-handed orchestration of fear, Stewart said, has cowed the nation. In the Carswell federal prison in Texas, the women's facility where she was incarcerated, she heard numerous accounts of gross injustices endured by poor women. She frequently asked these women why they had not demanded a trial rather than submit to a plea deal, or why they had not stood up and proclaimed their innocence. The answer, she said, was always the same: "I was afraid. I was afraid."

The right-wing Federalist Society, after its founding in 1982, unleashed a frontal assault on the legal system that has transformed it into a wholly owned subsidiary of the corporate state. After Stanford University asked Stewart to speak there in 2002, she arrived on campus to find that the Federalist Society had pressured the university into rescinding the invitation. Sympathetic students found her a place to talk, but Federalist Society members appeared at the event to jeer and ask caustic questions.

By the 1980s, she said, the federal government was "mopping up" the remnants of radical activists, many of whom had been underground for years. She and other civil rights attorneys were able to battle on behalf of these political radicals, but by the end of the 1980s the state had finished its hunt for underground activists. And lawyers, Stewart said, "were no longer part of the game."

The occasional victories that she and other civil rights lawyers were able to win before the attacks of 9/11 became nearly impossible to replicate afterward.

"The playing field suddenly changed, and everything favored the prosecution, certainly in federal cases," she said. "There was no level playing field anymore. It was like if you were the last guy standing and you had to keep them from making the goal. You were at the six-inch line trying to do it. It was impossible to stop them. They controlled it. They controlled what the charges were. They controlled whether an adjournment would be given. They determined whether the cooperation is worthy, and everybody must cooperate, and it changed into a very different system, certainly on the federal level."

In her own trial, the government presented audio recordings of her meetings with Abdel-Rahman in the prison in Rochester, Minnesota. The taping of that conversation before the federal Patriot Act would have violated attorney-client privilege, but now such tapings are legal.[5]

"We continue the facade that we are fair," she said, "that we have this Constitution we respect, and we can rely on, and that we can embrace. 'You can't do that, that's my constitutional rights, etc.' When really [our constitutional rights are] a puff of smoke. They don't really exist."

She began to reflect on the cost of being imprisoned, something she said she had not fully understood until she was locked up.

"I don't think I ever appreciated the unrelenting stress," she said about being in prison. "That you're always waiting for something to come down. That there's such arbitrary authority. Guard A says, 'Go down those stairs, use the stairs.' Guard B says, 'You can't use the stairs, you're not permitted on the stairs.' And you say, 'But Guard A just said—' 'I don't care what he said, this is *my* rule!' That kind of arbitrary thing, you're always guessing. What does this guy, what does this woman, want me to do? Where am I? Where is this? And that's 24/7."

"You're always on the cusp of doing the wrong thing, or getting in trouble for something," she said. "I wrote a letter for a woman, and in order to make a copy I emailed it to Ralph." She went on: "It was basically asking a judge to stay any decision because they were going to take all of her pension as payment for what she had done. And she wanted to get this letter in right away. So I emailed it to [Ralph,] and for that I lost, I think, about three months of commissary, and email."

"I found it virtually impossible to convince the women at Carswell that they should not be always thinking that what happened to them was personal," she said. "They should be looking at political answers, that where they ended up was not because of some personal lack or weakness, but because the political system has designated them to be there as one of the kick-arounds, as one of the not-for-consumption."

One of the saddest moments in prison was mail call. The names of those who had letters would be read. Some women "waited for their name to be called, and it never happened." Those who did not get mail or visits, Stewart said, "become more and more institutionalized. The world of the prison is the only world; the outside world does not exist for them anymore."

She no longer believes the working class has the ability or consciousness to revolt.

"I'm not waiting for the working class to make the revolution," she said. "I think that's a day long gone by. That might have happened in the thirties. It didn't. We have to look at a new way, some new force."

But at the same time she wants people to prepare.

"The most important thing is, don't let yourself get isolated," she said. "Don't feel that you're the only one in the room that thinks this way and you must be crazy or something, and they're going to get you because you're the only one. Find the other people who think like you. They're out there. There are people out there. There are groups. There's everyone from the raging grannies right up to the very serious lefties, but there's somebody out there, make sure you're not all alone. That's the worst part of what we face these days. As long as you're with other people, you have a fighting chance, and you can organize more people."

"This is a pretty loveless world we live in," she concluded. "We have lots of romantic love. We have lots of *Sex and the City*. But real love, love that is the kind that saves people, and makes the world better, and makes you go to bed with a smile on your face, that love is lacking greatly. You have to search for that."

The courts were perhaps the last institution that liberal reformers had faith in before they too fell victim to the demands of corporate power. There are no institutions left that provide the citizen with a voice.

————

My own dead end with the judicial system occurred in April 2014 when the US Supreme Court refused to hear *Hedges v. Obama*, the lawsuit I brought against Barack Obama concerning Section 1021(b)(2) of the National Defense Authorization Act (NDAA). This provision permits the military to seize US citizens and hold them indefinitely in military detention centers without due process.[6]

The refusal by the Supreme Court to hear the case means that extraordinary rendition by our government of US citizens on US soil is legal. It means that the courts, like the legislative and executive branches of government, are now exclusive servants of corporate power. It means that the consent of the governed—in a poll conducted by OpenCongress .com the NDAA provision had a 97 percent disapproval rating—is a cruel joke.[7] And it means that if we do not rapidly build militant mass movements to overthrow corporate tyranny, including breaking the back of the two-party duopoly that is the mask of corporate power, we will lose what remains of our liberty.

The attorneys Bruce Afran and Carl Mayer and I had brought the case to the US Southern District Court of New York in January 2012. I was later joined by coplaintiffs, the philosopher and linguist Noam Chomsky, Daniel Ellsberg, who leaked the Pentagon Papers; the journalist Alexa O'Brien; activist Tangerine Bolen; Icelandic parliamentarian Birgitta Jónsdóttir; and Occupy activist Kai Wargalla. US District Judge Katherine B. Forrest in 2012 declared Section 1021(b)(2) unconstitutional. The Obama administration not only appealed—we expected it to appeal—but demanded that the law be immediately put back into effect until the appeal was heard. Forrest, displaying the same judicial courage she showed with her ruling, refused to do this.

The government swiftly went to the US Court of Appeals for the Second Circuit. It asked, in the name of national security, that the court stay the district court's injunction until the government's appeal could be heard. The Second Circuit agreed. The law went back on the books. Afran, Mayer, and I surmised that the administration acted this quickly because it was already using the law to detain US citizens in black sites, most likely dual citizens with roots in countries such as Pakistan, Afghanistan, Somalia, and Yemen. The administration would have been in contempt of court if Forrest's ruling had been allowed to stand while the federal authorities detained US citizens under the statute. Government attorneys, when asked by Judge Forrest, refused to say whether or not the government was already using the law, buttressing our suspicion that it was in use.

The Second Circuit overturned Forrest's ruling in July 2013 in a decision that did not force it to rule on the actual constitutionality of

Section 1021(b)(2). It cited the Supreme Court ruling in *Clapper v. Amnesty International*, another case in which I was a plaintiff, to say that I had no standing, or right, to bring the NDAA case to court. *Clapper v. Amnesty International* had challenged the secret wiretapping of US citizens under the FISA Amendments Act of 2008. The Supreme Court had ruled in *Clapper* that our concern about government surveillance was "speculation." It said that we were required to prove to the court that the FISA Act would be used to monitor those we interviewed. The Court knew, of course, that the government does not disclose whom it is monitoring. And it knew we could not offer proof.

The documentation proving that we—and nearly all Americans—are victims of government surveillance had not yet been provided to the press by Edward Snowden. Snowden, who worked for the consulting firm Booz Allen Hamilton at a National Security Agency (NSA) center in Hawaii, fled the country before leaking thousands of classified documents that detailed the massive government surveillance operation within the United States and abroad. The Second Circuit used the spurious Supreme Court ruling to make its own spurious ruling. It said that because we could not show that the indefinite-detention law was about to be used against us, just as we could not prove government monitoring of our communications, we could not challenge the law. It was a dirty game of judicial avoidance on two egregious violations of the Constitution.

In refusing to hear our lawsuit, the courts have overturned nearly 150 years of case law that repeatedly holds that the military has no jurisdiction over civilians. Now a US citizen charged by the government with "substantially supporting" al-Qaeda, the Taliban, or those in the nebulous category of "associated forces"—some of the language of Section 1021(b)(2)—is lawfully subject to extraordinary rendition on US soil. And those seized and placed in military jails can be kept there until "the end of hostilities."

Judge Forrest, in her 112-page ruling against the section, noted that under this provision of the NDAA whole categories of Americans could be subject to seizure by the military. These might include Muslims, activists, Black Bloc anarchists—so named because they dress in black, obscure their faces, move as a unified mass, seek physical confrontations with police, and destroy property—and any other Americans labeled as domestic terrorists by the state. Forrest wrote that Section 1021(b)(2) echoed the 1944 Supreme Court ruling in *Korematsu v. United States,* which supported the government's use of the military to detain at least 110,000 Japanese Americans in internment camps without due process during World War II.[8]

When a citizenry no longer feels that it can find justice through the organs of power, when it feels that the organs of power are the enemies of freedom and economic advancement, it makes war on those organs. Those of us who are condemned as radicals, idealists, and dreamers call for basic reforms that, if enacted, would make peaceful reform possible. But corporate capitalists, now unchecked by state power and dismissive of the popular will, do not see the fires they are igniting. The Supreme Court ruling on our challenge, like the imprisonment of Lynne Stewart, is one more signpost on the road to revolt. The longer citizens are locked out of and abused by systems of power the more these systems become targets.

Section 1021(b)(2) is but one piece of the legal tyranny now in place, along with our wholesale surveillance, to ensure total corporate control. The state can order the assassination of US citizens. It has abolished habeas corpus. It uses secret evidence to imprison dissidents, such as the Palestinian academic Mazen Al-Najjar. It employs the Espionage Act to criminalize those who expose abuses of power. A ruling elite that accrues for itself this kind of total power, history has shown, eventually uses it. And at that point we cement into place a brutal corporate totalitarianism.

———

The cornerstone of control is the state's system of surveillance, exposed by Snowden. I saw the effect of blanket surveillance as a reporter in the Stasi state of Communist East Germany. I was followed by men, invariably with crew cuts and leather jackets, whom I presumed to be agents of the Stasi—the Ministry for State Security, which the ruling

Communist Party described as the "shield and sword" of the nation.[9] Stasi agents visited those I interviewed soon after I left their homes. My phone was bugged. Some of those I worked with were pressured to become informants. Fear hung like icicles over every conversation. People would whisper to me to convey the most banal pieces of information.

The Stasi did not set up massive death camps and gulags. It did not have to. Its network of as many as 2 million informants in a country of 17 million was everywhere. There were 102,000 secret police officers employed full-time to monitor the population—one for every 166 East Germans.[10] The Nazis broke bones. The Stasi broke souls. The East German security apparatus pioneered the psychological disintegration skills that torturers and interrogators in America's black sites, and within our prison system, have honed to a chilling perfection.

The goal of wholesale surveillance, as Hannah Arendt wrote in *The Origins of Totalitarianism,* is not, in the end, to discover crimes, "but to be on hand when the government decides to arrest a certain category of the population."[11] This is what happened to Stewart. And because Americans' emails, phone conversations, Web searches, and geographical movements are recorded and stored in perpetuity in government databases, there will be more than enough "evidence" to seize us should the state deem it necessary. This information waits like a dormant virus inside government vaults to be released against us. It does not matter how trivial or innocent that information is. In totalitarian states, justice, like truth, is irrelevant.

Any state that has the capacity to monitor all its citizenry, any state that has the ability to snuff out factual public debate through the control of information, any state that has the tools to instantly shut down all dissent, is totalitarian. The state may not use this power today. But it will use it if it feels threatened.

Those who sweep up all of our financial data, our tweets, our file transfers, our live chats, our medical data, our criminal and civil court records, those awash in billions upon billions of taxpayer dollars, those who have banks of sophisticated computer systems—along with biosensors, scanners, face recognition technologies, and miniature drones—are those who have obliterated our anonymity, our privacy, and our liberty.

No one who lives under constant surveillance, who is subject to detention anywhere at any time, whose conversations, proclivities, and habits are recorded, stored, and analyzed, can be described as free. This is the relationship of masters and slaves. Yet the state assures us that our rights are sacred, that government abides by the will of the people and the consent of the governed, that our right to privacy is protected. And so begins the surrealist nightmare that writers such as Bulgakov and Roth have chronicled. The vast distance between perceived reality and the official version of reality is characteristic of totalitarian systems. The state abolishes liberty and rights while claiming to uphold and defend them.

The most effective tyranny, as Arendt points out in *The Origins of Totalitarianism,* crushes its marginalized and harassed opponents and, through fear and the obliteration of privacy, incapacitates everyone else. The object of efficient totalitarian states, as George Orwell understood, is to create a climate in which people do not think of rebelling, a climate in which incarceration and state-sanctioned murder are used against only a handful of unmanageable renegades. The totalitarian state achieves this control, Arendt wrote, by systematically shutting down all human spontaneity—and by extension, human freedom—through fear. This fear and loss of spontaneity keep a population traumatized and immobilized and turn the courts, along with legislative bodies, into mechanisms that legalize the crimes of state.[12]

This legal sleight of hand is how our most basic constitutional rights have been obliterated. The Fourth and Fifth Amendments of the Constitution, which were established to protect us from unwarranted intrusion by the government into our private lives, may still technically be law but they have been judicially abolished. The Fourth Amendment was written in 1789 in direct response to the arbitrary and unchecked search powers that the British had exercised through general warrants called "writs of assistance," which played a significant part in fomenting the American Revolution. The amendment limits the state's ability to search and seize to a specific place, time, and event approved by a magistrate. It is impossible to square the bluntness of the Fourth Amendment with the arbitrary search and seizure of all our personal communications.

The courts and legislative bodies of the corporate state now routinely invert our most basic rights to justify corporate pillage and repression. They declare that massive and secret campaign donations—a form of legalized bribery—are protected speech under the First Amendment. They define corporate lobbying—under which corporations lavish funds on elected officials and write our legislation—as the people's right to petition the government. And according to new laws and legislation, we can be tortured or assassinated or locked up indefinitely by the military, be denied due process, and be spied upon without warrants. The US Constitution has not been rewritten, but steadily emasculated through a dirty system of judicial and legislative reinterpretation. We have been left with a fictitious shell of democracy and a totalitarian core.

Once the state has the power to intrude into the private lives of its citizens, it becomes omnipresent. It listens and collects everything, no matter how arcane or trivial. The NSA bugged the conclave that elected the new pope.[13] It bugged the phone of the German chancellor, Angela Merkel, and in fact it has bugged most of the leaders of Europe.[14] It intercepted the talking points of UN Secretary-General Ban Ki-moon ahead of a meeting with President Obama.[15] It bugged businesses like the Brazilian oil company Petrobras and acquired information regarding American law firms engaged in trade deals with Indochina for shrimp and clove cigarettes.[16]

The NSA, in conjunction with Australian intelligence, carried out a major eavesdropping effort focused on the United Nations Climate Change Conference in Bali in 2007.[17] NSA officials also bugged their own ex-lovers, wives, and girlfriends. A technical system of surveillance designed to monitor those considered to be a danger to the state has been "turned against you," in the words of the NSA whistle-blower William Binney. Thomas Paine described despotic government as a fungus growing out of a corrupt civil society.[18] This is what has happened to us.

But our corporate totalitarian rulers deceive themselves as often as they deceive the public. Politics, for them, is public relations. Lies are told not to achieve any discernible goal of public policy, but to protect the image of the state and its rulers. These lies have become a grotesque form of patriotism. James Clapper, the director of national intelligence, lied under oath to Congress about the pervasive state surveillance of the citizenry. This spectacle was a rare glimpse into the absurdist theater that now characterizes American political life. A congressional oversight committee holds public hearings. It is lied to. It knows it is being lied to. The person who lies knows the committee members know he is lying. And the committee members, to protect their security clearances, say and do nothing.[19]

The state's ability, through comprehensive surveillance, to prevent outside inquiry into the exercise of power engenders a terrifying intellectual and moral sclerosis within the ruling elite. Absurd notions—such as implanting "democracy" in Baghdad by force in order to spread it across the region, or terrorizing radical Islam into submission—are no longer checked by reality, experience, or factually grounded debate. Data and facts that do not fit into the whimsical theories of our political elites, generals, and intelligence chiefs are ignored and hidden from public view. The citizenry cannot take self-corrective measures because it is denied factual information. And when the unchallenged elites soon come to believe their own lies, the state descends into dysfunction, terror, and burlesque.

Totalitarian states use propaganda to orchestrate historical amnesia, a state-induced stupidity. The object is to make sure the populace does not remember what it means to be free. And once a population does not remember what it means to be free, it does not react when freedom is stripped from it.

The tightening of the corporate totalitarian noose would have continued without legal or public debate if Edward Snowden had not jolted the nation awake. Snowden revealed through his leaks of NSA documents evidence of what former vice president Al Gore said "appears to be crimes against the US Constitution."[20] Snowden's revelations triggered, for the first time, a genuine discussion about mass surveillance. Two judges finally passed rulings on the NSA's surveillance program. US District Judge Richard J. Leon, in December 2013, ruled that the bulk collection of metadata probably violates the Fourth Amendment (relating to unreasonable searches and seizures) and is "almost Orwellian" in its sweep.[21] The Justice Department appealed Judge Leon's ruling. US District Judge William Pauley, later that month, reversed Judge Leon's decision to rule that the National Security Agency's bulk collection of telephone records is legal.[22] A presidential panel criticized the agency's blanket surveillance and called for reform.

A *New York Times* editorial on January 1, 2014, argued that Snowden's revelations had done the country "a great service" and called for "some form of clemency that would allow him to return home." The editorial listed some of the crimes of government that Snowden had exposed:

- The NSA broke federal privacy laws, or exceeded its authority, thousands of times per year, according to the agency's own internal auditor.[23]
- The agency broke into the communications links of major data centers around the world and spied on hundreds of millions of user accounts, infuriating the Internet companies that own the centers.[24] Many of those companies are now scrambling to install systems that the NSA cannot yet penetrate.
- The NSA systematically undermined the basic encryption systems of the Internet, making it impossible to know whether sensitive banking and medical data is truly private and damaging businesses that depend on this trust.[25]
- James Clapper Jr., the director of national intelligence, lied to Congress when he testified in March 2013 that the NSA was not collecting data on millions of Americans.[26] (There has been no discussion of punishment for that lie.)
- The Foreign Intelligence Surveillance Court rebuked the NSA for repeatedly providing misleading information about its surveillance practices, according to a ruling made public because of the Snowden documents.[27] One of the practices violated the Constitution, according to the chief judge of the court.
- A federal district judge ruled in December 2013 that the phone records collection program probably violates the Fourth Amendment of the Constitution.[28] He called the program "almost Orwellian" and said there was no evidence that it had stopped any imminent act of terror.[29]

Before Snowden, we were not even able to get a hearing in court. Some members of Congress—although that body authorized the Patriot Act and its Section 215, which ostensibly permits this wholesale surveillance of the public—expressed dismay at the extent of the NSA's activities and the weakness of its promised reforms. Maybe they are lying. Maybe they are not. Maybe reforms will produce improvements, or maybe, as appears to be happening, they will be merely cosmetic. But before Snowden, we had nothing. Snowden's revelations made us conscious.

To rebel requires that elusive virtue that Snowden exemplifies and that Melville's Starbuck lacks—moral courage. I have been to war. I have seen physical courage. But this kind of courage is not moral courage. Very few of even the bravest warriors have moral courage. The person with moral courage defies the crowd, stands up as a solitary individual, shuns the intoxicating embrace of comradeship, and is disobedient to authority, even at the risk of his or her life, for a higher principle. And with moral courage comes persecution.

The US Army pilot Hugh Thompson had moral courage. He landed his helicopter between a platoon of US soldiers and ten terrified Vietnamese civilians during the My Lai massacre in 1968. He ordered his gunner to fire his M60 machine gun on the advancing US soldiers if they began to shoot the villagers. And for this act of moral courage, Thompson was hounded and reviled. Moral courage always looks like this. It is always defined by the state as treason—the Army attempted to cover up the massacre and threatened to court-martial Thompson. Moral courage is the courage to act and to speak the truth. Thompson had it. Daniel Ellsberg had it. Martin Luther King Jr. had it. What those in authority once said about them, they say today about Snowden.

We who have been fighting against mass state surveillance for years have made no headway by appealing to the traditional centers of power. It was only after Snowden methodically leaked documents disclosing the crimes committed by the state that genuine public debate began. Elected officials, for the first time, promised reform. None of this would have happened—none of it—without Snowden.

His critics argue that he could have reformed the system from the inside. He could have gone to his superiors or Congress or the courts.

But Snowden had numerous examples—including the persecution of the NSA whistle-blower Thomas Drake, who originally tried to go through so-called proper channels—to remind him that working within the system is fatal. Drake attempted to alert Congress and his superiors about waste, mismanagement, and possible constitutional violations at the NSA but was repeatedly rebuffed. He eventually provided information—none of it classified—to a reporter at *the Baltimore Sun* who was investigating a bungled $1.2 billion surveillance program called "Trailblazer." Drake was charged by the government under the Espionage Act and faced up to thirty-five years' imprisonment. When the government's case collapsed in court, Drake was able to plead to one misdemeanor count for exceeding authorized use of a computer.[30]

Snowden had watched as senior officials, including Obama, lied to the public about internal surveillance. He knew that the president was willfully dishonest when he assured Americans that the Foreign Intelligence Surveillance Court, which meets in secret and hears only from the government, is "transparent." He knew that the president's statement that Congress was "overseeing the entire program" was false. He knew that everything Director of National Intelligence James Clapper told the press, the Congress, and the public about the surveillance of Americans was a lie.

Snowden had access to the full roster of everyone working at the NSA. He could have made public the entire intelligence community and undercover assets worldwide. He could have exposed the locations of every clandestine station and their missions. He could have shut down the surveillance system, as he has said, "in an afternoon."[31] But this was never his intention. He wanted only to halt the wholesale surveillance that was being carried out, until he documented it, without our consent or knowledge.

He knew that the information he possessed could be made available to the public only through a few journalists whose integrity he could trust. There is no free press without the ability of reporters to protect the confidentiality of those who have the moral courage to make public the abuse of power. If we do not immediately dismantle the security and surveillance apparatus, there will be no investigative journalism or judicial oversight to address abuses of power. There will be no organized dissent. There will be no independent thought. Criticisms, however tepid, will be treated as acts of subversion.

Snowden had no choice, just as we now have no choice. He defied the formal institutions of government because they do not work. And all who seek reform must follow his example. Appealing to the judicial, legislative, or executive branches of government in the hope of reform is as realistic as accepting the offer made by the March Hare during the Mad Tea-Party in Lewis Carroll's *Alice in Wonderland*:

"Have some wine," the March Hare said in an encouraging tone.

Alice looked all round the table, but there was nothing on it but tea.

"I don't see any wine," she remarked.

"There isn't any," said the March Hare.[32]

The public's inability to grasp the pathology of our oligarchic corporate elite makes it difficult to organize effective resistance. Compliant politicians, entertainers, and our vapid, corporate-funded popular culture and news media hold up the elites as leaders to emulate. We are repeatedly assured that through diligence and hard work we can join them. We are taught to equate wealth with success. This narrative keeps us from seeing the truth.

"The rich are different from us," F. Scott Fitzgerald is said to have remarked to Ernest Hemingway, to which Hemingway allegedly replied, "Yes, they have more money."

The exchange, although it never took place, does sum up a wisdom Fitzgerald had that eluded Hemingway. The rich *are* different. The cocoon of wealth and privilege permits the rich to turn those around them into compliant and expendable workers, hangers-on, servants, and sycophants. Wealth, as Fitzgerald illustrated in his 1925 novel *The Great Gatsby*—a tome on the depravity of the rich in the giddy world of speculation that would lead to the Depression—as well as his short story "The Rich Boy," which appeared a year later, breeds a class of people for whom human beings are disposable commodities. Colleagues, business partners, clients, associates, shareholders, investors, employees, kitchen staff, servants, gardeners, tutors, personal trainers, even friends and family, bend to the whims of the wealthy or disappear. Once oligarchs achieve unchecked economic and political power, as they have in the United States, the citizens too become disposable. And that, in the eyes of the elite, is what we are.

"Let me tell you about the very rich," Fitzgerald writes in "The Rich Boy." "They are different from you and me. They possess and enjoy early, and it does something to them, makes them soft where we are hard, and cynical where we are trustful, in a way that, unless you were born rich, it is very difficult to understand. They think, deep in their hearts, that they are better than we are because we had to discover the compensations and refuges of life for ourselves. Even when they enter deep into our world or sink below us, they still think that they are better than we are. They are different."[33]

Aristotle, who saw extreme inequality as the fundamental cause of revolution, argues in *Politics* that the rise of an oligarchic state leads to one of two scenarios. The impoverished underclass can revolt and overthrow the oligarchs to rectify the imbalance of wealth and power, or it can submit to the tyranny of oligarchic rule.[34]

The public face of the oligarchic class is carefully crafted by publicists and a compliant media. It bears little resemblance to the private face. This is hard for those who have not been admitted into the intimate circles of the elite to grasp. I, like Fitzgerald, was thrown into the embrace of the upper crust as a boy. I was sent to an exclusive New England boarding school at the age of ten as a scholarship student. I had classmates whose fathers—fathers they rarely saw otherwise—arrived at the school in their limousines accompanied by personal photographers (and at times their mistresses), so the press could be fed images of rich and famous men playing the role of dutiful dads. I spent time in the mansions of the ultra-rich and powerful, watching my classmates, who were children, callously order around men and women who worked as their chauffeurs, cooks, nannies, and servants. When the sons and daughters of the rich get into serious trouble, there are always lawyers, publicists, and political personages to protect them—George W. Bush's life is a case study in the insidious affirmative action for the rich. The rich have a disdain for the poor—despite carefully publicized acts of philanthropy—and a haughty dislike of the middle class.

The lower classes are viewed as uncouth parasites, annoyances to be endured, sometimes placated, and always controlled in the quest to amass more power and money. My hatred of authority, along with my loathing for the pretensions, heartlessness, and sense of entitlement of the rich, comes from living among the privileged. It was a deeply unpleasant experience. I returned on summer breaks to the small town in Maine where my grandparents and relatives lived. They had more innate intelligence than most of my prep school classmates. I knew from a young age who my enemies were.

"They were careless people, Tom and Daisy," Fitzgerald writes of the wealthy couple at the center of Gatsby's life. "They smashed up things and creatures and then retreated back into their money or their vast carelessness, or whatever it was that kept them together, and let other people clean up the mess they had made."[35]

"Those who have too much of the goods of fortune, strength, wealth, friends, and the like, are neither willing nor able to submit to authority," Aristotle writes in *Politics*. "The evil begins at home; for when they are boys, by reason of the luxury in which they are brought up, they never learn, even at school, the habit of obedience."[36]

Oligarchs, as Aristotle, Machiavelli, Alexis de Tocqueville, Adam Smith, and Karl Marx knew, are schooled in the mechanisms of manipulation—subtle and overt repression and exploitation to protect their wealth and power. Foremost among their mechanisms of control is the control of ideas. Ruling elites ensure that the established intellectual class is subservient to an ideology—in this case, neoliberalism and globalization—that conveniently justifies their greed. "The ruling ideas are nothing more than the ideal expression of the dominant material relationships," Marx wrote, "the dominant material relationships grasped as ideas."[37]

The blanket dissemination of the ideology of neoliberalism through the media and the purging, especially in academia, of critical voices have permitted our oligarchs to orchestrate the industrial world's largest income inequality gap. Nobel Prize–winning economist Joseph Stiglitz, in a May 2011 article titled "Of the 1%, by the 1%, for the 1%" in *Vanity Fair,* warned of the damage caused by the extreme concentration of wealth in the hands of an oligarchic elite. "In our democracy, 1% of the people take nearly a quarter of the nation's income," he writes.

> In terms of wealth rather than income, the top 1% control 40%. . . . [As a result,] the top 1% have the best houses, the best educations, the best doctors, and the best lifestyles, but there is one thing that money doesn't seem to have bought: an understanding that their fate is bound up with how the other 99% live. Throughout history, this is something that the top 1% eventually do learn. Too late.[38]

For every $1 that the wealthiest 0.1 percent amassed in 1980, they had an additional $3 in yearly income in 2008, David Cay Johnston explains in his article "9 Things the Rich Don't Want You to Know About Taxes."[39] In the same period, the bottom 90 percent, Johnston says, added only one cent. Nearly half of the country is now classified as poor or low-income.[40] The real value of the minimum wage has fallen by $3.44 since 1968.[41]

Oligarchs do not believe in self-sacrifice for the common good. They never have. They never will. And now that they have full control of the economy and the legal system, as well as the legislative and executive branches of government, along with our media outlets, they use power as a blunt instrument for personal enrichment and domination.

"We Americans are not usually thought to be a submissive people, but of course we are," Wendell Berry writes.

> Why else would we allow our country to be destroyed? Why else would we be rewarding its destroyers? Why else would we all—by proxies we have given to greedy corporations and corrupt politicians—be participating in its destruction? Most of us are still too sane to piss in our own cistern, but we allow others to do so and we reward them for it. We reward them so well, in fact, that those who piss in our cistern

are wealthier than the rest of us. How do we submit? By not being radical enough. Or by not being thorough enough, which is the same thing.[42]

The ancient Greeks and Egyptians, the Romans, the Mayans, the Hapsburgs, even the inhabitants of Easter Island, all died because they were unable to control the appetites of their elites. The elites were able to exploit ecosystems and human beings until these civilizations self-destructed. The quest by a bankrupt elite in a civilization's final days to accumulate greater and greater wealth, as Marx observed, is modern society's version of primitive fetishism. As there is less and less to exploit, this quest leads to mounting repression, increased human suffering, infrastructure collapse, and, finally, death.

It is the self-deluded on Wall Street and among the political elite— those who entertain and inform us and those who lack the capacity to question the lusts that will ensure our self-annihilation—who are foolishly held up as exemplars of intelligence, success, and progress. This is the mark of a civilization that has gone insane. The National Alliance on Mental Illness calculates that "one in four adults—approximately 6.5 million Americans—experience mental illness in a given year," which seems a reasonable reaction to the future being constructed for us by our corporate masters.[43]

The rich, throughout history, have found methods and subterfuges to subjugate and resubjugate the working class. And workers have cyclically awoken throughout history to revolt. The founding fathers, largely wealthy slaveholders, feared direct democracy and enthusiastically embraced the slaughter of indigenous peoples to seize their land and resources. They rigged our political process to thwart popular rule and protect the property rights of the native aristocracy. The laboring classes were to be kept at bay. The electoral college, the original power of the states to appoint senators, and the disenfranchisement of women, Native Americans, African Americans, and men without property locked most people out of the democratic process at the beginning of the republic. We had to fight for our rights and our voice. Hundreds of workers attempting to form unions were killed and thousands were wounded in our labor wars. Tens of thousands more were fired and blacklisted.

The democratic openings we achieved were fought and paid for with the blood of abolitionists, African Americans, suffragists, workers, and antiwar and civil rights activists. Our radical movements, repressed and ruthlessly dismantled in the name of anticommunism, were the real engines of equality and social justice. Now that unions have been broken and sweatshops implanted in the developing world, the squalor and suffering inflicted on workers by the oligarchic class in the nineteenth century is mirrored in the present. Dissent is once again a criminal act. The Mellons, Rockefellers, and Carnegies at the turn of the last century sought to create a nation of masters and serfs. The modern corporate incarnation of this nineteenth-century oligarchic elite has created a worldwide neofeudalism under which workers across the planet toil in misery while corporate oligarchs amass hundreds of millions in personal wealth.

Rebellion against this global oligarchic elite, however, percolates across the planet.

The *China Labour Bulletin* estimates that there were at least 373 strikes in China from January to June 24, 2014,[44] and 1,171 strikes or worker protests from mid-2011 to 2013.[45] Workers carried out strikes at factories that made products for multinationals such as IBM, Pepsi, Wal-Mart, Nike, and Adidas.[46] In a single strike in April 2014, more than 40,000 workers walked off the job at a factory in Dongguan that produced shoes for Nike and Adidas.[47] The workers went on strike after they discovered that their work contracts were fraudulent and the company had been underpaying the social insurance to which they were legally entitled for at least two decades.[48] The monthly minimum wage for these production workers was 1,310 yuan, or $210.27, a month. Nike running shoes cost 1,469 yuan, or $235.79.[49]

Class struggle defines most of human history. Marx got this right. The seesaw of history has thrust the oligarchs upward. We sit humiliated and broken on the ground. It is an old battle. It has been fought over and over in human history. The only route left to us, as Aristotle knew, is either submission or revolt.

III / The Invisible Revolution

*The death of the contemporary forms of social order ought to glad-
den rather than trouble the soul. But what is frightening is that
the departing world leaves behind it not an heir, but a pregnant
widow. Between the death of one and the birth of the other, much
water will flow by, a long night of chaos and desolation will pass.*[1]

—ALEXANDER HERZEN, ON THE
FAILURE OF THE 1848 REVOLUTIONS

"Did you ever ask yourself how it happens that government and capitalism continue to exist in spite of all the evil and trouble they are
causing in the world?" the anarchist Alexander Berkman wrote in
his essay "The Idea Is the Thing." "If you did, then your answer must
have been that it is because the people support those institutions, and
that they support them because they believe in them."[2]

Revolutions, when they begin, are invisible, at least to the wider society. They start with the slow discrediting and dismantling of an old
ideology and an old language used to interpret reality and justify power.
Human societies are captive to and controlled by language. When the
old ideas are shattered, when it is clear that the official words and ideas
no longer match the reality, the institutions that buttress the ruling class
deflate and collapse. Our battle is a battle over what the experimental
psychologist and linguist Steven Pinker refers to as "mutual knowledge."[3]

"Human beings do not live in the objective world alone, nor alone in
the world of social activity as ordinarily understood, but are very much
at the mercy of the particular language which has become the medium
of expression for their society," the linguist Edward Sapir writes.

It is quite an illusion to imagine that one adjusts to reality essentially without the use of language and that language is merely an incidental means of solving specific problems of communication or reflection. The fact of the matter is that the "real world" is to a large extent unconsciously built up on the language habits of the group. . . . We see and hear and otherwise experience very largely as we do because the language habits of our community predispose certain choices of interpretation.[4]

Our inability, as citizens, to influence power in a system of corporate or inverted totalitarianism, along with the loss of our civil liberties, weakens the traditional political vocabulary of a capitalist democracy. The descent of nearly half the country into poverty or near-poverty diminishes the effectiveness of the rhetoric about limitless growth and ceaseless material progress. It undermines the myth of American prosperity. The truths are dimly apparent. But we have yet to sever ourselves from the old way of speaking and formulate a new language to explain us to ourselves. Until this happens, the corporate state can harness the old language like a weapon and employ the institutions of power and organs of state security to perpetuate itself.

In the *Prison Notebooks*, Antonio Gramsci calls such a moment in history an "interregnum"—a time when the reigning ideology is bankrupt but has yet to be replaced by a new one. "The crisis consists precisely in the fact that the old is dying and the new cannot be born, [and] in this interregnum a great variety of morbid symptoms appear," Gramsci writes.[5]

We have been captivated in the modern age by what John Ralston Saul calls "a theology of pure power" built on "organization, technology and information." Our new priest, he writes, is the technocrat, "the man who understands the organization, makes use of the technology and controls access to the information, which is a compendium of facts." These technocrats have "rendered powerless the law," which is no longer used, as it was designed, "to protect the individual from the unreasonable actions of others, especially those in power." It is a weapon of injustice wielded by those who have married "the state and the means of production." This marriage, Saul notes, makes it "almost impossible for the law to judge illegal that which is wrong."[6]

The cult of rationality in the hands of technocrats has become an absolutist ideology. Technocrats, Saul notes, are "slaves to dogma" and "hedonists of power." This cult presents itself as the solution to the problems it perpetuates—as if the fossil fuel industry could solve the energy crisis or global banks the financial crisis. Saul warns that if we do not free ourselves from this cult—and like Pinker and Berkman, he believes that this is only possible once we develop a new language to describe reality—we will be vanquished by these technocrats. "Their obsession with structures and their inability or unwillingness to link these to the public good make this power an abstract force—a force that works, more often than not, at cross-purposes to the real needs of a painfully real world," he writes.[7]

The Austrian writer Stefan Zweig, in his 1942 novella *Chess Story*, chronicles the arcane specializations that have created technocrats unable to question the systems they serve, as well as a society that foolishly reveres them. Mirko Czentovic, the world chess champion, represents the technocrat. His mental energy is invested solely in the sixty-four squares on a chessboard. Apart from the game, he is a dolt, a "momomaniac" like all monomaniacs, who "burrow like termites into their own particular material to construct, in miniature, a strange and utterly individual image of the world." When Czentovic "senses an educated person he crawls into his shell. That way no one will ever be able to boast of having heard him say something stupid or of having plunged the depths of his seemingly boundless ignorance."[8]

An Austrian lawyer known as Dr. B, who had been held by the Gestapo for many months in solitary confinement, challenges Czentovic to a game of chess. During his confinement, the lawyer's only reading material was a chess manual, which he memorized. He reconstructed games in his head. Forced in captivity to replicate the single-minded obsession of the technocrat Czentovic, Dr. B also became trapped inside a specialized world, but unlike Czentovic, he went insane focusing on a tiny, specialized piece of human activity. His insanity returns once he challenges the chess champion.

Zweig, who mourned for the broad liberal culture of educated Europe swallowed up by fascism and modern bureaucracy, warns of the absurdity and danger of a world run by technocrats. For Zweig, the rise of the industrial age and the industrial man and woman is a terrifying metamorphosis in the relationship of human beings to the world. As specialists and bureaucrats, human beings become tools, able to make systems of exploitation and even terror function efficiently without the slightest sense of personal responsibility or understanding. They retreat into the arcane language of all specialists to mask what they are doing and give to their work a sanitized, clinical veneer.

This is Hannah Arendt's central point in *Eichmann in Jerusalem.* Technocratic human beings are spiritually dead. They are capable of anything, no matter how heinous, because they do not reflect upon or question the ultimate goal. "The longer one listened to him," Arendt writes of Eichmann on trial, "the more obvious it became that his inability to speak was closely connected with an inability to *think,* namely, to think from the standpoint of somebody else. No communication was possible with him, not because he lied but because he was surrounded by the most reliable of all safeguards against the words and presence of others, and hence against reality as such."[9]

Zweig, horrified by a world run by technocrats, committed suicide with his wife in 1942. He knew that, from then on, it was the Czentovics who would be exalted in the service of state and corporate monstrosities.

Resistance, as Berkman points out, is first about learning to speak differently and abandoning the vocabulary of the "rational" technocrats who rule. Once we discover new words and ideas through which to perceive and explain reality, we free ourselves from neoliberalism, which functions, as Benjamin knew, like a state religion. This effort will take place outside the boundaries of popular culture and academia, where the deadening weight of the dominant ideology curtails creativity and independent thought.

———

Subcomandante Insurgente Marcos, the spokesman for the Zapatistas (Ejército Zapatista de Liberación Nacional, or EZLN), announced in May 2014 that his rebel persona no longer existed. He had gone, he said, from being a "spokesman to a distraction." His persona had fed an easy and cheap media narrative and turned a social revolution into a cartoon for the mass media, he explained. This persona had allowed the commercial press and the outside world to ignore traditional community leaders and indigenous commanders and wrap a movement around a fictitious personality. His persona, Marcos said, had trivialized a movement.

"The entire system, but above all its media, plays the game of creating celebrities who it later destroys if they don't yield to its designs," Marcos declared.[10]

The Zapatistas formed the most important resistance movement of the last two decades. They were a refreshing departure from the dreary, jargon-filled rhetoric of the Stalinist/Third Worldist sections of the old radical left. The Zapatistas recaptured the language of poetry, art, lyricism, and humor and became a visible counterweight to the despoiling of the planet and the subjugation of the poor by global capitalism. They repeatedly reinvented themselves—as Marcos did—to survive. The Zapatistas gave global resistance movements a new language, drawn in part from the indigenous communal Mayan culture, as well as from the writings of figures such as Eduardo Galeano and Gabriel García Márquez. Offering a new paradigm for action, they understood that corporate capitalism has launched a war against us. And they showed us how to fight back.

"Neoliberalism, this doctrine that makes it possible for stupidity and cynicism to govern in diverse parts of the earth, does not allow for inclusion other than that of subjection to genocide," Marcos wrote in an open letter in May 12, 1995.

"Die as a social group, as a culture, and above all as a resistance. Then you can be part of modernity," say the great capitalists, from the seats of government, to the indigenous campesinos. These indigenous people irritate the modernizing logic of neo-mercantilism. Their rebellion, their defiance, their resistance, irritates them. The anachronism of their existence within a project of globalization, an economic and political project that, soon, will decide that poor people, all the people in opposition, which is to say, the majority of the population, are obstacles. The armed character of "We are here!" of the Zapatista indigenous people does not matter much to them nor does it keep them awake (a little fire and lead will be enough to end such "imprudent" defiance). What matters to them, and bothers them, is that their very existence, in the moment that they [the indigenous Zapatistas] speak out and are heard, is converted into a reminder of an embarrassing omission of "neoliberal modernity": "These Indians should not exist today, we should have put an end to them BEFORE. Now annihilating them will be more difficult, which is to say, more expensive." This is the burden which weighs upon neo-liberalism made government in Mexico.

"Let's resolve the causes of the uprising," say the negotiators of the government (leftists of yesterday, the shamed of today) as if they were saying: "All of you should not exist, all of this is an unfortunate error of modern history." . . . "Let's resolve the causes" is the elegant synonym of "we will eliminate them." For this system which concentrates wealth and power and distributes death and poverty, the campesinos, the in-digenous, do not fit in the plans and projects. They have to be gotten rid of, just like the herons . . . and the eagles . . . have to be gotten rid of.[11]

The Zapatistas began by using violence, but they soon abandoned it for the slow, laborious work of building thirty-two autonomous, self-governing municipalities. Local representatives from the Juntas de Buen Gobierno (Councils of Good Government), which is not rec-ognized by the Mexican government, preside over these independent Zapatista communities. The councils oversee community programs that distribute food, set up clinics and schools, and collect taxes. Resources are for those who live in the communities, not for the corporations that come to exploit them. And in this the Zapatistas allow us to see the future—a future where we have a chance of surviving.

———————

"This figure was created, and now its creators, the Zapatistas, are de-stroying it," Subcomandante Marcos said to roughly 1,000 people who turned out late in the evening of May 24, 2014, in the village of La Realidad for a memorial for a Zapatista teacher, José Luis Solís López, who had been murdered by Mexican paramilitary members. "And we saw that now, the full-size puppet, the character, the hologram, was no longer necessary. Time and time again we planned this, and time and time again we waited for the right moment—the right calendar and geography to show what we really are to those who truly are."[12]

The murder of the teacher—known by his nom de guerre as "Galeano"—three weeks earlier, on May 2, appears to have been part of a drive by a government-allied paramilitary group, CIOAC-H, to assassinate rural Zapatista leaders and destroy the self-governing Zapatista enclaves. The Fray Bartolome Human Rights Center said that fifteen unarmed Zapatista civilians were wounded on May 2. In other attacks that day, a Zapatista clinic was destroyed and a school and three vehicles were damaged.[13]

The address was the first public appearance by Marcos since 2009. In a downpour, he spoke to the crowd into the early hours of May 25. He has been the public face of the Zapatistas since the group emerged as an insurrectionary force on January 1, 1994, in Chiapas, the southernmost state of Mexico. Marcos, who is mestizo rather than Mayan, spoke about his rise as a media figure following the uprising and how the movement had catered to the demands for an identifiable leader by a press that distorts reality to fit into its familiar narratives.

Just a few days later [after the uprising], with the blood of our fallen soldiers still fresh in the city streets, we realized that those from outside did not see us.

Accustomed to looking at the indigenous from above, they did not raise their eyes to look at us.

Accustomed to seeing us humiliated, their heart did not understand our dignified rebellion.

Their eyes were fixed on the only mestizo they saw with a balaclava, that is to say, one they did not look at.

Our bosses told us:

"They only see their own smallness, let's make someone as small as them, so they may see him and through him they may see us."

A complex maneuver of distraction began then, a terrible and marvelous magic trick, a malicious play of the indigenous heart that we are, the indigenous knowledge challenging modernity in one of its bastions: the media.

The character called "Marcos" started then to be built.

The clandestine movement began, like all rebellions, with a handful of idealists.[14]

"When the first group arrived in 1983, 1984, we were in the densest part of the jungle," Marcos said in *Remembering Ten Years of Zapatismo,* a documentary produced by the Chiapas Independent Media Center and Free Speech Radio News. "We are talking about a group of four or five, six people that repeated to themselves every day 'this is the right thing to do,' 'the right thing to do.' There was nothing in the world telling us this was the right thing to do. We were dreaming that someday all of this would be worth something."[15]

Early on January 1, 1994, armed rebels took over five major towns in Chiapas. It was the day the North American Free Trade Agreement (NAFTA) came into effect. The EZLN announced that it no longer recognized the legitimacy of the Mexican government. In denouncing NAFTA as a new vehicle to widen the inequality between the global poor and the rich, the EZLN showed an understanding of free trade agreements that many in the United States lacked. It said it had resorted to violence because peaceful means of protest had failed. The Mexican government, alarmed and surprised, sent several thousand members of the military and police to Chiapas to crush the uprising. The military handed out food to the impoverished peasants. It also detained scores of men. Many were tortured. Some were killed. In twelve days of heavy fighting, about two hundred people died. By February, the Zapatistas, who had hoped to ignite a nationwide revolution and who were reeling under the military assault, agreed to negotiate. Most had retreated into the surrounding jungle. The insurgency, Marcos said at the memorial for his assassinated comrade, had faced a fundamental existential choice at that point:

Should we prepare those who come after us for the path of death?
   Should we develop more and better soldiers?
   Invest our efforts in improving our battered war machine?
   Simulate dialogues and a disposition toward peace while preparing new attacks?
   Kill or die as the only destiny?

Or should we reconstruct the path of life, that which those from above had broken and continue breaking?

. . . Should we have adorned with our blood the path that others have charted to Power, or should we have turned our heart and gazed toward who we are, toward those who are what we are—that is, the indigenous people, guardians of the earth and of memory?

Nobody listened then, but in the first babblings that were our words we made note that our dilemma was not between negotiating and fighting, but between dying and living.

. . . And we chose.

And rather than dedicating ourselves to training guerrillas, soldiers, and squadrons, we developed education and health promoters, who went about building the foundations of autonomy that today amaze the world.

Instead of constructing barracks, improving our weapons, and building walls and trenches, we built schools, hospitals and health centers; improving our living conditions.

Instead of fighting for a place in the Parthenon of individualized deaths of those from below, we chose to construct life.

All this in the midst of a war that was no less lethal because it was silent.[16]

The movement's shift from violence to nonviolent civil disobedience—a shift that also took place within the African National Congress (ANC)—was evidenced during the memorial. Zapatista leaders said they knew the identities of the vigilantes who had carried out the attacks. But those in the crowd were cautioned not to seek vengeance against the killers, who, they were told, had been manipulated to murder in the service of the state. The focus had to remain on dismantling the system of global capitalism itself.

As happened with the ANC half a world away, the shift from violence to nonviolence was what gave the Zapatistas their resiliency and strength. Marcos stressed this point:

Small justice looks so much like revenge. Small justice is what distributes impunity; as it punishes one, it absolves others.

What we want, what we fight for, does not end with finding Galeano's murderers and seeing that they receive their punishment (make no mistake this is what will happen).

The patient and obstinate search seeks truth, not the relief of resignation.

True justice has to do with the buried *compañero* Galeano.

Because we ask ourselves not what do we do with his death, but what do we do with his life.[17]

This transformation by the EZLN is one that is crucial to remember as we search for mechanisms to sever ourselves from the corporate state and build self-governing communities. The goal is not to destroy but to transform. And this is why violence is counterproductive. We too must work to create a radical shift in consciousness. We must, as the Zapatista slogan insisted, "Be a Zapatista wherever you are." And this will take time, drawing larger and larger numbers of people into acts of civil disobedience. We too must work to make citizens aware of the mechanisms of power. An adherence to nonviolence will not save us from the violence of the state or from the state's hired goons and vigilantes. But nonviolence makes conversion, even among our oppressors, possible. And it is conversion that is our goal. As Marcos said:

Maybe it's true. Maybe we were wrong in choosing to cultivate life instead of worshipping death.

But we made the choice without listening to those on the outside. Without listening to those who always demand and insist on a fight to the death, as long as others will be the ones to do the dying.

We made the choice while looking and listening inward, as the collective Votán that we are.

We chose rebellion, that is to say, life.[18]

———

It was a brisk February morning in Oxford, England, when I left the Macdonald Randolph Hotel, a stately Victorian Gothic building, on Beaumont Street. I walked along the narrow cobblestone streets, past the storied colleges with resplendent lawns and Gothic stone spires, to meet Avner Offer, an economic historian and Chichele Professor Emeritus of Economic History at Oxford University.

Offer, author of *The Challenge of Affluence: Self-control and Well-being in the United States and Britain Since 1950* (2006), has explored for twenty-five years the cavernous gap between our economic and social reality and our ruling economic ideology. According to Offer, our ideology of neoclassical economics—the belief that, as E. Roy Weintraub wrote, "people have rational choices among outcomes" that can be identified and associated with values, that "individuals maximize utility and firms maximize profits," and that "people act independently on the basis of full and relevant information"—is a *"just-world" theory.*[19] "A just-world theory posits that the world is just. People get what they deserve. If you believe that the world is fair, you explain or rationalize away injustice, usually by blaming the victim."

But, he warned, if we continue down a path of mounting scarcities, along with economic stagnation and decline, this neoclassical model becomes ominous.

"Major ways of thinking about the world constitute just-world theories," he said. "The Catholic Church is a just-world theory. If the Inquisition burned heretics, they only got what they deserved. Bolshevism was a just-world theory. If Kulaks were starved and exiled, they got what they deserved. Fascism was a just-world theory. If Jews died in the concentration camps, they got what they deserved. The point is not that the good people get the good things, but the bad people get the bad things. Neoclassical economics, our principal source of policy norms, is a just-world theory."

Offer quoted the economist Milton Friedman: "The ethical principle that would directly justify the distribution of income in a free market society is, 'To each according to what he and the instruments he owns produces.'"

"So," Offer went on, "everyone gets what he or she deserves, either for his or her effort or for his or her property. No one asks how he or she got this property. And if they don't have it, they probably don't deserve it. The point about just-world theory is not that it dispenses justice, but that it provides a warrant for inflicting pain."

Offer, a transplanted Israeli who came to Oxford after serving as a soldier in the 1967 war, said that the effectiveness of an ideology is measured by the amount of coercion it takes to keep a ruling elite in power. Reality, when it does not conform to the reigning ideology, he said, has to be "forcibly aligned." The amount of coercion needed to make society adhere to the model is "a rough measure of the model's validity."

"That the Soviet Union had to use so much coercion undermined the credibility of communism as a model of reality," he said. "It is perhaps symptomatic that the USA, a society that elevates freedom to the highest position among its values, is also the one that has one of the very largest penal systems in the world relative to its population. It also inflicts violence all over the world. It tolerates a great deal of gun violence, and a health service that excludes large numbers of people."

As larger and larger segments of society are forced because of declining economies to become outsiders, the use of coercion, under our current model, will probably become more widespread.

"There are two core doctrines in economics," Offer said. "One is individual self-interest. The other is the invisible hand, the idea that the pursuit of individual self-interest aggregates or builds up for the good of society as a whole. This is a logical proposition that has never been proven. If we take the centrality of self-interest in economics, then it is not clear on what basis economics should be promoting the public good. This is not a norm that is part of economics itself; in fact, economics tells us the opposite. Economics tells us that everything anyone says should be motivated by strategic self-interest. And when economists use the word 'strategic,' they mean cheating."

Offer argued that "a silent revolution" took place in economics in the 1970s. That was a time when "economists discovered opportunism—a polite term for cheating," he said. "Before that, economics had been a just-world defense of the status quo. But when the status quo became the welfare state, suddenly economics became all about cheating. Game theory was about cheating. Public-choice theory was about cheating. Asymmetric information was about cheating. The invisible-hand doctrine tells us there is only one outcome, and that outcome is the best. But once you enter a world of cheating, there is no longer one outcome. It is what economists call 'multiple equilibria,' which means there is not a deterministic outcome. The outcome depends on how successful the cheating is. And one of the consequences of this is that economists are not in a strong position to tell society what to do."

The problem, he said, is that the old norms of economics continue to inform our policies, as if the cheating norm had never been introduced.

"Let's take the doctrine of optimal taxation," he said. "If you assume a world of perfect competition, where every person gets their marginal products, then you can deduce a tax distribution where high progressive taxation is inefficient. This doctrine has been one of the drivers to reduce progressive taxation. But looking at the historical record, this has not been accompanied by any great surge in productivity; rather, it has produced a great surge in inequality. So once again, there is a gap between what the model tells us should happen and what actually happens. In this case, the model works, but only in the model—only if all the assumptions are satisfied. Reality is more complicated."

Offer brought up one of the issues to consider: "When those in authority, whether political, academic, or civic, are expounding their doctrines through Enlightenment idioms . . . we must ask, is this being done in good faith? And here I think the genuine insight provided by the economics of opportunism is that we cannot assume it is being done in good faith."

According to Offer, "economics, political science, and even philosophy, ever since rational choice swept through the American social sciences, have embraced the idea that an individual has no responsibility towards anyone except himself or herself. A responsibility to anyone else is optional. The public discourse, for this reason, has become a hall of mirrors."

Our current economic model, he said, will be of little use to us in an age of ecological deterioration and growing scarcities. Energy shortages, global warming, population increases, and increasing scarceness of water and food will create an urgent need for new models of distribution. Our two options, he said, will be "hanging together or falling apart." Offer argues that we cannot be certain that growth will continue. If standards of living stagnate or decline, he said, we must consider other models for the economy.

Offer, who studied the rationing systems set up in the countries that took part in World War I, suggested that we examine how past societies coped successfully with scarcity. He held up these war economies, with their heavy rationing, as a possible model for collective action in a contracting economy. In an age of scarcity, it will be imperative to set up new, more egalitarian models of distribution. Clinging to the old neoclassical model, he argued, could erode and perhaps destroy social cohesion and require the state to engage in greater forms of coercion.

"What you had [in World War I] was a very sudden transition to a serious scarcity economy that was underpinned by the necessity for sharing," he said. "Ordinary people were required to sacrifice their lives. They needed some guarantee for those they left at home. These war economies were relatively egalitarian. These economics were based on the safety net principle. If continued growth in the medium run is not feasible, and that is a contingency we need to think about, then these rationing societies provide quite a successful model. On the Allied side, people did not starve, society held together."

Adam Smith, he noted, "wrote that what drives us is not, in the end, individual selfishness but reciprocal obligation. We care about other people's good opinions. This generates a reciprocal cycle. Reciprocity is not altruistic. That part of the economic core doctrine is preserved. But if we depend on other people for our self-worth, then we are not truly self-sufficient. We depend on the sympathy of others for our own well-being. Therefore, obligation to others means that we do not always seek to maximize economic advantage. Intrinsic motivations, such as obligation, compassion, and public spirit, crowd out financial ones. This model can also motivate a different type of political and economic aspiration."

However, if we cling to our current economic model—which Offer labels "every man for himself"—then, he said, "it will require serious repression."

He concluded: "There is not a free market solution to a peaceful decline."

———

The revolutionary theorists of the past invested tremendous energy in looking for the triggers of revolt, although nearly all were caught off guard by the eruption of the revolutions they championed and organized. Lenin said in January 1917, six weeks before the revolution that would bring him to power: "We of the older generation may not see the decisive battles of this coming revolution." It is impossible, as Lenin discovered, to "predict the time and progress of revolution. It is governed by its own more or less mysterious laws. But when it comes, it moves irresistibly."[20]

"The history of human thought recalls the swinging of a pendulum which takes centuries to swing," the Russian anarchist Peter Kropotkin said.

> After a long period of slumber comes a moment of awakening. Then thought frees herself from the chains with which those interested— rulers, lawyers, clerics—have carefully enwound her. She shatters the chains. She subjects to severe criticism all that has been taught her, and lays bare the emptiness of the religious, political, legal, and social prejudices amid which she has vegetated. She starts research in new paths, enriches our knowledge with new discoveries, creates new sciences. But the inveterate enemies of thought—the government, the lawgiver, and the priest—soon recover from their defeat. By degrees they gather together their scattered forces, and remodel their faith and their code of laws to adapt them to the new needs.[21]

Lenin placed his faith in a violent uprising, in a professional, disciplined revolutionary vanguard freed from moral constraints, and (like Marx) in the inevitable emergence of the workers' state. Pierre-Joseph Proudhon insisted that gradual change would be accomplished as enlightened workers took over production and educated and converted the rest of the proletariat. Mikhail Bakunin predicted the catastrophic breakdown of the capitalist order—something we are likely to witness in our lifetimes—and new autonomous worker federations rising up out of the chaos. Kropotkin, like Proudhon, believed in an evolutionary process that would hammer out the new society.[22]

Emma Goldman, along with Kropotkin, came to be very wary of both the efficacy of violence and the revolutionary potential of the masses. "The mass," Goldman wrote bitterly, echoing Marx, "clings to its masters, loves the whip, and is the first to cry Crucify!"[23]

The revolutionists of history counted on a mobilized base of enlightened industrial workers or common laborers. The building blocks of revolt, they believed, relied on the tool of the general strike—the ability of workers to cripple the mechanisms of production. Strikes could be sustained with the support of political parties, strike funds, and union halls. Workers without these support mechanisms had to replicate the infrastructure of parties and unions if they wanted to put prolonged pressure on the bosses and the state. But today, with the decimation of the US manufacturing base and the dismantling of our unions and opposition parties, we will have to search for different instruments of rebellion, as Lynne Stewart correctly observed.

Our family farms have been destroyed by agro-businesses, and most manufacturing jobs have disappeared as our manufacturing base has moved overseas; of those that remain, fewer than 12 percent are unionized.[24] Unlike past revolutionary struggles in industrial societies, we cannot rely today on the industrial or agrarian muscle of workers. The dispossessed working poor, along with unemployed college graduates and students and unemployed journalists, artists, lawyers, and teachers, will form our movement, while workers in Asia and the global south— where our manufacturing is now located—will have to organize and fight the industrialists through the traditional tactics of strikes, work stoppages, and unionizing. The fight for a higher minimum wage is crucial to uniting service workers with the alienated college-educated sons and daughters of the old middle class in the United States. Bakunin would have recognized these pivotal déclassé intellectuals in the Occupy movement.

Once they unite, those who have had their expectations dashed and concluded that they will not be able to rise economically and socially will become our triggers of revolt. This consciousness is part of the self-knowledge of service workers and fast-food workers. It is also part of the consciousness of the swelling population of college graduates caught in a vise of low-paying jobs and obscene amounts of debt.

Many of the urban poor have been crippled and broken by a rewriting of laws, especially drug laws, that has permitted courts, probation officers, parole boards, and police to randomly seize poor people of color, especially African American men, without just cause and lock them in cages for years. In many of our most impoverished urban centers—our "internal colonies," as Malcolm X called them—mobilization will be difficult. Many African Americans, especially the urban poor, are in prison, on probation, or living under some kind of legal restraint. Charges can be stacked against them, and they have little hope for redress in the courts, especially as 97 percent of all federal cases and 94 percent of all state cases are resolved by guilty pleas rather than trials. A *New York Times* editorial recently said that the pressure employed by state and federal prosecutors to make defendants accept guilty pleas, which often include waiving the right to appeal to a higher court, is "closer to coercion" than to bargaining.[25]

Poor people of color are subject to daily abuse by omnipotent police forces. Police are permitted to strip them of their most basic rights and are either authorized to use deadly force or protected by their departments and the legal system in most cases when they do, even against unarmed suspects. The law professor Michelle Alexander, author of *The New Jim Crow: Mass Incarceration in the Age of Colorblindness,* argues that we have created a criminal "caste system." This caste system controls the lives of not only the 2.3 million people who are incarcerated but the 4.8 million people on probation or parole.[26] Millions more people are forced into "permanent second-class citizenship" by their criminal records, which make employment, higher education, and public assistance difficult or impossible.[27]

A Department of Defense program known as "1033," begun in the 1990s and authorized by the National Defense Authorization Act, and federal homeland security grants to the states have provided a total of $4.3 billion in military equipment to local police forces, either for free or on permanent loan, the magazine *Mother Jones* reported. The militarization of the police, which includes outfitting police departments with heavy machine guns, magazines, night vision equipment, aircraft, and armored vehicles, has effectively turned urban police, and increasingly rural police as well, into quasi-military forces of occupation. "Police conduct up to 80,000 SWAT raids a year in the US, up from 3,000 a year in the early '80s," writes Hanqing Chen, the magazine's reporter. The American Civil Liberties Union, cited in the article, found that "almost 80 percent of SWAT team raids are linked to search warrants to investigate potential criminal suspects, not for high-stakes 'hostage, barricade, or active shooter scenarios.' The ACLU also noted that SWAT tactics are used disproportionately against people of color."[28]

The urban poor are already in chains. These chains are being readied for the rest of us.

Maria J. Stephan and Erica Chenoweth examine 100 years of violent and nonviolent resistance movements in their 2008 article "Why Civil Resistance Works: The Strategic Logic of Nonviolent Conflict." They conclude that nonviolent movements succeed twice as often as violent uprisings. Nonviolent movements appeal to those employed within the power structure, especially the police and civil servants, who are cognizant of the corruption and decadence of the power elite and are willing to abandon them. And, the authors point out, with as little as 3.5 percent of the population who are organized and disciplined, it is possible to bring down even the most ruthless totalitarian structures.

While governments "easily justify violent counterattacks against armed insurgents, regime violence against nonviolent movements is more likely to backfire against the regime," Stephan and Chenoweth write. "Potentially sympathetic publics perceive violent militants as having maximalist or extremist goals beyond accommodation, but they perceive nonviolent resistance groups as less extreme, thereby enhancing their appeal and facilitating the extraction of concessions through bargaining."[29]

The ability to draw those within the systems of power into the movement creates paralysis and crippling divisions within the ruling elite. And this is fundamental to all successful revolts. "Internally, members of a regime—including civil servants, security forces, and members of the judiciary—are more likely to shift loyalty toward nonviolent opposition groups than toward violent opposition groups," they write.

> The coercive power of any resistance campaign is enhanced by its tendency to prompt disobedience and defections by members of the opponent's security forces, who are more likely to consider the negative

political and personal consequences of using repressive violence against unarmed demonstrators than against armed insurgents. Divisions are more likely to result among erstwhile regime supporters, who are not as prepared to deal with mass civil resistance as they are with armed insurgents. Regime repression can also backfire through increased public mobilization. Actively involving a relatively larger number of people in the nonviolent campaign may bring greater and more sustained pressure to bear on the target, whereas the public may eschew violent insurgencies because of physical or moral barriers.[30]

Although it appears, as I write this book, that political ferment is dormant in the United States, this is incorrect. Revolutions, when they erupt, are to the wider public sudden and unexpected, because the real work of revolutionary ferment and consciousness is, as Berkman observed, invisible. Revolutions expose their face only after revolutionary ferment has largely been completed.

Throughout history, those who have sought radical change have always had to begin by discrediting the ideas used to prop up ruling elites and constructing alternative ideas and language. Once ideas shift for a large portion of a population, once the vision of a new society grips the popular imagination, once the old vocabulary no longer holds currency, the power elite is finished, although outwardly it may appear that nothing has changed. But this process is difficult to see and often takes years. Those in power are completely unaware that the shift is taking place. They will speak, like all dying elites, in the old language until they finally become figures of ridicule.

In the United States today, no person or movement can program the ignition of this tinder. No one knows where or when the eruption will take place. No one knows the form it will take. But a popular revolt is coming. The refusal by the corporate state to address even the minimal grievances of the citizenry, its abject failure to remedy the mounting state repression, the chronic unemployment and underemployment and the massive debt peonage[31] that is crippling millions of Americans, and the widespread despair and loss of hope, along with the collapse of institutions meant to carry piecemeal and incremental reforms, including the courts, make blowback inevitable.

"Because revolution is evolution at its boiling point you cannot 'make' a real revolution any more than you can hasten the boiling of a tea kettle," Berkman wrote. "It is the fire underneath that makes it boil: how quickly it will come to the boiling point will depend on how strong the fire is."[32]

If a nonviolent popular movement is able to ideologically disarm the bureaucrats, civil servants, and police—to get them, in essence, to defect—nonviolent revolution is possible. But if the state can organize effective and prolonged violence against dissent, then state violence can spawn reactive revolutionary violence, or what the state calls "terrorism." Violent uprisings are always tragic, and violent revolutions always empower revolutionaries, such as Lenin and the Bolsheviks, who are as ruthless as their adversaries. Violence inevitably becomes the principal form of coercion on both sides of the divide. Social upheaval without clear definition and direction, without ideas behind it, swiftly descends into nihilism, terrorism, and chaos. It consumes itself. This is the minefield we will have to cross.

"[The] tyrant and his subjects are in somewhat symmetrical positions," wrote Thomas Schelling.

> They can deny him most of what he wants—they can, that is, if they have the disciplined organization to refuse collaboration. And he can deny them just about everything they want—he can deny it by using force at his command. . . . They can deny him the satisfaction of ruling a disciplined country, he can deny them the satisfaction of ruling themselves. . . . It is a bargaining situation in which either side, if adequately disciplined and organized, can deny most of what the other wants, and it remains to see who wins.[33]

By the time ruling elites are openly defied, there has already been a nearly total loss of faith in the ideas—in our case, neoclassical economics and globalization—that sustain their structures of power. The process of understanding this can take years, but once people do understand it, "the slow, quiet, and peaceful social evolution becomes quick, militant, and violent," as Berkman explained. "Evolution becomes revolution."[34]

I prefer the gradual reforms of a functioning, liberal democracy. I fear the process of massive social engineering. I detest the poison of violence. I would rather live in a system in which our social institutions permit the citizenry to nonviolently dismiss those in authority and promote the common good, a system in which institutions are independent and not captive to corporate power. But we do not live in such a system. We live in a system that is incapable of reforming itself. The first step to dismantling that system is to dismantle the ideas that give it legitimacy. Once that is done, though the system may be able to cling to power through coercion and fear for years, it will have been given a mortal blow.

"Many ideas, once held to be true, have come to be regarded as wrong and evil," Berkman wrote.

Thus the ideas of the divine right of kings, of slavery and serfdom. There was a time when the whole world believed those institutions to be right, just, and unchangeable. In the measure that those superstitions and false beliefs were fought by advanced thinkers, they became discredited and lost their hold upon the people, and finally the institutions that incorporated those ideas were abolished. Highbrows will tell you that they had "outlived their usefulness" and therefore they "died." But how did they "outlive" their "usefulness"? To whom were they useful, and how did they "die"? We know already that they were useful only to the master class, and they were done away with by popular uprisings and revolutions.[35]

IV/Conversion

Independence is my happiness, and I view things as they are, without regard to place or person; my country is the world, and my religion is to do good.[1]

—THOMAS PAINE, *THE RIGHTS OF MAN*

Ronnie Kasrils, white, middle-class, and Jewish, was working as a twenty-two-year-old scriptwriter for a South African film company called Alpha Film Studios in March 1960 when the Sharpeville Massacre took place. Sixty-nine unarmed blacks who had been protesting the apartheid regime's restrictive pass laws were gunned down by white South African police, with 180 seriously wounded.[2] Many were shot in the back as they fled.[3]

He approached some black workers at the studio to commiserate. They told him: "This is South Africa. *Amapoyisa yi'zinja.* [The police are dogs]." Groups of white English and Afrikaans were also gathering in separate groups. The massacre, everyone knew, signaled the start of a new phase in blacks' battle for liberation in apartheid South Africa. One of the white men told Kasrils: "*Moe'nie* [Don't] worry, mate, you'll be in the trenches with the rest of us. *Ons wit ous* [us white guys] have to sink or swim together."[4]

But his white coworkers were wrong. Something snapped in Kasrils. He underwent a conversion—the rite of passage of all revolutionaries. During the next few days, he argued passionately with family and friends about the gross injustice that had taken place, but found that "outside my immediate circle, few whites showed any sensitivity—the general view being: 'we should machinegun the lot of them.'"[5]

He watched enraged blacks burn their passbooks in defiance and get arrested. The apartheid government declared a state of emergency. It outlawed the African National Congress (ANC) and its rival, the Pan African Congress (PAC). British-made Saracen armored cars, with their mounted .30 caliber machine guns, rumbled down the streets of the Alexandra Township, where most of the black workers at the film studio lived. Kasrils was no longer able to be a passive accomplice in a system of such gross injustice. He took time off from his job and went to Durban, where he met Rowley Arenstein, a radical lawyer who was being hunted by the police. Arenstein urged Kasrils to join what he called "the movement," predicting that the ruling National Party government would not last six more months in power—a prediction that was off by three decades. Kasrils became Arenstein's driver. He chauffeured the lawyer to various safe houses around Durban. He met others also being hunted by the police.

Kasrils returned to his job, but at night he drafted and printed leaflets for the underground movement calling for the release of all detainees, the lifting of the state of emergency, and a democratic government for blacks and whites. He painted anti-apartheid slogans on walls at night. He eventually committed himself totally to the struggle. Turning his back on his job, his class, his government, and his race, Kasrils joined the South African Communist Party and the African National Congress. He became a founding member, along with Nelson Mandela, of Umkhonto we Sizwe (MK), or Spear of the Nation, the armed wing of the ANC. Kasrils became a rebel.

Such a decision to engage in open defiance, abandoning all that is safe, familiar, and secure for a precarious life of resistance, is often triggered by a singular traumatic experience. Lenin was radicalized when his older brother, Aleksandr Ilyich Ulyanov, was executed after being involved in a plot to assassinate the Czar and he began to read his dead brother's radical books.[6] The trip taken by the twenty-two-year-old medical student Ernesto "Che" Guevara—like Kasrils and Lenin, a member of the middle class—into the poor backwaters of South America allowed him to place himself in the shoes of the oppressed. Such conversions have more to do with the heart than the head. Empathy is the most important asset. Guevara, like Kasrils and Lenin, would use his empathy to justify violence—a dangerous transformation when all action, even murder, becomes acceptable in the name of the coming utopia. But the sentiments engendered at the moment of conversion are real. Albert Camus said that no rebellion can take place without this "strange form of love."[7]

When I met with Kasrils in New York, he spoke of an incident in 1984 involving a South African death squad led by the notorious killer and former police colonel Eugene de Kock. De Kock was the commanding officer of C1, a counterinsurgency unit of the South African police that in the 1980s and 1990s kidnapped, tortured, and murdered hundreds of anti-apartheid activists and ANC leaders. He and his hit squad had recently assassinated three of Kasrils's ANC comrades. Kasrils tracked de Kock, nicknamed "Prime Evil"—and now serving a life sentence in South Africa—and his squad of killers to a motel in Swaziland. Kasrils organized a group of ANC insurgents to gun down the members of the hit squad. De Kock and his men had left, however, before Kasrils and his armed group burst into the room where they had been. I asked Kasrils whether, should the situation be repeated today, he would organize an armed group to kill de Kock and his henchmen.

"I see this as similar to the French Resistance and the resistance in Europe against the Nazis," he said. "So, you know there were the battles in the open, but most of the battles were by stealth. I don't think there's anything morally wrong in the battle of stealth against power when you are engaged in a war. They had killed, murdered in cold blood, three of our people in Swaziland. You've got to take harsh decisions at times, and this is in the context of an ongoing war there. . . . I put it within the context of a revolutionary war."

Nevertheless, he said that "when I look back and I meet some of these people who we fought before, and I hear from them how they knew someone who died, I wish that that person didn't have to die."

Kasrils served as the commander of the Natal Regional Command and in 1964 underwent military training in Odessa in the Soviet Union. As a leader in the MK, Kasrils carried out sabotage and bombings of state infrastructure and industrial sites. The attacks took an inevitable toll on unarmed white civilians. A 1983 MK guerrilla attack left nine-teen dead. A 1986 raid killed three and injured seventy-three.[8] Kasrils was unrepentant. Blacks, he pointed out, paid a far higher price. Tens of thousands were slaughtered by the apartheid state.

Kasrils, a stocky bull of a man, argued that all rebels are driven by an instinctive compassion, concern for others, and a tendency toward "standing up for the underdog." These impulses are often present in children, he said, but they are muted or crushed by the institutions of social control, including the family and school. Kasrils, although an atheist, said he saw the rebel in Jesus Christ, as well as in the thunderous denunciations of evil and oppression by the Hebrew prophets of the Bible. He said that those who endure oppression, such as Mandela, and rise up to resist are better described as revolutionaries. The rebel, he said, is one who often enjoys certain "liberties" but who is "prepared to give up his class or her class, or tribe." Rebels, he said, turn their back on their own.

Kasrils spoke about a discussion he had on the nature of the rebel with Jack Simons, a retired university professor who was teaching ANC recruits in Angola and who had been a leader in the South African Communist Party before it was outlawed in 1950.

"Unconventional thought is a force for development," Simons told Kasrils. "It is wrong to suppress it. The likes of you and I were thrown to the lions in Roman times and burnt at the stake in the Middle Ages as heretics."

It was in post-apartheid South Africa that Kasrils fully realized Si-mons's wisdom. Kasrils's relentless quest for political and economic justice eventually turned him into a fierce critic of the two organiza-tions to which he had dedicated himself for fifty years—the African National Congress and the Communist Party. The failure of these two organizations to ameliorate the suffering of the poor, the rampant cor-ruption that he said exists within the leadership of the ANC, and the Marikana Massacre of 2012, in which thirty-four striking miners were gunned down by the South African Police Service—the country's most lethal single assault on unarmed civilians since the 1960 Sharpeville massacre—left him alienated, once again, from the centers of power.[9]

Camus observed that "every revolutionary [who achieves power] ends by becoming either an oppressor or a heretic."[10]

"I have to speak up," Kasrils said. "It's deep within me."

Kasrils said that the ANC's fatal mistake, which he concedes was partly his fault, was its decision during the transition to power in 1994 to shelve its socialist economic agenda, known as the Freedom Charter. Written in 1955, the charter had wide popular appeal. It demanded the end of the exploitation by the white oligarchic elite, who treated black laborers as serfs on farms, in mines, and on factory floors. It called for the right to work, freedom of expression, access to decent housing and land for all South Africans, and the sharing of South African wealth, especially its mineral resources. Banks, industries, and mines were to be nationalized.

Kasrils and other ANC leaders believed that they could deal with economic injustice later. They were fearful of defying Western imperialism and, as Kasrils put it, "neoliberal global economy market fundamentals." But the ANC's capitulation to global pressure to adopt a free market economy has proved to be a disaster. South Africa continues to be one of the most unequal societies on the planet. Whites, although they number less than 10 percent of the nation's population, earn 7.7 times more on average than their black counterparts. Only a few thousand of the country's 41 million blacks earn more than $5,000 a year. It is apartheid by another name.[11] "[A] true rebel would not have accepted that," Kasrils said.

———

The goal of the counterrevolutionary is to physically eradicate the insurgents' logistical base of operations, disrupt their communication, and shatter their organization. Counterrevolutionaries seek to dry up popular, financial, and material support for the revolutionaries. They hunt down and decapitate leaders. Counterrevolutionaries create rival organizations to discredit and purge the rebel leadership and infiltrate the movement to foster internal divisions and rivalries. They provoke the movement by forming front groups that carry out repugnant acts to

alienate the wider populace from the insurgency. Meanwhile, the counterrevolutionaries churn out shadowy propaganda that the mainstream
press often runs uncritically. Finally, they offer a political alternative
that appears reformist but is ultimately under the control of the state.

The tools to break resistance are similar whether those movements
are violent or nonviolent. The physical eradication of the Occupy encampments, the attempt to marginalize the protesters from the wider
society, the use of figures such as Anthony Kapel "Van" Jones to co-opt
the language of the Occupy movement and funnel energy into a dys-
functional electoral process—all these strategies fit the classic outline of
a counterrevolutionary agenda.

Counterinsurgency campaigns, although they involve arms and
weapons, are primarily, as in the old cliché, about hearts and minds.
The goal is to win back, or at least render passive, a disaffected population. And the tactics employed by our intelligence operatives abroad
are not dissimilar from those employed by our intelligence operatives at
home. In fact, these operatives are frequently the same people.

But once violence is added to the mix, whether to defend the state or
destroy it, something poisonous and insidious takes place. Violence is directed against society not to convert but to eradicate. All aspects of civic
life are targeted—political, religious, educational, familial, economic,
and traditional. The goal—as we see in Iraq and Afghanistan—is not to
control territory but to control populations. Terror, assassination, imprisonment, and death become the glue that replaces the tissue of social
cohesion. Society is mutilated. Civic life is destroyed. And in wartime
each side uses violence to attempt to shape civil society to its own ends.

We do not have the tools or the wealth of the state. We cannot beat
it at its own game. We cannot ferret out infiltrators. The legal system is
almost always on the state's side. If we attempt to replicate the elaborate
security apparatus of our oppressors, even on a small scale, we unleash
paranoia and fracture those who build movements. If we retreat into anonymity, hiding behind masks, then we provide an opening for *agents
provocateurs* who deny their identities while disrupting the movement.
If we fight pitched battles in the streets, we give authorities an excuse to
fire their weapons and demonize the movement to the public.

All we have, as Vaclav Havel wrote, is our powerlessness. And that powerlessness is our strength. The ability of the movement to overthrow the corporate state depends on embracing this powerlessness. It depends on two of our most important assets—utter and complete transparency, and a rigid adherence to nonviolence, including respect for private property. These assets permit us, as Havel puts it in his classic 1978 essay "The Power of the Powerless," to live in truth. And by living in truth, we expose a corrupt corporate state that perpetrates lies and functions by deceit.

Havel, who would become the first president of the Czech Republic in 1993, reflects in the essay on the mind of a greengrocer who, as instructed, puts up a poster "among the onions and carrots" that reads: "Workers of the World, Unite!" He displays the poster partly out of habit, partly because everyone else is doing it, and partly out of fear of the consequences for not following the rules. Havel notes that the greengrocer would not display a poster saying, "I am afraid and therefore unquestioningly obedient."[12] This, for Havel, was the difference between the terror of a Joseph Stalin or an Adolf Hitler and the collective charade between the rulers and the ruled that by the 1970s had gripped Communist Czechoslovakia.

"Imagine that one day something in our greengrocer snaps and he stops putting up the slogans merely to ingratiate himself," Havel writes.

> He stops voting in elections he knows are a farce. He begins to say what he really thinks at political meetings. And he even finds the strength in himself to express solidarity with those whom his conscience commands him to support. In this revolt the greengrocer steps out of living within the lie. He rejects the ritual and breaks the rules of the game. He discovers once more his suppressed identity and dignity. He gives his freedom a concrete significance. His revolt is an attempt to live within the truth.[13]

This attempt to "live within the truth" brings with it ostracism and retribution. Punishment, Havel points out, is imposed in bankrupt systems because of the necessity for compliance, not out of any genuine conviction. And the real crime committed is not the crime of speaking out or defying the rules, but the crime of exposing the charade. "By breaking the rules of the game, he has disrupted the game as such, he has exposed it as a mere game," Havel says of his greengrocer.

> He has shattered the world of appearances, the fundamental pillar of the system. He has upset the power structure by tearing apart what holds it together. He has demonstrated that living a lie is living a lie. He has broken through the exalted facade of the system and exposed the real, base foundations of power. He has said that the emperor is naked. And because the emperor is in fact naked, something extremely dangerous has happened: by his action, the greengrocer has addressed the world. He has enabled everyone to peer behind the curtain. He has shown everyone that it is possible to live within the truth. Living within the lie can constitute the system only if it is universal. The principle must embrace and permeate everything. There are no terms whatsoever on which it can coexist with living within the truth, and therefore everyone who steps out of line *denies it in principle and threatens it in its entirety.*[14]

Those who do not carve out spaces separate from the state and its systems of power, those who cannot find room to become autonomous, or who do not "live in truth," inevitably become compromised. Kasrils understood this during the Sharpeville Massacre. By refusing to act, he was part of the system of oppression.

Movements that call on followers to "live in truth" do not always succeed. They failed in Nicaragua, El Salvador, and Guatemala in the 1970s and 1980s, as well as in Yugoslavia in the 1990s, triggering armed insurgencies and blood-drenched civil wars. They have failed so far in Iran, the Israeli-occupied territories, and Syria. China has a movement modeled after Havel's Charter 77—which was formed in 1977 to pressure the Czech government to abide by human rights guarantees enshrined in the Constitution and honor international human rights accords that the Communist government had signed—called Charter 08. But the Chinese opposition to the state has been effectively suppressed, even though its principal author, Liu Xiaobo—currently serving an eleven-year prison term for "incitement of subversion of state power"[15]—was awarded the 2010 Nobel Peace Prize.[16]

Power elites who stubbornly refuse to heed popular will and resort to harsher and harsher forms of state control provoke counterviolence. The first Palestinian uprising, which lasted from 1987 to 1992, saw crowds of demonstrators throw rocks at Israeli soldiers, but it was largely a nonviolent movement. The second uprising, or intifada, which erupted in 2000 and endured for five years, included armed attacks on Israeli soldiers and civilians. And the clashes during the summer of 2014 saw Hamas launching rockets into Israel from Gaza and carrying out armed assaults in Israeli territory via tunnels it had constructed. History is dotted with brutal fratricides spawned by calcified and repressive regimes that ignored the legitimate grievances of their citizens and continued to visit injustices upon them—or in the case of Israel, upon the people it occupies and whose peaceful protests it crushes.

A resistance movement's most powerful asset, however, is that it articulates a fundamental truth. As this truth is understood by the mainstream—"the 99 percent"—it gathers a force that jeopardizes the credibility of ruling elites. If the resistance movement is effectively severed from the mainstream—which is the primary goal of the counterinsurgency effort by the Department of Homeland Security, city police departments, and the FBI—it is crippled and easily contained. Other, more militant groups may rise and even flourish, but if a mass movement is to retain its hold over the majority, it has to fight within self-imposed limitations of nonviolence.

"We would not have a movement if violence or property damage were used from the outset," Kevin Zeese, one of the first activists to call for an Occupy movement, told me. "People are not drawn to violent movement[s]. Such tactics will shrink rather than expand our base of support. Property damage justifies police violence to many Americans. There is a wide range of diversity of tactics within a nonviolent strategy. Disciplined nonviolence is often more difficult because anger and emotion lead people to want to strike back at the police when they are violent, but disciplined nonviolence is the tactic that is most effective against the violence of the state."

The organizer Lisa Fithian is one of the authors of a concise argument for nonviolence, "An Open Letter to the Occupy Movement." The essay points out that without agreements that enshrine nonviolence, "the young [are privileged] over the old, the loud voices over the soft, the fast over the slow, the able-bodied over those with disabilities, the citizen over the immigrant, white folks over people of color, those who can do damage and flee the scene over those who are left to face the consequences."[17]

Of the slogan used by the Black Bloc anarchists, Fithian and her coauthors write: "'Diversity of tactics' becomes an easy way to avoid wrestling with questions of strategy and accountability. It lets us off the hook from doing the hard work of debating our positions and coming to agreements about how we want to act together. It becomes a code for 'anything goes,' and makes it impossible for our movements to hold anyone accountable for their actions.

"The Occupy movement includes people from a broad diversity of backgrounds, life experiences and political philosophies," the article goes on. "Some of us want to reform the system and some of us want to tear it down and replace it with something better. Our one great point of agreement is our call for transparency and accountability. We stand against the corrupt institutions that broker power behind closed doors. We call to account the financial manipulators that have bilked billions out of the poor and the middle classes.

"Just as we call for accountability and transparency, we ourselves must be accountable and transparent," the authors write. "Some tactics are incompatible with those goals, even if in other situations they might be useful, honorable or appropriate. We can't be transparent behind masks. We can't be accountable for actions we run away from. We can't maintain the security culture necessary for planning and carrying out attacks on property and also maintain the openness that can continue to invite in a true diversity of new people. We can't make alliances with groups from impacted communities, such as immigrants, if we can't make agreements about what tactics we will employ in any given action."[18]

By the 1980s, Mandela and the ANC leadership had recognized that as the struggle against apartheid evolved, it was the strikes and boycotts, along with the organizing work by nonviolent groups such as the United Democratic Front (UDF), the ANC's political wing, that were the best instruments for crippling the apartheid regime. The ANC's tiny rebel bands were increasingly ineffectual. South Africa heavily patrolled its borders and stymied most cross-border infiltrations and attacks. Armed attacks frightened white liberals—who were natural allies in the anti-apartheid movement—and were used by the apartheid regime to justify state violence. It was the growing use of "noncooperation" by the black majority that brought the economic engines of the country to a halt.

The tactic of nonviolent protest also garnered support from the international community, which eventually imposed sanctions. If the ANC had invested all its energy in an armed movement rather than mass mobilization, it would have never triumphed. Mandela, although he never renounced violence, understood by this time that the movement had become a civil insurrection rather than an armed insurrection. And it was this transformation—and his ability as a leader to recognize and respect the transformation—that allowed the movement to triumph.

Mandela was open about the inner moral struggle that accompanied his foray into violence and then his retreat from violence. In an excerpt from a 1979 letter to his former wife Winnie, included in his last book, *Conversations with Myself*, he wrote:

Habits die hard and they leave their unmistakable marks, the invisible scars that are engraved in our bones and that flow in our blood, that do havoc to the principal actors beyond repair. . . . Such scars portray people as they are and bring out into the full glare of public scrutiny the embarrassing contradictions in which individuals live out their lives.

We are told that a saint is a sinner who keeps on trying to be clean. One may be a villain for three-quarters of his life and be canonized because he lived a holy life for the remaining quarter of that life.

In real life we deal, not with gods, but with ordinary humans like ourselves: men and women who are full of contradictions, who are stable and fickle, strong and weak, famous and infamous, people in whose bloodstream the muckworm battles daily with potent pesticides.[19]

As societies unravel, as desperation becomes worldwide, it may happen that neither nonviolence nor violence will do very much to alter our impending self-destruction. Violence, in moments when we face near certain annihilation, can become a final affirmation of human dignity. But by then the game is over.

———————

Hanna Krall's book *Shielding the Flame* drew on the experience of Dr. Marek Edelman, who before he died in 2009 was the sole survivor of the five-person command that led the April 1943 Warsaw Ghetto Uprising. Edelman, who was twenty-three years old when he helped lead the uprising, refused to hold up his actions as more moral than the actions of those who walked with their children to the gas chambers. After all, he said, by the time of the uprising he and the other resistance fighters knew that death was for most of them inevitable. In the apocalypse of the Warsaw Ghetto, armed resistance was morally justified, as even Edelman pointed out, but it was not the only choice.

The uprising, started by mostly young Jews, lasted three weeks. They formed the Zydowska Organizacja Bojowa (ZOB), or Jewish Fighting Combat Organization. The uprising ended when the Germans burned and razed the ghetto. Edelman escaped through the sewers and was carried away from the ghetto on a stretcher by members of the underground posing as members of the Polish Red Cross. A sign reading TYPHUS was placed on his body. German soldiers' fear of contracting typhus ensured his easy passage through checkpoints. One of the women carrying the stretcher, Alina Margolis, later became Edelman's wife. In the 1980s, during part of the war in El Salvador, Margolis, a pediatrician, lived in my house in San Salvador. She was working in a refugee camp for Médecins Sans Frontières (Doctors Without Borders).

She and Edelman were socialists. They did not support the Zionist leadership's decision during World War II to negotiate with the Nazis so Jews could leave Europe for Palestine. Edelman and Margolis were committed to building societies where Jews could remain in Europe. They sought to foster a solidarity and common cause with all anti-Nazi forces, rather than retreating into the exclusive Zionist call for a Jewish state. They believed that capitalism was the problem. Edelman and Margolis, horrified by the slaughter and mass displacement of Palestinians when Israel was created in 1948, denounced Israel's occupation. They defended the right of Palestinian people to resist that occupation, even through violence. They saw in the Palestinian struggle their own fight against German occupation during the war.

Poland's Jewish population of 3 million was largely obliterated in mass executions and concentration camps. This population comprised half of all the Jews murdered in the Nazi Holocaust. But Edelman, who witnessed two-thirds of the Warsaw ghetto population being taken away without resistance in cattle cars to the extermination camps, had little time for those who criticized these families for walking meekly to slaughter. He saw how starvation had broken the will of those around him. He saved his venom for those on the Jewish councils and the Jewish police, who knew about the mass exterminations and nevertheless did the Nazis' bidding and herded their fellow Jews into the cattle cars. Starvation drove thousands of families into the hands of the Nazis who passed out oblong, brown loaves of rye bread to those who boarded the trains, trains that took them, unknowingly, to the Nazi death camp Treblinka.[20]

Death, in moments of extremity, was about retaining one's dignity.

"To die in a gas chamber is by no means worse than to die in battle. . . . The only undignified death is when one attempts to survive at the expense of somebody else," Edelman told Krall. Being deported was "infinitely more difficult than to go out shooting. After all, it is much easier to die firing—for us it was much easier to die than it was for someone who first boarded a train car, then rode the train, then dug a hole, then undressed naked."[21]

To be totally alone, even for those who faced certain death, was to be drained of purpose and meaning. There was a ferocious struggle to cling to life.

One would [secrete] oneself somewhere with the other person—in a bed, in a basement, anywhere—and until the next action one was not alone anymore. One person had had his mother taken away, somebody else's father had been shot and killed, or a sister taken away in a shipment. So if someone, somehow, by some miracle escaped and was still alive, he had to stick to some other living human being. People were drawn to one another as never before, as never in normal life. During the last liquidation action they would run to the Jewish Council in search of a rabbi or anybody who could marry them, and then they would go to the Umschlagplatz [where Jews were forced to gather for transportation to the death camps] as a married couple.[22]

He described a friend he called "Adam" who had graduated before the war from military college and who took part in the September 1939 fight against the German forces that invaded Poland. "He was famous for his courage," Edelman told Krall. "For many years he was a real idol of mine." One day the two men were walking down Leszno Street in the ghetto, and "all of a sudden some SS [men] started shooting." He went on:

The crowd scrambled away desperately. And so did he.

You know, I had never before suspected that he could be afraid of anything. And there he was, my idol, running away.

Because he was used to always having a weapon by his side: in the military college, later in the defense of Warsaw in September, and in Modlin. The others had weapons, but he had a weapon, too, so therefore he could be brave. But when it happened that the others were firing their arms and he couldn't shoot, he became another man.

It all actually happened without a single word, [from] one day to the next: he simply quit all activity. And when the first meeting of the command group was about to be held, he was useless for participating in it. So I went instead.

He [had] a girlfriend, Ania. One day, they took her to Pawiak Prison—she managed to get out later—but the day they took her, he broke down completely. He came to see us, leaned his hands on the table, and started telling us that we were all lost, that they would slaughter us all, and that since we were young we should escape to the forest and join the partisans instead of attempting to form an underground here in the city.

Nobody interrupted him.

After he'd left, somebody said: "It's because they have taken her away. He has no reason to live anymore. Now he will get killed."[23]

The tragedy of the ghetto, of violence and counterviolence, extended to the hated Jewish police, who collaborated with the Nazis to maintain control and hunt down the underground resistance. The underground assassinated Jacob Lejkin, a senior Jewish police officer who zealously helped the Nazis organize the deportations, in October 1942. But even Lejkin had a story. He had a child, born after seventeen years of marriage, and he hoped by joining the police to save the child's life.[24]

Edelman noted the collective self-delusion that prohibited the Jews in the ghetto—as it prohibits us—from facing their fate, even after it became clear that the transports were taking thousands daily to Treblinka. In 1942 the underground resistance sent a spy to follow the trains. He returned to the ghetto and reported that freight trains loaded with people entered Treblinka and returned empty. He noted that food supplies were never sent to the death camp. The spy's account was written up in the underground ghetto newspaper, but as Edelman remarked, "nobody believed it." "'Have you gone insane?' people would say when we were trying to convince them that they were not being taken to work," Edelman remembered. "'Would they be sending us to death with bread? So much bread would be wasted!'"[25]

Edelman condemned Adam Czerniaków, the Jewish leader of the ghetto, for committing suicide by swallowing cyanide on July 23, 1942, the day after the mass deportation of the Jews to Treblinka began. Czerniaków, Edelman said, should have informed everyone in the ghetto of the deportations. He should have dissolved all public institutions, especially the Jewish police. "They would have believed him," Edelman said. "But he had committed suicide. That wasn't right: one should die with a bang. At that time this bang was most needed—one should die only after having called other people into the struggle." Edelman went on to say that Czerniaków's suicide was the "only thing we reproach him for."

"We?" Krall asked.

"Me and my friends," Edelman said. "The dead ones. We reproach him for having made his death his own private business. We were convinced that it was necessary to die [publicly], under the world's eyes."[26]

Traditional concepts of right and wrong, Edelman pointed out, collapse in moments of extremity. Edelman spoke to Krall about a doctor in the ghetto hospital who poisoned the sick children on her ward as the Germans entered the building. She saved children from the gas chamber. She became, to those who remained in the ghetto, "a hero."

"So what, then, in that world turned upside down, was heroism?" Krall asked. "Or honor? Or dignity? And where was God?"

"God," Edelman said, "was on the side of the persecutors. A malicious God."²⁷

Edelman said that as a heart surgeon in Poland after the war, he felt that he was always battling against this malevolent deity who sought to extinguish life.

> God is trying to blow out the candle and I'm quickly trying to shield the flame, taking advantage of His brief inattention. To keep the flame flickering, even if only for a little while longer than He would wish. It is important: He is not terribly just. It can also be very satisfying, because whenever something does work out, it means you have, after all, fooled Him.²⁸

Edelman came upon a crowd of people on Zelazna Street in Warsaw after the occupation but before the ghetto was established. The crowd was standing around a "simple wooden barrel with a Jew on top of it. He was old and short, and he had a long beard." Edelman went on:

> Next to him were two German officers. (Two beautiful, tall men next to this small, bowed Jew.) And those Germans, tuft by tuft, were chopping off this Jew's long beard with huge tailor's shears, splitting their sides with laughter all the while.
>
> The surrounding crowd was also laughing. Because, objectively, it really was funny: a little man on a wooden barrel with his beard growing shorter by the moment as it disappeared under the tailor's shears. Just like a movie gag.
>
> At that time the Ghetto did not exist yet, and one might [not] have sensed the grim premonition in that scene. After all, nothing really horrible was happening to that Jew: only that it was now possible to put him on a barrel with impunity, that people were beginning to realize that such activity wouldn't be punished and that it provoked laughter.

But you know what?

At that moment I realized that the most important thing on earth was going to be never letting myself be pushed onto the top of the barrel. Never, by anybody. Do you understand?

Everything I was to do later, I was doing in order not to let myself get pushed up there.[29]

There will be no moral hierarchy to resistance. We will be pulled one way or another by fate and love. And these different routes of resistance will all be legitimate as long as we do not, as Edelman said, attempt "to survive at the expense of somebody else." Many of those in the developing world, as climate change makes human habitation where they live difficult and then impossible, will be faced with the terrible moral quandary endured by Edelman. They will be denied the luxury of nonviolence. But if the ecosystem continues to disintegrate, we will all have to grapple with forms of resistance that, in the end, will permit us only to protect our dignity until the inevitable comes.

"The majority of us favored an uprising," Edelman told Krall. "After all, humanity had agreed that dying with arms was more beautiful than without arms. Therefore we followed this consensus. In the Jewish Combat Organization there were only two hundred and twenty of us left. Can you even call that an uprising? All it was about, finally, was that we not just let them slaughter us when our turn came. It was only a choice as to the manner of dying."[30]

V/The Rebel Caged

*The most valuable blacks are those in prison, those who have the
warrior spirit, who had a sense of being African. They got for their
women and children what they needed when all other avenues
were closed to them.*

*The greatest spirit of resistance among blacks [is] found among
those in prison.*[1]

—AUGUST WILSON, INTERVIEW WITH
BILL MOYERS, OCTOBER 20, 1988

*If I were a member of the class that rules, I would post men in all
the neighborhoods of the nation, not to spy upon or club rebel-
lious workers, not to break strikes or disrupt unions; but to ferret
out those who no longer respond to the system in which they live.
I would make it known that the real danger does not stem from
those who seek to grab their share of wealth through force, or from
those who seek to defend their property through violence, for both
of these groups, by their affirmative acts, support the values of the
system in which they live. The millions that I would fear are those
who do not dream of the prizes that the nation holds forth, for it
is in them, though they may not know it, that a revolution has
taken place and is biding its time to translate itself into a new and
strange way of life.*[2]

—RICHARD WRIGHT, *BLACK BOY*

drove four hours one rainy, cold morning to SCI (State Correctional
Institution) Mahanoy in Frackville, Pennsylvania, from my home in
Princeton, New Jersey, to see the black revolutionary Mumia Abu-Jamal,

America's best-known political prisoner. We met in the reception area for the prisoners and their families. He sat hunched forward on the gray plastic table, his dreadlocks cascading down the sides of his face. The room resembled a high school cafeteria. It had vending machines on the wall by the entrance, which the prisoners were not allowed to operate, plastic chairs, a few tables, and a booth for the corrections officers. Small children, visiting their fathers or brothers, raced around the floor or wailed in their mothers' arms.

Abu-Jamal, like the other prisoners in the room, was wearing a brown jumpsuit bearing the letters DOC—Department of Corrections. We dove immediately into a discussion about books. He spoke intently about the nature of empire, which he was currently reading voraciously about, and effective forms of resistance to tyranny throughout history.

Abu-Jamal was transferred in January 2012 to the general prison population after nearly thirty years in solitary confinement on death row. During those three decades, he was barred from physical contact with his wife, his children, and other visitors. He had been sentenced to death in 1982 for the December 9, 1981, killing of Philadelphia police officer Daniel Faulkner. His sentence was amended to life without parole. The misconduct of the judge, flagrant irregularities in his trial, and tainted evidence have been criticized by numerous human rights organizations, including Amnesty International.[3] Abu-Jamal, who was a young activist in the Black Panthers and later one of the most important radical journalists in Philadelphia, a city that a few decades earlier produced I. F. Stone, has long been the bête noire of the state. The FBI opened a file on him when he started working with the local chapter of the Black Panthers at the age of fifteen. He was suspended from his Philadelphia high school when he campaigned to rename the school for Malcolm X and distributed "black revolutionary student power" literature. Abu-Jamal has published seven books in prison, including his best-selling *Live from Death Row*, and he was at work on an eighth. Dick Gregory says in *Mumia: Long Distance Revolutionary*, the documentary about Abu-Jamal, that he has single-handedly brought "dignity to the whole death row." The late historian Manning Marable is quoted in the film saying: "The voice of black journalism in the struggle for the

liberation of African American people has always proved to be decisive throughout black history. When you listen to Mumia Abu-Jamal,
you hear the echoes of David Walker, Frederick Douglass, W.E.B. Du
Bois, Paul Robeson, and the sisters and brothers who kept the faith with
struggle, who kept the faith with resistance."[4]

The authorities, as they did before he was convicted, have attempted
to silence him in prison. Pennsylvania banned all recorded interviews
with Abu-Jamal after 1996. In response to protests over the singling out
of one inmate in the Pennsylvania correction system, the state banned recorded access to all its inmates. The ban is nicknamed "the Mumia Rule."
And the state did not stop there. In October 2014, days after Abu-Jamal
gave a pre-recorded commencement address to graduates of Goddard
College, the governor of Pennsylvania, Tom Corbett, signed into law the
Revictimization Relief Act. The law permits crime victims and prosecutors to go to court to prevent prisoners from making public statements
that cause mental anguish. Governor Corbett was surrounded by police
officers, victims' advocates, and Faulkner's widow, Maureen Faulkner, at
the signing. He said that Mrs. Faulkner "has been taunted by the obscene
celebrity that her husband's killer has orchestrated from behind bars.
This unrepentant cop killer has tested the limits of decency, while gull-
ible activists and celebrities have continued to feed this killer's ego at the
expense of his victims." In November 2014, Abu-Jamal and supporters
filed a federal lawsuit in an attempt to overturn the law.[5]

"I was punished for communicating," Abu-Jamal said.

Philosopher Cornel West says in the documentary, "The state is very
clever in terms of keeping track, especially [of] the courageous and visionary ones, the ones [who] are long-distance runners. You can keep
track of them, absorb 'em, dilute 'em, or outright kill 'em—you don't
have to worry about opposition to 'em.

"If you tell them the truth about the operation of our power, this is
what happens to you," he goes on. "Like Jesus on the cross. This is what
happens to you."

I was not permitted a pencil or paper during my four-and-a-half-
hour conversation with Abu-Jamal. I wrote down his quotes immediately after I left the prison. These restrictions mirror the wider pattern of

a society where the poor and the destitute, and especially those who rise up in rebellion, are rendered invisible and voiceless.

The breadth of Abu-Jamal's reading, which along with his writing and 3,000 radio broadcasts has kept his mind and soul intact, was staggering. His own books are banned in the prison. In conversation he swung from discussions of the Opium Wars between 1839 and 1860 to the Black Panthers to the Palestinian-Israeli conflict to the series of legislative betrayals of the poor and people of color by Bill Clinton, Barack Obama, and the Democratic Party.

He quoted Frederick Douglass, W.E.B. Du Bois, Huey P. Newton, Assata Shakur, Eric Foner, Gore Vidal, Cornel West, Howard Zinn, James Cone, and Dave Zirin. We talked about Nat Turner, Gabriel Prosser, Joseph Cinqué, Harriet Tubman, Charles Deslondes, Denmark Vesey, and Sojourner Truth. He was simultaneously reading *Masters of War* by Clara Nieto, *How the World Works* by Noam Chomsky, *The Face of Imperialism* by Michael Parenti, and *Now and Then* by Gil Scott-Heron. He wondered what shape the collapse of empire will take. And he despaired of the political unconsciousness among many incoming prisoners, some young enough to be his children.

"When I first got out in the yard," he said, "and I heard groups of men talking about how Sarah was going to marry Jim or how Frank had betrayed Susan, I thought, *Damn, these cats all know each other and their families. That's odd.* But after a few minutes I realized they were talking about soap operas. Television in prison is the great pacifier. They love *Basketball Wives* because it is 'T and A' with women of color. They know how many cars Jay-Z has. But they don't know their own history. They don't understand how they got here. They don't know what is being done to them. I tell them they have to read, and they say, 'Man, I don't do books.' And that is just how the empire wants it. You can't fight power if you don't understand it. And you can't understand it if you don't experience it and then dissect it."

Abu-Jamal's venom is reserved for liberal politicians such as Bill Clinton and Barack Obama, whom he excoriates for callously disempowering the poor and the working class on behalf of their corporate patrons. And he has little time for those who support them.

"It was Clinton that made possible the explosion of the prison-industrial complex," he said, speaking of the 1994 Omnibus Crime Bill.

He looked around the visiting area at the thirty-odd prisoners with their families.

"Most of these people wouldn't be here if it weren't for Bill Clinton," he said. "He and Barack Obama haven't done anything for poor people but lock them up. And if our first African American president isn't going to halt the growth of the prison-industrial complex, no president after him is going to do it. This prison system is here to stay. The poor and the destitute feed it. It is the empire's solution to the economic crisis. Those who are powerless, who have no access to diminishing resources, get locked away. And the prison business is booming. It is one of the few growth industries left. It used to be that towns didn't want prisons. Now these poor rural communities beg for them. You look down the list of the names of the guards and see two or three with the same last names. This is because fathers, brothers, spouses, work here together. These small towns don't have anything else."

The United States has the highest documented incarceration rate in the world—743 adults per 100,000.[6] Of the 2.3 million adults incarcerated in federal and state prisons and local jails, nearly 60 percent are nonwhite.[7] He who has not been in jail does not know what the state is, Leo Tolstoy said.[8]

The Omnibus Crime Bill, pushed through the Senate with the help of Joe Biden, appropriated $30 billion to expand the nation's prison program, state and local law enforcement, and border patrols over a six-year period.[9] It gave $10.8 billion in federal matching funds to local governments to hire 100,000 new police officers over five years.[10] It provided nearly $10 billion for the construction of new federal prisons.[11] It instituted the three-strikes proposal that mandates a life sentence for anyone convicted of three "violent" felonies. The bill permitted children as young as thirteen to be tried as adults. It authorized the use of secret evidence. The prison population during the Clinton presidency jumped from 1.4 million to 2 million.[12] Between 1982 and 2001, total state corrections expenditures increased each year, rising from $15.0 billion to $53.5 billion in real dollars, according to the Department of

Justice (DOJ). Between 2002 and 2010, according to the DOJ, expenditures fluctuated annually between $53.4 billion and $48.4 billion.[13]

Abu-Jamal talked about being a Black Panther and the use of violence as a form of political resistance throughout history. He remembered visiting the Chicago apartment where Black Panther leader Fred Hampton was shot to death by Chicago police and the FBI while he slept on December 4, 1969. He called Hampton, who was twenty-one when he was killed, "one of the bright lights." Abu-Jamal choked up and his eyes glistened with tears. "Fred . . . ," he said as his voice trailed off.

"It used to be that a politician promised jobs, a chicken in every pot," Abu-Jamal went on. "But in our new national security state, they promise law and order. They get elected by saying they will be tough on crime and by calling for the death penalty. Death sells. Fear sells. What was a crime by the state in the 1960s is now legal. The state can wiretap, eavesdrop, listen to phone calls, and break into homes. And there is nothing we can do about it. The mass incarceration and the mass repression impact every community to make people afraid and compliant."

Abu-Jamal has written: "In this place, a dark temple of fear, an altar of political ambition, death is a campaign poster, a stepping-stone to public office. . . . In this space and time, in this dark hour, how many of us are not on death row?"[14]

"The brutality of the empire was exposed under George W. Bush," he said to me. "The empire desperately needed a new face, a black face, to seduce the public. This is the role of Barack Obama. He is the black face of empire. He was pitched to us during the most recent presidential campaign by Bill Clinton, the same Clinton who gave us NAFTA in 1994 and abolished good-paying manufacturing jobs for millions of workers. The same Clinton who locked us up. Clinton and Obama represent the politics of betrayal at the heart of the corporatist machinery. And they have fooled a lot of people, especially black people. During slavery, and even post-Reconstruction, there were always a few black people who served the system. The role of these black servants to white power was to teach passivity in the face of repression. This is why Obama is president. Nothing has changed."

Abu-Jamal saw hope in the Occupy movement, largely because white middle-class youths were beginning to experience the cruelty of capitalism and state repression that had long been visited on poor people of color. But, he added, we must recover our past if we are going to effectively resist. We must connect ourselves to the revolutionaries, radicals, and prophets who fought injustice before us. We must defy the historical amnesia that the corporate state seeks to cement into our consciousness. His book *Faith of Our Fathers: An Examination of the Spiritual Life of African and African-American People* sets out to do precisely this, to recover a past intellectual and spiritual life for African Americans that has been trivialized, ignored, or censored by the dominant culture.[15] He was worried that the mindless diversions of popular culture and the assault by corporate power on education are keeping many from grasping not only what is happening but the continuity between modern systems of oppression and older systems of oppression.

"We would not be who we are as African Americans of this date were it not for the Reverend, the Prophet, Nat Turner—who brilliantly merged the religious with the political," Abu-Jamal said in the film. "Who didn't just talk about the world to come but fought to transform the world that is. You know, [Nat Turner] is honored and revered today—not because he could quote the Bible well, he could do that, but because he worked in the fields of life to get the slave master off of his neck, off of all of our necks."

The vending machines in the reception area dispensed White Castle hamburgers, soda, candy, and Tastykake cupcakes. I dropped in the prepaid tokens—no money is allowed inside the prison—and the fast food tumbled into the vent. For Abu-Jamal, forced to eat prison food for decades, it was a treat, especially the Hershey's bar. He watched as a boy darted past him toward his father.

"I didn't see children for thirty years on death row," he said quietly. "It is a delight to see them here. They are what is most precious, what the struggle is finally about."

The effort to silence Abu-Jamal is part of the cultural drive to crush the remnants of the black prophetic tradition. This tradition, which stretches back to Sojourner Truth and Frederick Douglass, has consistently named and damned the cruelty of imperialism and white supremacy. It has been our most astute critique of empire. The black prophetic tradition expressed radical truths with a clarity and moral force that have eluded most other critics of American capitalism. Obama first displayed his fear of this tradition when he betrayed his pastor, the Reverend Jeremiah Wright, abetting the brutal character assassination of one of the nation's most prophetic voices. And Obama has sustained this assault, largely through black surrogates such as the Rev. Al Sharpton, Tom Joyner, and Steve Harvey, in vicious attacks on Cornel West.

"Jeremiah Wright was the canary in the mine," West told me when we spoke in Princeton, New Jersey, where we both live. "The black prophetic tradition has been emptied out. Its leaders have either been murdered or incarcerated. . . . A lot of political prisoners who represent the black prophetic tradition [are] in jail. They have been in there for decades. Or we have leaders who have completely sold out. They have been co-opted. And these are the three major developments. With sold-out leaders, you get a pacified followership or people who are scared.

"The black prophetic tradition has been the leaven in the American democratic loaf," West said. "What has kept American democracy from going fascist or authoritarian or autocratic has been the legacy of Frederick Douglass, Harriet Tubman, Sojourner Truth, Martin King, Fannie Lou Hamer. This is not because black people have a monopoly on truth, goodness, or beauty. It is because the black freedom movement puts pressure on the American empire in the name of integrity, decency, honesty, and virtue."

The tradition is sustained by a handful of beleaguered writers and intellectuals, including Glen Ford and his Black Agenda Report, James Cone, Carl Dix, Bruce Dixon, Boyce Watkins, Yvette Carnell, Robin Kelley, Margaret Kimberley, Nellie Bailey, the Rev. Michael Pfleger, Maulana Karenga, Ajamu Baraka, and Jeremiah Wright, but none have the public profile of West, who is relentlessly attacked by Obama's black supporters as a "race traitor"—the equivalent of a "self-hating Jew" to hard-line supporters of Israel.

It is understandable why this tradition frightens Obama. It exposes him for what he is—the ideological heir of Booker T. Washington, a black accommodationist whose core message to black people was, in the words of W.E.B. Du Bois, "adjustment and submission." Obama's message to the black underclass in the midst of the corporate rape of the nation is drawn verbatim from the Booker T. Washington playbook. He tells them to work harder—as if anyone works harder than the working poor in this country—to get an education, and to obey the law.

"Obama is the highest manifestation of the co-optation that took place," West said. "It shifted to the black political class. The black political class, more and more, found itself unable to tell the truth, or if they began to tell some of the truth, they were [put] under surveillance, attacked, and demonized. Forty percent of our babies are living in poverty, living without enough food, and Obama comes to us and says quit whining. He doesn't say that to the Business Roundtable. He doesn't say that to the corporate elites. He doesn't say that to AIPAC, the conservative Jewish brothers and sisters who will do anything to support the Israeli occupation against Palestinians. This kind of neglect in policy is coupled with disrespect in his speeches to black folk, which the mainstream calls tough love.

"He is a shell of a man," West said of Obama. "There is no deep conviction. There is no connection to something bigger than him. It is a sad spectacle, sad if he were not the head of an empire that is in such decline and so dangerous. This is a nadir. William Trotter and Du Bois, along with Ida B. Wells-Barnett, were going at Booker T tooth and nail. Look at the fights between [Marcus] Garvey and Du Bois, or Garvey and A. Philip Randolph. But now if you criticize Obama the way Randolph criticized Garvey, you become a race traitor and an Uncle Tom. A lot of that comes out of the Obama machine, the Obama plantation.

"The most pernicious development is the incorporation of the black prophetic tradition into the Obama imperial project," West told me. "Obama used [Martin Luther] King's Bible during his inauguration, but under the National Defense Authorization Act, King would be detained without due process. He would be under surveillance every day because of his association with Nelson Mandela, who was the head of a 'terrorist' organization, the African National Congress. We see the richest prophetic tradition in America desecrated in the name of a neoliberal worldview, a worldview King would be in direct opposition to. Martin would be against Obama because of his neglect of the poor and the working class and because of the [aerial] drones, because he is a war president, because he draws up kill lists. And Martin King would have nothing to do with that.

"We are talking about crimes against humanity—Wall Street crimes, war crimes, the crimes of the criminal justice system in the form of Jim Crow, the crimes against our working poor that have their backs pushed against the wall because of stagnant wages and corporate profits going up," West explained. "Abraham Heschel said that the distinctive feature of any empire in decline is its indifference to criminality. That is a fundamental feature of our time, an indifference to criminality, especially on top, wickedness in high places.

"This is not personal," West said. "This was true for [George W.] Bush. It was true for [Bill] Clinton. We are talking about an imperial system, manifest in Obama's robust effort to bomb Syria [in 2013]. War crimes against Syrian children do not justify US war crimes. We are talking about a corporate state and a massive surveillance and national security state. It operates according to its own logic. Profit, on the one hand, and secrecy to hide imperial policy, on the other. Jesse [Jackson] was the head house Negro on the Clinton plantation, just as Sharpton is the head house Negro on the Obama plantation. But there is a difference. Jesse was willing to oppose Clinton on a variety of issues. He marched, for example, against the welfare bill. But Sharpton loves the plantation. He will not say a critical word. It is sad and pathetic. We are living in the age of the sellout.

"Garvey used to say that as long as black people were in America the masses of black people, the poor and the working class, would never be treated with respect, decency, or fairness," West noted. "That has always been a skeleton in the closet, the fundamental challenge to the black prophetic tradition. It may very well be that black people will never be free in America. But I believe, and the black prophetic tradition believes, that we proceed because black people are worthy of being free, just as poor people of all colors are worthy of being free, even if they never will be free. That is the existential leap of faith. There is no doubt that with a black president the black masses are still treated unfairly, from stop-and-frisk to high unemployment, indecent housing, and decrepit education.

"It is a spiritual issue," West said. "What kind of person do you choose to be? People say, 'Well, Brother West, since the mass of black folk will never be free, then let me just get mine.' That is the dominant response. 'I am wasting my time fighting a battle that can't be won.' But that is not what the black prophetic tradition is about. History is a mystery. Yes, it doesn't look good. But the masses of black folk *must* be respected. Malcolm X used to say, as long as they are not respected, you could show me all the individual respect you want, but I know it's empty. That is the fundamental divide between the prophetic tradition and the sellouts."

The tradition has been diminished by what West called the "emaciation" of the black press that once amplified the voices of black radicals. The decline of the black press and the consolidation of the media, especially the electronic media, into the hands of a few corporations has shut out those who have remained faithful to this tradition. West does not appear on MSNBC, where the black and white hosts serve as giddy cheerleaders for Obama, and was abruptly dropped as a scheduled guest on an episode of CBS's *Face the Nation* that aired after the fiftieth anniversary of the march on Washington. Because the black prophetic tradition is rarely taught in schools, including primarily African American schools, it is at risk of being extinguished.

The black prophetic tradition, West observed, "no longer has a legitimacy or significant foothold in the minds of the black masses. With corporate media and the narrowing of the imagination of all Americans, including black people, there is an erasure of memory. This is the near-death of the black prophetic tradition. It is a grave issue. It is a matter of life and death. It means that the major roadblock to American fascism, which has been the black prophetic tradition, is gone. To imagine America without the black prophetic tradition, from Frederick Douglass to Fannie Lou Hamer, means an American authoritarian regime, American fascism. We already have the infrastructure in place for the police state.

"Black intelligence and black suspicion is still there among the masses," West said. "Black people are not stupid. We are not completely duped. We are just scared. We don't think there is any alternative. This is re-niggerization of the black professional class. They have big money, nice positions, comfort and convenience, but are scared, intimidated, afraid to tell the truth, and will not bear witness to justice. Those who are incorporated into the black professional and political class are willing to tolerate disrespect for the black masses and sip their tea and accept their checks and gain access to power. That is what niggerization is—keeping people afraid and intimidated."

————

Bonnie Kerness, with a bun of blond hair, sat behind a desk in her cramped office in Newark where she runs the American Friends Service Committee's Prison Watch. Mass incarceration, which she called "the war at home," is the latest physical mutation of systems of social control to thwart black radicalism and silence the black prophetic tradition. The infrastructure within prisons, she said, is designed to contain and silence black radicals and will be used to contain anyone who decides to resist the corporate state.

"There are no *former* Jim Crow systems," Kerness said. "The transition from slavery to Black Codes to convict leasing to the Jim Crow laws to the wars on poverty, veterans, youth, and political activism in the 1960s has been a seamless evolution of political and social incapacitation of poor people of color. The sophisticated fascism of the practices of stop-and-frisk, charging people in inner cities with 'wandering,' driving and walking while black, ZIP code racism—these and many other de facto practices all serve to keep our prisons full. In a system where 60 percent of those who are imprisoned are people of color, where students of color face harsher punishments in school than their white peers, where 58 percent of African American youth . . . are sent to adult prisons, where women of color are 69 percent more likely to be imprisoned, and where offenders of color receive longer sentences, the concept of color blindness doesn't exist. The racism around me is palpable.

"The 1960s, when the last of the Jim Crow laws were reversed, this whole new set of practices accepted by law enforcement was designed to continue to feed the money-generating prison system, which has neo-slavery at its core," she said. "Until we deeply recognize that the system's bottom line is social control and creating a business from bodies of color and the poor, nothing can change." She noted that more than half of those in the prison system have never physically harmed another person, but that "just about all of these people have been harmed themselves." And not only does the criminal justice system sweep up the poor and people of color, but slavery within the prison system is permitted by the Thirteenth Amendment to the US Constitution, which reads: "Neither slavery nor involuntary servitude, except as punishment for crime whereof the party shall have been duly convicted, shall exist within the United States."

This provision, Kerness said, "is at the core of how the labor of slaves was transformed into what people in prison call neo-slavery." Neo-slavery is an integral part of the prison-industrial complex, in which hundreds of thousands of the nation's prisoners, primarily people of color, are forced to work at involuntary labor for pennies an hour. "If you call the New Jersey Bureau of Tourism, you are most likely talking to a prisoner at the Edna Mahan Correctional Institution for Women who is earning 23 cents an hour who has no ability to negotiate working hours or working conditions," she said. The bodies of poor, unemployed youths are worth little on the streets but become valuable commodities once they are behind bars.

Marie Gottschalk in *Caught: The Prison State and the Lockdown of American Politics* points out, like Alexander, that prisons, or what she calls "the carceral state," extends far beyond those trapped inside prison walls. "It encompasses the more than eight million people—or one in twenty-three adults—who are under some form of state control, including jail, prison, probation, parole, community sanctions, drug courts, immigrant detention, and other forms of government supervision," she writes. "It includes the millions of people who are booked into jail each year—perhaps nearly seven million—and the estimated 7.5 percent of all adults who are felons or ex-felons."[16]

Prison affects the lives of millions of people who have never been arrested. There are, Gottschalk points out, an estimated eight million minors—or one in ten children—who have a parent incarcerated. Two million children have a mother or father in prison. Millions of Americans have, she writes, been condemned to "civil death," stripped of their voting rights, rendered ineligible for student loans, food stamps, and public housing, because of criminal convictions. And the explosion of the penal system, accompanied by expanding rural poverty, means that it is no longer a black-white issue or a form solely of racial control. There are mounting incarceration rates for women—the fastest-growing segment of the prison population—poor whites, Latinos, and immigrants.[17] The carceral state, unable to satiate itself with black bodies, is consuming other groups and ethnicities.

"People have said to me that the criminal justice system doesn't work," Kerness said. "I've come to believe exactly the opposite—that it works perfectly, just as slavery did, as a matter of economic and political policy. How is it that a fifteen-year-old in Newark who the country labels worthless to the economy, who has no hope of getting a job or affording college, can suddenly generate $20,000 to $30,000 a year once trapped in the criminal justice system? The expansion of prisons, parole, probation, the court, and police systems has resulted in an enormous bureaucracy which has been a boon to everyone from architects to food vendors, all with one thing in common—a paycheck earned by keeping human beings in cages. The criminalization of poverty is a lucrative business, and we have replaced the social safety net with a dragnet."

––––––––––

In 1913 Philadelphia's Eastern State Penitentiary discontinued its isolation cages, which had driven prisoners insane.[18] Prisoners within the US prison system would not be held in prolonged isolation again in large numbers until the turmoil of the 1960s. The rise of the antiwar and civil rights movements, along with the emergence of radical groups such as the Black Panthers, the Black Liberation Army, the Puerto Rican independence movement, and the American Indian movement, saw a return to systematized abuse within the prison system.[19] In 1975 Trenton State Prison (now New Jersey State Prison) established a Management Control Unit, or isolation unit, for political prisoners—mostly black radicals such as Ojore Lutalo, a leader in the Black Liberation Army, whom the state wanted to segregate from the wider prison population.[20] Those held in the isolation unit were rarely there because they had violated prison rules. They were there because of their revolutionary beliefs—beliefs that the prison authorities feared might resonate with other prisoners.

In 1983 the federal prison in Marion, Illinois, instituted a permanent lockdown, creating, in essence, a prisonwide "control unit."[21] By 1994 the Federal Bureau of Prisons, using the Marion model, had built its maximum-security prison in Florence, Colorado.[22] The use of prolonged isolation and sensory deprivation exploded. "Special Housing Units" were used for the mentally ill. "Security Threat Group Management Units" were formed for those accused of gang activity.[23] "Communication Management Units" were formed to isolate Muslims labeled as terrorists.[24] Voluntary and involuntary protective custody units were formed. Administrative segregation punishment units were formed to isolate prisoners said to be psychologically troubled. All were established in open violation of the United Nations Convention Against Torture and the UN's International Covenant on Civil and Political Rights.[25]

Once you disappear behind prison walls, you become prey. Rape. Torture. Beatings. Prolonged isolation. Sensory deprivation. Racial profiling. Chain gangs. Forced labor. Rancid food. Children sentenced and imprisoned as adults. Prisoners forced to take medications to induce lethargy. Inadequate heating and ventilation. Poor health care. Draconian sentences for nonviolent crimes. Endemic violence.

Lutalo endured his prolonged isolation by methodically tearing up the few magazines and newspapers he was allowed to read and making political collages that kept alive his defiance and his dignity—an example of Havel's advice to break the rules of the game to preserve one's identity. "Prisons: America's Finest Slave Plantation" read one. "Blessed are those who struggle. Oppression is worse than the grave. Better to die for a noble cause than to live and die a slave," read another, a quote from The Last Poets. "One of the worst places on earth" read yet another.

Lutalo wrote to Bonnie Kerness in 1986 while he was a prisoner at Trenton State Prison. He described to her the bleak and degrading world of solitary confinement, the world of the prisoners like him held in the so-called management control unit, which he called "a prison within a prison."

Before being released in 2009, Lutalo was in the Management Control Unit for twenty-two of the twenty-eight years he served for the second of two convictions—the first for a bank robbery and the second for a gun battle with a drug dealer. He kept his sanity, he told me, by following a strict regime of exercising in his tiny cell, writing, meditating, and putting together his collages to portray his prison conditions.

"The guards in riot gear would suddenly wake you up at 1:00 AM, force you to strip, and make you grab all your things and move you to another cell just to harass you," he said when we spoke in Kerness's Newark office. "They had attack dogs with them that were trained to go for your genitals. You spent twenty-four hours alone one day in your cell and twenty-two the next. If you do not have a strong sense of purpose, you don't survive psychologically. Isolation is designed to defeat prisoners mentally, and I saw a lot of prisoners defeated."

Lutalo's letter was Kerness's first indication that the US prison system was creating something new—special detention facilities that under international law are a form of torture. Lutalo wrote to her, "How does one go about articulating desperation to another who is not desperate? How does one go about articulating the psychological stress of knowing that people are waiting for me to self-destruct?"

The techniques of sensory deprivation and prolonged isolation were pioneered by the Central Intelligence Agency to break prisoners during the Cold War. Alfred McCoy, in *A Question of Torture: CIA Interrogation, from the Cold War to the War on Terror*, writes that "interrogators had found that mere physical pain, no matter how extreme, often produced heightened resistance." So the intelligence agency turned to the more effective mechanisms of "sensory disorientation" and "self-inflicted pain," McCoy notes in his book.[26]

One example of self-inflicted pain is to force a prisoner to stand without moving or to hold some other stressful bodily position for a long period. The combination, government psychologists argued, would cause victims *to feel responsible for their own suffering* and accelerate psychological disintegration. Sensory disorientation combines extreme sensory overload with extreme sensory deprivation. Prolonged isolation is followed by intense interrogation. Extreme heat is followed by extreme cold. Glaring light is followed by total darkness. Loud and sustained noise is followed by silence. "The fusion of these two techniques, sensory disorientation and self-inflicted pain, creates a synergy of physical and psychological trauma whose sum is a hammer-blow to the existential platforms of personal identity," McCoy writes.[27]

After hearing from Lutalo, Kerness became a fierce advocate for him and other prisoners held in isolation units. She published through her office a survivor's manual for those held in isolation as well as a booklet titled "Torture in United States Prisons."[28] And she began to collect the stories of prisoners held in isolation.

"My food trays have been sprayed with mace or cleaning agents, . . . human feces and urine put into them by guards who deliver trays to my breakfast, lunch, and dinner," a prisoner in isolation in the Wabash Valley Correctional Facility in Carlisle, Indiana, was quoted as saying in "Torture in United States Prisons."

I have witnessed sane men of character become self-mutilators, suffer paranoia, panic attacks, hostile fantasies about revenge. One prisoner would swallow packs of AA batteries, and stick a pencil in his penis. They would cut on themselves to gain contact with staff nurses or just to draw attention to themselves. These men made slinging human feces "body waste" daily like it was a recognized sport. Some would eat it or rub it all over themselves as if it was body lotion. . . . Prisoncrats use a form of restraint, a bed crafted to strap men in four point Velcro straps. Both hands to the wrist and both feet to the ankles and secured. Prisoners have been kept like this for 3–6 hours at a time. Most times they would remove all their clothes. The Special Confinement Unit used [water hoses] on these men also. . . . When prisons become overcrowded, prisoncrats will do forced double bunking. Over-crowding issues present an assortment of problems many of which results in violence. . . . Prisoncrats will purposely house a "sex offender" in a cell with prisoners with sole intentions of having him beaten up or even killed.[29]

Prisons are at once hugely expensive and, as Kerness pointed out, hugely profitable. Prisons function in the same way the military-industrial complex functions: the money is public and the profits are private. "Privatization in the prison-industrial complex includes companies which run prisons for profit while at the same time gleaning profits from forced labor," she said. "In the state of New Jersey, food and medical services are provided by corporations, which have a profit motive. One recent explosion of private industry is the partnering of Corrections Corporation of America with the federal government to detain close to 1 million undocumented people. Using public monies to enrich private citizens is the history of capitalism at its most exploitive."

Those released from prison are woefully unprepared for reentry. They bear the years of trauma they endured and often suffer from the endemic health problems that come with long incarceration, including hepatitis C, tuberculosis, and HIV.[30] Many of them lack access to medications upon release to treat their physical and mental illnesses.[31] Finding work is difficult, and they feel alienated and are often estranged from friends and family. More than 60 percent end up back in prison.[32]

"How do you teach someone to rid themselves of degradation?" Kerness asked. "How long does it take to teach people to feel safe, a sense of empowerment in a world where they often come home emotionally and physically damaged and unemployable? There are many reasons that ex-prisoners do not make it—paramount among them is that they are not supposed to succeed."

Kerness grew up asking different questions. In 1961, at the age of nineteen, she left New York to work for a decade in Tennessee in the civil rights struggle, including a year at Tennessee's Highlander Research and Education Center, where Rosa Parks and other civil rights leaders were trained. By the 1970s, she was involved in housing campaigns for the poor in New Jersey. She kept running into families with incarcerated loved ones. This led her to found Prison Watch.

The letters that pour into her office are disturbing. Female prisoners routinely complain of being sexually abused by guards. One prisoner wrote to her office: "That was not part of my sentence to perform oral sex with officers." Other prisoners write on behalf of the mentally ill who have been left to deteriorate in the prison system. One California prisoner told of a mentally ill man spreading feces over himself and the guards then dumping him into a scalding bath that took skin off 30 percent of his body.

Kerness said the letters she receives from prisoners collectively present a litany of "inhumane conditions including cold, filth, callous medical care, extended isolation often lasting years, use of devices of torture, harassment, brutality, and racism." Prisoners send her drawings of "four- and five-point restraints, restraint hoods, restraint belts, restraint beds, stun grenades, stun guns, stun belts, spit hoods, tethers, and waist and leg chains." But the worst torment, prisoners tell her, is the psychological pain caused by "no-touch torture," which includes "humiliation, sleep deprivation, sensory disorientation, extreme light or dark, extreme cold or heat," and "extended solitary confinement." These techniques, she said, are consciously designed to carry out "a systematic attack on all human stimuli."

Sensory deprivation is used against Islamic militants, jailhouse lawyers, and the some 150 political prisoners, many part of radical black underground movements in the 1960s that advocated violence. A few, such as Leonard Peltier and Abu-Jamal, are well known, but most have little public visibility—among them are Sundiata Acoli, Mutulu Shakur, Imam Jamil Al-Amin (known as H. Rap Brown when he was the chairman of the Student Nonviolent Coordinating Committee, or SNCC, in the 1960s), Jalil Bottom, Sekou Odinga, Abdul Majid, Tom Manning, and Bill Dunne.

Those within the system who attempt to resist the abuse and mistreatment are dealt with severely. Prisoners in the overcrowded Southern Ohio Correctional Facility, a maximum-security prison in Lucasville, Ohio, staged a revolt in 1993 after years of beatings, degrading rituals of public humiliation, and the alleged murders of prisoners by guards. Approximately 450 prisoners were able to unite antagonistic prison factions, including the Aryan Brotherhood and the Black Gangster

Disciples, and hold out for eleven days by holding guards hostage. It was one of the longest prison rebellions in US history. Nine prisoners and a guard were killed by the prisoners during the revolt.

The state responded with characteristic fury. It singled out about forty prisoners and eventually shipped them to Ohio State Penitentiary (OSP), a supermax facility outside Youngstown.[33] There prisoners are held in solitary confinement twenty-three hours a day in seven-by-eleven-foot cells. Prisoners at OSP almost never see the sun or have human contact. Some of those charged with participating in the uprising have been held in these punitive conditions at OSP or other facilities since the 1993 revolt. Five prisoners involved in the uprising—Bomani Shakur, Siddique Abdullah Hasan, Jason Robb, George Skatzes, and Namir Abdul Mateen—were charged with murder. They are being held in isolation on death row.[34]

Kerness said that the for-profit prison companies have created an entrepreneurial class like that of the Southern slaveholders, one "dependent on the poor and on bodies of color as a source for income," and she described federal and state departments of corrections as "a state of mind." This state of mind, she said in the interview, "led to Abu Ghraib, Bagram, and Guantánamo, and what is going on in US prisons right this moment."

As long as profit remains an incentive to incarcerate human beings and our corporate state abounds in superfluous labor, there is little chance that the prison system will be reformed. Our prisons serve the engine of corporate capitalism, transferring state money to private corporations. These corporations will continue to stymie rational prison reform because the system, however inhumane and unjust, feeds corporate bank accounts. At bottom, the problem is not race, although race plays a huge part in incarceration rates, nor is it ultimately poverty. It is the predatory nature of corporate capitalism itself. And until we slay the beast of corporate capitalism, until we wrest power back from corporations, until we build social institutions and a system of governance designed not to profit the few but to foster the common good, our prison industry and the horror it perpetuates will only expand.

———

African American radicals were targeted first. Muslim radicals were targeted next, especially after the attacks of 9/11. Their stories differ little from those of Abu-Jamal or Lutalo.

Syed Fahad Hashmi, a US citizen, is serving a fifteen-year sentence in Guantánamo-like conditions in the supermax ADX (Administrative Maximum) facility in Terre Haute, Indiana. He is isolated in a small cell for twenty-two to twenty-three hours a day. He has only extremely limited contact with his mother, father, and brother, often going weeks without any communication. He was charged by the government with two counts of providing and conspiring to provide material support to al-Qaeda and two counts of making and conspiring to make a contribution of goods or services to al-Qaeda. He accepted a plea bargain on one count of conspiracy to provide material support to terrorism. If he had gone to trial, he would have faced the possibility of a seventy-year sentence.[35]

The best the US government could offer as evidence of Hashmi's crimes was that an acquaintance who stayed in his apartment with him in early 2004 while he was a graduate student in London, Junaid Babar, also an American citizen, had raincoats, ponchos, and waterproof socks in his luggage that were to be handed over to a member of al-Qaeda in south Waziristan, Pakistan. Hashmi also allegedly permitted Babar to use his cell phone to contact others who were planning acts of terrorism.[36] Babar, who was arrested in 2004 and pled guilty to five counts of material support for al-Qaeda, also faced up to seventy years in prison. But he agreed to serve as a government witness against Hashmi, as well as in other terror trials, in exchange for a reduced sentence.

I doubt that the government was overly concerned about a suitcase full of waterproof socks that were being taken to Pakistan. The reason Hashmi was targeted was because, like the Palestinian activist Dr. Sami Al-Arian, he was fearless and zealous in his defense of those being bombed, shot, terrorized, and killed throughout the Muslim world.[37] The government planned to introduce tapes of Hashmi's political talks while he was a student at Brooklyn College, during which time Hashmi was a member of the New York political group Al Muhajiroun. He made numerous provocative statements, including calling America "the biggest terrorist in the world," but Al Muhajiroun is not defined by the government as a terrorist organization. Membership in the group is not illegal. And our complicity in massive acts of state terror is a historical fact.[38] Hashmi had a right to express these sentiments. More important, he had a right to expect freedom from persecution and imprisonment because of his opinions.

I spoke to Hashmi's father, Syed Anwar Hashmi, in June 2011. The elder Hashmi came to the United States from Pakistan when Fahad was three and his other son, Faisal, was four. He worked for more than two decades as an accountant for the city of New York. Anwar came, as most immigrants do, for his children. He believed in America, in its fairness, its chances for opportunity, its freedoms. And then it all crumbled when the state proved as capricious and cruel as the Pakistani dictatorship he had left behind. On the day of his son's arrest, he said, "my American dream became an American nightmare."

Three law enforcement officials appeared at his home in Flushing, Queens, on June 6, 2006, to inform him that his son, who had been in London completing a master's degree in international relations, had been arrested at Heathrow Airport on terrorism charges. Hashmi, after fighting the order for eleven months while in Belmarsh Prison in London, was the first American citizen extradited under the post-9/11 laws. He was taken in May 2007 to the Metropolitan Correctional Center in lower Manhattan and placed in solitary confinement. Like so many of those arrested during the Bush years, Hashmi was briefly a poster child in the "war on terror." His arrest was the top story on the CBS and NBC nightly news programs, which used graphics that read "Terror Trail" and "Web of Terror."[39]

"I came to this country from Pakistan nearly thirty years ago, in 1982, with my wife and two young boys," his father said. "Coming from a Third World country, we were full of hope and looked towards America for liberty and opportunity. I had an American dream to work hard and give my sons good educations. I worked as an assistant accountant for the city of New York, six days a week, nine hours a day, including overtime, to support my family and to send both my kids through college. We all became US citizens, and my sons fulfilled my dreams by completing their undergraduate and postgraduate education. I was very proud of them.

"In high school and then as a student at Brooklyn College, Fahad became a political activist, concerned about the plight of Muslims around the world and the civil liberties of Muslims in America," he went on. "Growing up here in America, Fahad did not fear expressing his views. But I was scared for him and urged him not to speak out. He would remind me that everything he did was under the law. But having grown up in a Third World country, I had seen that it did not always work this way, and so I worried. He was monitored by law enforcement and quoted in *Time* magazine. But he kept speaking out. And then, with his arrest, my fears came true."

Judge Loretta Preska, who would later oversee the case of the hacker Jeremy Hammond, denied Hashmi bail. His family and friends, who sat crowded together in the courtroom, listened in stunned silence. And then, after five months in jail, Hashmi, already isolated in solitary confinement, was suddenly put under "special administrative measures." SAMs are the state's legal weapon of choice when it seeks to isolate and break prisoners. They were bequeathed to us by the Clinton administration, which justified SAMs as a way to prevent Mafia and other gang leaders from ordering hits from inside prison. The use of SAMs expanded widely after the attacks of 2001. They are frequently used to isolate terrorism case detainees before trial. SAMs, which were renewed by Barack Obama, severely restrict a prisoner's communication with the outside world. They end calls, letters, and visits with anyone except attorneys and sharply limit contact with family members.[40]

Hashmi, once in this legal straitjacket, was not permitted to see much of the evidence against him under a law called the Classified Information Procedures Act, or CIPA. CIPA, begun under the Reagan administration, allows evidence in a trial to be classified and withheld from those being prosecuted.[41]

The weekly visits that Hashmi's family had made to the jail in Manhattan were canceled. A single family member was permitted to visit only once every two weeks, and on a number of occasions the family member was inexplicably denied admittance. During the last five months of the trial, Hashmi's family was barred from visiting him. Anyone who has contact with a prisoner under SAMs is prohibited by law from disclosing any information learned from the detainee. This requirement, in a twist that Kafka would have relished, makes it illegal for those who have contact with an inmate under SAMs—including attorneys—to speak about his or her physical and psychological condition. The measures were imposed because of Hashmi's "proclivity for violence," although he had not been charged with or convicted of committing an act of violence.[42]

Once the SAMs were imposed, "he wrote us occasionally—one letter on no more than three pages at a time—but he was allowed no correspondence or contact with anyone else," his father said of his son. "In addition, because of Fahad's SAMs, we were not allowed to discuss anything we heard from him, including his health or any details of his detention or what he was experiencing, with anyone else. It was like being suffocated."

In a pretrial motion, Hashmi's lawyer presented the extensive medical and scholarly research that demonstrates the severe impact of solitary confinement on human beings, which often leaves them incapable of defending themselves during their trial. It did not sway the judge. Before ever being sentenced, Hashmi lived in a universe where he had no fresh air and was subjected to twenty-three-hour lockdown and constant electronic surveillance, including when he showered or relieved himself. He was barred from group prayer. He exercised alone in a solitary cage. He was denied access to television or a radio. His newspapers were cut up by censors. And this was all *before* trial.

"These years have brought deep disillusionment for my family in the American justice system," Syed Anwar Hashmi said. "Fahad was restricted in reviewing much of the evidence against him, and even his attorney could not discuss much of the evidence with him. Secret evidence is something we knew from back home. The judge accepted the prosecutor's motion to introduce Fahad's political activities and speeches into the trial to demonstrate his mind-set. Where was the First Amendment to protect Fahad's speech? Two days before the trial was set to begin, Judge Preska agreed to the prosecutor's motion to keep the jury anonymous and kept under extra security—even though this could have frightened the jury and affected how they viewed Fahad."

"On the day before trial [April 27, 2010], nearly four years since he had been arrested, I had just returned from dropping off clothes for

Fahad to wear to court when I received a call from my attorney," his father said. "The government had offered a deal to drop three of the four charges against Fahad if he accepted one charge which carried a fifteen-year sentence, and Fahad had agreed to this plea bargain. I was shocked by my son's decision on the eve of his trial, but after I thought more, I wondered how anyone could have decided differently in his situation. Fahad had been in solitary confinement, under SAMs, for nearly three years. The judge had in every instance sided with the government in pretrial motions. If convicted, Fahad faced a possible seventy-year sentence."

Fahad is serving his sentence at the federal supermax in Florence, Colorado. Hashmi's father added, "The US government is concerned about human rights in China and Iran. I wonder about Fahad's rights, and how they have been blatantly violated in this great land. It seems like 'innocent until proven guilty' is only a saying. My son was treated as guilty until proven innocent."

"The Muslim community supported my son by offering prayers, particularly in the month of Ramadan," he said. "But they were initially afraid to raise their voices against injustice. This reminds me of the fear the Chinese have under Communist rule, or Iranians under Ahmadinejad. As a citizen, I now have developed fear of my own government."

"For one charge for luggage storing socks, ponchos, and raincoats in his apartment, he is serving a fifteen-year sentence in the harshest federal prison in the country, still in solitary confinement, still under SAMs," his father said. "The cooperating witness in the case, the one who brought and delivered the luggage, is now free and able to enjoy his life and family."

The despair and bewilderment of Hashmi's father are a reflection of the wider despair and bewilderment that have gripped the lives of many Muslims.

"There are many things I'd like to be able to say about the visit and my son's continuing detention, but because of Fahad's SAMs, I am forbidden," Hashmi's father said. "Everything has changed for my family. Our first grandchild was born nineteen days after Fahad's arrest, our second two years later. But now everything has a cloud over it—graduations, birthdays, holidays, going to the store or the park or visiting family or running errands, and particularly the Eid day. In other words, we have lost our happiness."

The extreme sensory deprivation used on Hashmi and other political prisoners is far more effective in breaking and disorienting detainees than physical abuse is. It is torture as science, the dark art of gradual psychological disintegration. By the time Hashmi was hauled into court, it was questionable whether he had the mental and psychological capability to defend himself or make rational judgments. He was told to stop speaking so quickly at his sentencing; he apologized to the court, saying he had spoken little during his years in isolation, and then burst into tears. This is what the system is designed to do.

Constitutionally protected statements, beliefs, and associations are now a crime. Dissidents, even those who break no laws, can be stripped of their rights and imprisoned without due process. It is the legal equivalent of preemptive war. The state can detain and prosecute people not for what they have done, or even for what they are planning to do, but for holding religious or political beliefs that the state deems seditious.

There will be more Hashmis. In 2006 the Justice Department, planning for future detentions, set up a segregated facility, the Communication Management Unit, at the federal prison in Terre Haute, Indiana. Nearly all the inmates transferred to Terre Haute are Muslims. A second facility has been set up at Marion, Illinois, where the inmates, again, are mostly Muslim but also have included a sprinkling of animal rights and environmental activists, among them Daniel McGowan, who was charged with two counts of arson at logging operations in Oregon. His sentence was given "terrorism enhancements" under the Patriot Act. Amnesty International has called the Marion prison facility "inhumane."[43] All calls and mail are monitored in these two Communication Management Units. Communication among prisoners is required to be only in English. These facilities replicate the conditions for most of those held at Guantánamo.[44]

In Franz Kafka's short story "Before the Law," a tireless supplicant spends his life praying for admittance into the courts of justice. He sits outside the law court for days, months, and years. He makes many attempts to be admitted. He sacrifices everything he owns to sway or bribe the stern doorkeeper. He ages, grows feeble and finally childish. He is told as he nears death that the entrance was constructed solely for him and it will now be closed.[45]

Justice has become as unattainable for Muslim activists and black radicals in the United States as it was for Kafka's frustrated petitioner. The draconian legal mechanisms that condemn African Americans and Muslim Americans who speak out publicly about the outrages we commit in our impoverished urban ghettos and the Middle East have left many, including Abu-Jamal and Hashmi, wasting away in cages. The state has no intention of limiting its persecution to African Americans and Muslims. They were the first. We are next.

———

Cecily McMillan sat in a plastic chair wearing a baggy, oversized gray prison jumpsuit, cheap brown plastic sandals, and horn-rim glasses. Other women, also dressed in prison-issued gray jumpsuits, sat nearby in the narrow, concrete-walled visitation room at Rikers Island in New York. Most were clutching their children, tears streaming down their faces. The children, bewildered, had their arms wrapped tightly around their mothers' necks. It looked like the disaster scene it was.

"It's all out in the open here," said the twenty-five-year-old graduate student at the New School of Social Research in New York City. I spoke with her the day before she was sentenced in a New York criminal court, on May 19, 2014, to three months in jail and five years' probation. "The cruelty of power can't hide like it does on the outside. You get America, everything America has become, especially for poor people of color in prison. My lawyers think I will get two years. But two years is nothing compared to what these women, who never went to trial, never had the possibility of a trial with adequate legal representation, face. There are women in my dorm who, because they have such a poor command of English, do not even understand their charges. I spent a lot of time trying to explain the charges to them."

McMillan endured the last criminal case originating from the Occupy Wall Street protest movement. It is also one of the most emblematic. The state, after the coordinated nationwide eradication of Occupy encampments, relentlessly used the courts to harass and neutralize Occupy activists, often handing out long probation terms that came with activists' forced acceptance of felony charges. A felony charge makes it harder to find employment and bars those with such convictions from serving on juries or working for law enforcement. Most important, the long probation terms effectively prohibit further activism by turning any arrest into a parole violation. McMillan, one of the few who refused to accept a plea deal and have a felony charge on her record, went to court.

The Occupy Wall Street movement was not only about battling back against the rise of a corporate oligarchy. It was also about our right to peaceful protest. The police in cities across the country were deployed to short-circuit this right.[46] I watched New York City police during the Occupy protests yank people from sidewalks into the street, where they would be arrested. I saw police routinely shove protesters and beat them with batons. I saw activists slammed against police cars. I saw groups of protesters suddenly herded like sheep to be confined within police barricades. I saw, and was caught up in, mass arrests in which those around me were handcuffed and then thrown violently onto the sidewalk. The police often blasted pepper spray into faces from inches away, temporarily blinding the victims.

This violence, carried out against nonviolent protesters, came amid draconian city ordinances that effectively outlawed protest and banned demonstrators from public spaces. It was buttressed by heavy police infiltration and surveillance of the movement. When the press or activists attempted to document the abuse by police, they often were assaulted or otherwise blocked from taking photographs or videos. The message the state delivered was clear: *Do not dissent.* And the McMillan trial was part of the message.

McMillan, who spent part of her childhood living in a trailer park in rural Texas, found herself with several hundred other activists at Zuccotti Park in Manhattan in March 2012 to mark the six-month an-

niversary of the start of Occupy Wall Street. The city, fearing the reestab-
lishment of an encampment, deployed large numbers of police officers
to clear the park just before midnight of March 17. The police, heavily
shielded, stormed into the gathering in fast-moving lines. Activists, as
Democracy Now! reported, were shoved, hit, knocked to the ground,
and cuffed. Some ran for safety. More than 100 people were arrested on
the anniversary. After the violence, numerous activists would call the
police aggression perhaps the worst experienced by the Occupy movement. In the mayhem, McMillan—whose bruises were photographed
and subsequently displayed to Amy Goodman on *Democracy Now!*—
was manhandled by a police officer later identified as Grantley Bovell.

Bovell, who was in plainclothes and who, according to McMillan,
did not identify himself as a policeman, allegedly came up from behind
and grabbed McMillan's breast—a perverse form of assault by New
York City police that other female activists also suffered during Occupy
protests. McMillan's elbow made contact with his face, just below the
eye, in what she says appeared to be a reaction to the grope. She says
she has no memory of the incident. By the end of the confrontation, she
was lying on the ground, bruised and convulsing, after being beaten by
the police. She was taken to a hospital emergency room, where police
handcuffed her to a bed.

Had McMillan not been an Occupy activist, the trial that came out of
this beating would have been about her receiving restitution from New
York City for police abuse. Instead, she was charged with felony assault
in the second degree and faced up to seven years in prison.

McMillan's journey from a rural Texas backwater to Rikers Island
was a journey of political awakening. Her parents, divorced when she
was small, had little money. At times she lived with her mother, who
worked in a Dillard's department store, as an accountant for a pool
hall, and later, after earning a degree, as a registered nurse doing weekly
shifts of sixty to seventy hours in hospitals and nursing homes. There
were also painful stretches of unemployment.

Her mother was from Mexico, and she was circumspect about reveal-
ing her ethnicity in the deeply white conservative community, one in
which blacks and other minorities were not welcome. She never taught

her son and daughter Spanish. As a girl, McMillan saw her mother struggle with severe depression, and in one terrifying instance, she was taken to a hospital after she passed out from an overdose of prescription pills. For periods, McMillan, her brother, and her mother survived on welfare, and they moved often: she attended thirteen schools, including five high schools. Her father worked at a Domino's Pizza shop, striving in vain to become a manager.

Racism was endemic in the area. There was a sign in the nearby town of Vidor, not far from the Louisiana state line, that read: IF YOU ARE DARK GET OUT BEFORE DARK. It had replaced an earlier sign that said: DON'T LET THE SUN SET ON YOUR ASS NIGGER.

The families around the McMillans struggled with all the problems that come with poverty—alcoholism, drug abuse, domestic and sexual violence, and despair. Cecily's younger brother was serving a seven-year sentence for drug possession in Texas.

"I grew up around the violence of poverty," she said. "It was normative."

Her parents worked hard to fit into the culture of rural Texas. Mc-Millan said she competed as a child in a beauty pageant called Tiny Miss Valentines of Texas. She was on a cheerleading team. She ran track.

"My parents tried," McMillan said. "They wanted to give us everything. They wanted us to have a lifestyle we could be proud of. My parents, because we were . . . at times poor, were ashamed of who we were. I asked my mother to buy Tommy Hilfiger clothes at the Salvation Army and cut off the insignias and sew them onto my old clothes. I was afraid of being made fun of at school. My mother got up at five in the morning before work and made us pigs in a blanket, putting the little sausages into croissants. She wanted my brother and myself to be proud of her. She really did a lot with so very little."

McMillan spent most of her summers with her paternal grandmother in Atlanta. Those visits opened up another world for her. She attended a Spanish-language camp. She went to blues and jazz festivals. She attended a theater summer camp called Seven Stages that focused on cultural and political perspectives. When she was a teenager, Mc-Millan wrote collective theater pieces, including one in which she wore the American flag as a burka and sang "The Star-Spangled Banner" as a character dressed as Darth Vader walked onto the stage. "My father was horrified," she said. "He walked out of the theater." As a thirteen-year-old, she was in a play called *I Hate Anne Frank*. "It was about American sensationalism," she said. "It asked how the entire experience of the Holocaust could be turned for many people into a girl's positive narrative, a disgusting false optimism. It was not well received."

In Atlanta, art, and especially theater, awakened her to the realities endured by others, from Muslims in the Middle East to the black underclass in the United States. And unlike in the Texas towns where she grew up, she made black friends in Atlanta. She began to wonder about the lives of the African Americans who lived near her in rural Texas. What was it like for them? How did they endure racism? Did black women suffer the way her mother suffered? She began to openly question and challenge the conventions and assumptions of the white community around her. She read extensively, falling in love with the work of Albert Camus.

"I would miss bus stops because I would be reading *The Stranger* or *The Plague*," she said. "Existentialism to me was beautiful. It said the world is shit. It said this is the lot humanity is given. But human beings have to try their best. They swim and they swim and they swim against the waves until they can't swim any longer. You can choose to view these waves as personal attacks against you and give up, or you can swim. And Camus said you should not sell out for a lifeboat. These forces are impersonal. They are structural. I learned from Camus how to live and how to die with dignity."

She attended Lawrence University in Appleton, Wisconsin, through a partial scholarship and loans. As an undergraduate, she worked as a student teacher in inner-city schools in Chicago and joined the Young Democratic Socialists, the youth chapter of Democratic Socialists of America. In the fall of 2011, she enrolled at the New School for Social Research in New York City, where she planned to write a master's thesis on Jane Addams, Hull House, and the settlement movement. The Occupy Wall Street demonstrations began in the city six days after she arrived at the school.

McMillan said that at first she was disappointed with the Occupy encampment in Zuccotti Park and felt that it lacked political maturity. She had participated in the political protests in Madison, Wisconsin, in early 2011, and the solidarity of government workers, including police, that she saw there deeply influenced her feelings about activism.[47] She came away strongly committed to nonviolence.

"Police officers sat down to occupy with us," she said of the protests in Madison. "It was unprecedented. We were with teachers, the fire department, police, and students. You walked around saying thank you to the police. You embraced police. [But then] I went to Occupy in New York and saw drum circles and people walking around naked. There was yoga. I thought, *What is this?* I thought for many protesters this was just some social experiment they would go back to their academic institutions and write about. Where I come from people are hungry. Women are getting raped. Fathers and stepfathers beat the shit out of children. People die. . . . Some people would rather not live.

"At first I looked at the Occupiers and thought they were so bourgeois," she went on. "I thought they were trying to dress down their class by wearing all black. I was disgusted. But in the end I was wrong. I wasn't meeting them where they were. These were kids, some of whom had been to Harvard, Yale, or Princeton, [who] were the jewels of their family's legacy. They were doing something radical. They had never been given the opportunity to have their voices heard, to have their own agency. They weren't clowns, like I first thought. They were really brave. We learned to have conversations. And that was beautiful. And these people are my friends today."

She joined Occupy Wall Street's Demands Working Group, which attempted to draw up a list of core demands that the movement could endorse. She continued with her academic work at the New School for Social Research and also worked part-time. McMillan was visiting her grandmother, who was terminally ill in Atlanta, in November 2011 when the police cleared out the Zuccotti Park encampment. When she returned to the New School, she took part in the occupation of school buildings, but some Occupiers trashed the property, leading to a bitter disagreement between her and other activists. Radical elements in the movement who supported the property destruction held a "shadow trial" and condemned her as a "bureaucratic provocateur."

"I started putting together an affinity group after the New School occupation," she said. "I realized there was a serious problem between anarchists and socialists and democratic socialists. I wanted, like Bayard Rustin, to bring everyone together. I wanted to repair the fractured left. I wanted to build coalitions."

Judge Ronald A. Zweibel was caustic and hostile to McMillan and her defense team when I attended the trial. Her defense lawyers said he barred video evidence that would have helped her case. He issued a gag order that forbade the defense lawyers, Martin Stolar and Rebecca Heinegg, from communicating with the press. The jury was also barred from being made aware of the widespread and indiscriminate violence that took place in the park that night, much of it photographed. And the judge denied her bail.

Bovell, the policeman who McMillan says beat her, had been investigated at least twice by the Internal Affairs Bureau of the New York City Police Department, according to the British newspaper *The Guardian*. Stolar's motion requesting access to Bovell's NYPD personnel file was rejected by Judge Zweibel, who said the attorney had "failed to even establish that 'prior misconduct' of any sort has been found, or documented, by the NYPD against Officer Bovell."[48] In one of these cases, Bovell and his partner were sued for allegedly using an unmarked police car to strike a seventeen-year-old fleeing on a dirt bike. The teenager said his nose was broken, two teeth were knocked out, and his forehead was lacerated. The case was settled out of court. The officer was allegedly also captured on a video that appeared to show him kicking a suspect on the floor of a Bronx grocery, according to Stolar. Stolar also said he had seen documents that implicated Bovell in a ticket-fixing scandal in his Bronx precinct.

Austin Guest, a thirty-three-year-old graduate of Harvard University who was arrested at Zuccotti Park on the night McMillan was assaulted, was at the time suing Bovell for allegedly intentionally banging his head on the internal stairs of an MTA bus that took him and other activists in for processing. The judge ruled that Bovell's involvement in the cases stemming from the chasing of the youth on the dirt bike and the Guest arrest could not be presented as evidence in the McMillan case, according to *The Guardian*.[49] The corporate state, unwilling to address the grievances and injustices endured by the underclass, is extremely nervous about the mass movements that have swept the country in recent years. And if protests erupt again—as I think they will—the state hopes it will have neutralized much of the potential leadership. Being an activist in a peaceful mass protest was the only real "crime" McMillan committed.

"This was never about justice," she said. "Just as it is not about justice for these other women. One mother was put in here for shoplifting after she lost her job and her house and needed to feed her children. There is another prisoner, a preschool teacher with a one-year-old son she was breast-feeding, who let her cousin stay with her after her cousin was evicted. It turns out the cousin sold drugs. The cops found money, not drugs, that the cousin kept in the house and took the mother. They told her to leave her child with the neighbors. There is story after story in here like this. It wakes you up."

McMillan, who was released on July 2, 2014, has since worked to organize outside support for those in Rikers who endure abuse and mistreatment.

Her case stood in contrast with the blanket impunity given to the criminals of Wall Street. Some 8,000 nonviolent Occupy protesters were arrested across the nation. Not one banker or investor went to jail for causing the 2008 financial meltdown. The disparity of justice mirrored the disparity in incomes and the disparity in power.[50]

"I am deeply committed to nonviolence, especially in the face of all the violence around me inside and outside this prison," McMillan said. "I could not accept [the plea deal]. I had to fight back. That is why I am an activist. Being branded as someone who was violent was intolerable."

The case galvanized many activists, who saw in McMillan's persecution the persecution of movements across the globe struggling for nonviolent democratic change. McMillan was visited in Rikers by some of the Russian human rights campaigners from the dissident group Pussy Riot.[51] Hundreds of people, including nine of the twelve jurors and some New York City Council members, urged Judge Zweibel to be lenient.

An online petition signed by 195,949 people called on Mayor Bill de Blasio and Governor Andrew Cuomo to intervene on her behalf.[52]

"I am very conscious of how privileged I am, especially in here," McMillan told me. "When you are in prison, white privilege works against you. You tend to react when you come out of white privilege by saying, 'You can't do that,' when prison authorities force you to do something arbitrary and meaningless. But the poor understand the system. They know it is absurd, capricious, and senseless, that it is all about being forced to pay deference to power. If you react out of white privilege, it sets you apart. I have learned to respond as a collective, to speak to authority in a unified voice. And this has been good for me. I needed this.

"We can talk about movement theory all we want," she went on. "We can read Michel Foucault or Pierre Bourdieu, but at a certain point it becomes a game. You have to get out and live it. You have to actually build a movement. And if we don't get to work to build a movement now, there will be no one studying movement theory in a decade because there will be no movements. I can do this in prison. I can do this out of prison. It is all one struggle."

When I saw McMillan, she was in Rikers' Rose M. Singer Center with about forty other women. They slept in rows of cots. Nearly all the women were poor mothers of color, most of them black, Hispanic, or Chinese. McMillan was giving lessons in English in exchange for lessons in Spanish.

She had bonded with an African American woman known as "Fat Baby" who ogled her and told her she had nice legs. Fat Baby threw out a couple of lame pickup lines that, McMillan said, "sounded as if she was a construction worker. I told her I would teach her some pickup lines that were a little more subtle."

McMillan, who was required to have a prison activity, participated in the drug rehabilitation program, although she did not use drugs. She was critical of the instructor's feeding of "positive" and Christian thinking to the inmates, some of whom were Muslims. "It is all about the power of positive thinking, about how they made mistakes and bad choices in life, and now they can correct those mistakes by taking another road, a Christian road, to a new life," she said. "This focus on happy thoughts pervades the prison. There is little analysis of the structural causes for poverty and oppression. It is as if it was all about decisions we made, not that were made for us. And this is how those in power want it. This kind of thinking induces passivity."

McMillan was receiving dozens of letters daily at Rikers, but during the week before my visit she was told every day that she had none. She suspected the prison had cut off the flow of mail to her.

My pens and paper were confiscated during the two-hour process it took to enter Rikers Island. I had to reconstruct the notes from our conversation, which lasted an hour and a half. The entry process is normal for visitors, who on weekends stand in long lines in metal chutes outside the prison. My body was searched, and my clothing was minutely inspected for contraband. I had to go through two metal detectors.

"It is hard to read, it is hard to write," she went on. "There is constant movement and constant noise." McMillan had just finished writing a message to supporters who planned to rally in her support the afternoon before her sentencing. She told them:

> Oppression is rampant. Take a moment to try & really see, hear, feel the suffering of the many around you. Now imagine the power of your collective love ethic to stand against it.
>
> Only through the pervasive spread of such a love ethic by the many for the many—not just the privileged few—will we *finally* have ourselves a movement.

McMillan took comfort from her supporters and her family and from those of her heroes who endured prison for a just cause. She had read and reread the speech the Socialist Eugene V. Debs made to a federal court in Cleveland before he went to prison for opposing the draft in World War I. His words, she said, had become her own.

"Your honor, years ago I recognized my kinship with all living beings, and I made up my mind that I was not one bit better than the meanest on earth," Debs said. "I said it then, as I say it now, that while there is a lower class, I am in it, and while there is a criminal element I am of it, and while there is a soul in prison, I am not free."[53]

VI / Vigilante Violence

It is not permissible that the authors of devastation should also be innocent. It is the innocence which constitutes the crime.[1]

—JAMES BALDWIN, *THE FIRE NEXT TIME*

My mother's family arrived in Watertown, Massachusetts, in 1633, in the figure of John Prince, a Puritan fleeing Britain. My father's family landed with William Hedges, a tanner and also a Puritan refugee, in East Hampton, New York, in 1650. As time passed, the huge tributaries of these two families intersected with every major event in American life. My forebears included soldiers, whalers and sea captains, farmers, a few writers and scholars, and a smattering of political leaders who ascended to governorships. By the time of the Civil War, the family included a Union general and a colonel in the elite Iron Brigade on one side, and a Confederate spy on the other. A couple of my ancestors took part in the brutal Indian wars. One was a scout for General Philip Sheridan on the Western plains. Lakota warriors murdered him, a fate he appears to have deserved, given the drunken, murderous rampages against Indian encampments he describes in letters home to Maine. Other ancestors were sober, dour-looking Anglican ministers, teachers, and abolitionists.

A distant relative of my father's family became the largest landowner in Cuba after 1898, when it was seized by force from the Spanish. A few of this family's descendants worked with the CIA in the fight against Fidel Castro, in the waning days of the Batista dictatorship. My maternal grandfather, who worked most of his life in a small-town post office, served as a master sergeant in the Maine Army National Guard in the

1930s. He and other Guardsmen regularly waded into the crowds of striking textile and mill workers to violently break up labor unrest. He kept his Army-issued truncheon in his barn; it had twenty-three small nicks he had made with his penknife. "One nick," he told me, "for every Communist I hit."

My father and most of my uncles fought in World War II. One uncle was severely maimed, physically and psychologically, in the South Pacific and drank himself to death. I was in Central America in the 1980s during the proxy wars waged by Washington. I accompanied a Marine Corps battalion as it battled Iraqi troops into Kuwait during the first Gulf War. My family history intersects with the persistent patterns of violence that are a constant in American life, both at home and abroad.

Any rebellion must contend with this endemic American violence, especially vigilante violence, as well as the sickness of the gun culture that is its natural expression. As it has done throughout American history, the state, under siege, will turn to extrajudicial groups of armed thugs to repress populist movements. Radical change in America is paid for with blood.

There are some 310 million firearms in the United States, including 114 million handguns, 110 million rifles, and 86 million shotguns. There is no reliable data on the number of military-style assault weapons in private hands, but the working estimate is about 1.5 million. The United States has the highest rate of gun ownership in the world—an average of 89 per 100 people, according to the 2007 Small Arms Survey. By comparison, Canada has 31 per 100 people.[2] Canada usually sees under 200 gun-related homicides a year.[3] Our addiction to violence and bloodletting—which will continue to grow—marks a nation in terminal decline.

The view of ourselves as divine agents of purification anointed by God and progress to reconfigure the world around us is a myth that remains firmly embedded in the American psyche. Most of our historians, with only a few exceptions—such as Eric Foner, Howard Zinn, Richard Hofstadter, and Richard Slotkin—studiously avoid addressing these patterns of violence. They examine a single foreign war. They chronicle an isolated incident, such as the draft riots in New York during the

Civil War. They write about the Indian wars. They detail the cruelty of Jim Crow and lynching. They do not see in the totality of our military adventures—including our bloody occupation of the Philippines, when General Jacob H. Smith ordered his troops to kill every Filipino over the age of ten and turn the island of Samar into "a howling wilderness"[4]—a universal truth about the American soul and the naturalness with which we turn to violence at home and abroad. We suffer from a dangerous historical amnesia and self-delusional fantasies about the virtues and goodness of ourselves and of empire. We have masked our cultural propensity for widespread and indiscriminate murder. "The essential American soul is hard, isolate, stoic, and a killer," D. H. Lawrence wrote. "It has never yet melted."[5]

Violence in America is not restricted to state violence. There is a tradition of vigilante violence that is used, usually with the state's tacit if unofficial blessing, to crush dissent, to keep repressed minorities in a state of fear, or to exact revenge on those the state has branded as traitors. It is a product of hatred, not hope. It is directed against the weak, not the strong. And it is deeply ingrained in the American psyche.

America has been formed and shaped by slave patrols, gunslingers, Pinkerton and Baldwin-Felts detectives, gangs of strikebreakers, hired gun thugs, company militias, and the American Legion—originally right-wing World War I veterans who attacked union agitators, especially those belonging to the Industrial Workers of the World (the "Wobblies"). The influence on the country of the White Citizens' Council, the White League—which carried out public military drills and functioned as the armed wing of the Democratic Party in the South—the Knights of the White Camelia, and the Ku Klux Klan—which boasted more than 3 million members between 1915 and 1944 and took over the governance of some states—has been equally profound.[6] More recently, heavily armed mercenary paramilitaries, violent Cuban exile groups, and armed militias such as the Oath Keepers and the anti-immigration extremist group Ranch Rescue have perpetuated America's seamless tradition of vigilantism.

These vigilante groups have been tolerated, and often encouraged and utilized, by the ruling elite. And roaming the landscape along with these vigilante groups have been lone gunmen and mass killers who murder for money or power or to appease their own personal demons.

Vigilante groups in America do not trade violence for violence. They are mostly white men who often prey on people of color and radicals. They are capitalism's ideological vanguard, its shock troops used to break populist movements and tyrannize the oppressed. And they will be unleashed against any mass movement that seriously threatens the structures of capitalist power and calls for rebellion. Imagine if, instead of right-wing militias, so-called ecoterrorists—who have never been found responsible for taking a single American life—had showed up armed in Nevada on April 12, 2014, to challenge the federal government's attempt to thwart rancher Cliven Bundy from continuing to graze his cattle on public land. How would the authorities have responded if those carrying guns had been from the environmental group Earth First? What if they had been black?

The long struggle to abolish slavery, then to free blacks from the reign of terror after the Civil War, and to build labor unions and organize for workers' rights—these movements flushed from the bowels of American society the thugs who found a sense of self-worth and intoxicating power in their role as armed vigilantes. In America, such thugs have always worked for minimal pay and the license to use indiscriminate violence against those branded as anti-American.

It was armed vigilantes who in 1914 attacked a tent encampment of workers in Ludlow, Colorado. The vigilantes set tents on fire, burning to death eleven children and two women.[7] This brutality characterized the labor wars of the early twentieth century. Vigilante groups working on behalf of coal, steel, and mining concerns gunned down hundreds of unarmed labor organizers. Thousands more were wounded. The United States had the most violent labor wars in the industrialized world, as the scholars Philip Taft and Philip Ross have documented.[8] And murderous rampages by these vigilante groups, almost always in the pay of companies or oligarchs, were sanctioned even though no American labor union ever publicly called for an armed uprising. There is no American immigrant group, from Chinese laborers to the Irish, who have not suffered the wrath of armed vigilantes. And African Americans know too intimately how judicial systems work to protect white vigilantes and police who gun down unarmed black men, women, and children. There is a long, tragic continuum from the murders and lynching of blacks following Emancipation to the strangulation on July 17, 2014, of Eric Garner in Staten Island by police who charged him with selling loose, untaxed cigarettes, as well as the shooting to death on August 9, 2014, in Ferguson, Missouri, of an unarmed African American teenager, Michael Brown, by a white police officer. It is lynching by another name. The police officers who carried out these murders, offering a window into a court system that routinely ignores black suffering and murder, were never charged with a crime. And the longer this continues the more likely become random and violent acts of retaliation, which the state will label terrorism and use to justify odious forms of repression. Once this eruption happens, as American history has illustrated, white vigilantes, along with the organs of state security, are given carte blanche to attack and even murder those who are demonized as enemies of the state.

Vigilante thugs serve the interests of the power elites, as in the case involving the Nevada rancher who made war, in essence, on behalf of corporations that seek to eradicate public ownership of land. These vigilantes revel in a demented hypermasculinity. They champion a racist nationalism and sexism. And they have huge megaphones on the airwaves, funded by the most retrograde forces in American capitalism. The gang violence in poor, urban neighborhoods in cities like Chicago or Detroit credentializes these vigilante groups and stokes the inchoate fear of blacks among whites that lies at the core of the gun culture and American vigilantism.

The *raison d'être* given by vigilante groups for the need to bear arms is that guns protect us from tyranny. Guns keep us safe in our homes. Guns are the bulwark of liberty. But history does not support this contention. The Communist Party during the rise of fascism in Nazi Germany did not lack for weapons. Throughout the dictatorship of Saddam Hussein in Iraq, citizens had assault weapons in their homes. During the war in Yugoslavia, AK-47 assault rifles were almost as common in households as stoves. I watched in Iraq and Yugoslavia as heavily armed units encircled houses and those inside walked out with their hands in the air, leaving their assault rifles behind.

American vigilantes will act no differently if members of the US Army or SWAT teams surround their homes. When 10,000 armed coal miners at Blair Mountain in West Virginia rose up in 1921 for the right to form unions and held gun thugs and company militias at bay for five days, the government called in the Army.[9] The miners were not suicidal. When the Army arrived, they disbanded. And faced with the full weight of the US military, armed vigilante groups today will disband as well. The militias in Nevada might have gotten the Bureau of Land Management to back down, but they would have scattered like a flock of frightened crows if the government had sent in the 101st Airborne.

The engine of vigilante violence is not fear of government. It is the fear by white people of the black underclass and of the radicals who champion the cause of the oppressed. The black underclass has been enslaved, lynched, imprisoned, and impoverished for centuries. The white vigilantes do not acknowledge the reality of this oppression, but at the same time they are deeply worried about retribution directed against whites. Guns, for this reason, are made easily available to white people, while gun ownership is largely criminalized for blacks. The hatred expressed by vigilante groups for people of color, along with Jews and Muslims, is matched by their hatred for the college-educated elite. The vigilantes see people of color, along with those who espouse the liberal social values of the college-educated elites, including gun control, as contaminants to society.

Richard Rorty, in *Achieving Our Country: Leftist Thought in Twentieth-Century America*, fears that a breakdown will be inevitable once workers realize that the government has no genuine interest in raising low and substandard wages, halting the exportation of jobs overseas, or curbing crippling personal debt. White-collar workers, who are also being downsized, will turn to the far right, he writes, and refuse to be taxed to provide social benefits:

At that point, something will crack. The nonsuburban electorate will decide that the system has failed and start looking for a strongman to vote for—someone willing to assure them that, once he is elected, the smug bureaucrats, tricky lawyers, overpaid bond salesmen, and postmodern professors will no longer be calling the shots. A scenario like that of Sinclair Lewis' novel *It Can't Happen Here* may then be played out. For once such a strongman takes office, nobody can predict what will happen. In 1932, most of the predictions made about what would happen if Hindenburg named Hitler chancellor were wildly overoptimistic.

One thing that is very likely to happen is that the gains made in the past forty years by black and brown Americans, and by homosexuals, will be wiped out. Jocular contempt for women will come back into fashion. The words "nigger" and "kike" will once again be heard in the workplace. All the sadism which the academic Left tried to make unacceptable to its students will come flooding back. All the resentment which badly educated Americans feel about having their manners dictated to them by college graduates will find an outlet.[10]

America's episodic violence, while dwarfed by the campaigns of genocide and mass extermination carried out by totalitarian systems led by the Nazis, Joseph Stalin, and Mao Tse-tung, is nevertheless, as the black activist H. Rap Brown once said, "as American as cherry pie."[11] We have always mythologized, even idolized, our vigilante killers. The Indian fighters, gunslingers, and outlaws on the frontier, as well as the mobsters and the feuding clans such as the Hatfields and McCoys, color our history.

Vigilantes and lone avengers are the popular heroes in American culture. They are celebrated on television and in Hollywood movies. Audiences, especially as they feel economic and political power slipping from their hands, yearn for the violent authority embodied in rogue cops in films such as *Dirty Harry* or in unrepentant killers such as Bradley Cooper in *American Sniper*. D. W. Griffith's 1915 film *The Birth of a Nation,* inspired by and adapted, in part, from Thomas Dixon Jr.'s novel *The Clansman,* was the prototype for the filmic celebrations of American vigilante violence.

President Woodrow Wilson held a screening of *The Birth of a Nation*. It was the first motion picture shown at the White House. Wilson praised Griffith's portrayal of savage, animalistic black men—portrayed by white actors in blackface—humiliating noble Southern men and carrying out sexual assaults on white women. "It is like writing history with lightning, and my only regret is that it is all so terribly true," Wilson reportedly said.[12] The film swept the nation. White audiences, including in the North, cheered the white vigilantes. The ranks of the Ku Klux Klan exploded by a few million following the film's release.

> The really rapid growth of the Klan did *not* occur in the early years when *The Birth of a Nation* was at the peak of its influence and availability. By 1919, the Klan had only a few thousand members. Not until the summer of 1920 [five years after the film's release] . . . did the real expansion of the Klan begin. By the summer of 1921, it had around 100,000 members. . . . By the middle years of the 1920s, the Klan, according to Nancy Maclean, may have reached a peak of 5 million members spread across the nation. . . . It is impossible to say with any certainty what the precise role of *The Birth of a Nation* was in encouraging this increase; but as African-American scholar Lawrence Reddick noted in 1944, "Its glorification of the Ku Klux Klan was at least one factor which enabled the Klan to enter upon its period of greatest expansion." James Baldwin called the film "an elaborate justification of mass murder."[13]

A century later, our culture's long infatuation with guns and acquiescence to vigilante killings continue to inspire the lone vigilantism of gunmen such as George Zimmerman, who followed an unarmed black teenager, Trayvon Martin, through a gated community in Florida and killed him. That state's "stand your ground" law that allowed Zimmerman to be acquitted of murder is the judicial sanction of vigilante violence.

In 1984 Bernhard Goetz, in one of the most celebrated cases of vigilante violence, used an unlicensed gun to shoot four black teenagers in a New York subway car. He claimed the black men were trying to mug him. The National Rifle Association (NRA) was linked to Goetz's legal defense, and one of the NRA's daughter organizations, the Fire Arms Civil Rights Legal Defense, provided funds. Goetz was acquitted of attempted murder and convicted only of illegal possession of a firearm, for which he spent eight months in jail.[14] The case strengthened arguments for less restrictive "concealed carry" laws. It was because of Goetz and the NRA that Zimmerman was legally permitted to carry the concealed Kel-Tec PF-9 pistol he used to murder an unarmed seventeen-year-old boy.

In December 2012, twenty first-graders and six adults were gunned down in an elementary school in Newtown, Connecticut, yet the Senate will not pass legislation imposing stiffer background checks on gun purchasers, nor a ban on assault weapons. On average, 32 Americans are murdered with guns every day. Another 140 are treated for a gun assault in an emergency room.[15] Some 30,000 Americans die each year from gunfire—and about two-thirds of the shootings are suicides.[16] But Newtown, like the mass shootings at a movie theater in Aurora, Colorado (12 dead), at Virginia Tech in Blacksburg, Virginia (33 dead), at the immigration center in Binghamton, New York (14 dead), and at Columbine High School in Littleton, Colorado (15 dead), has had no discernible effect on mitigating our gun culture. There has been a school shooting on average every ten days since the Newtown massacre.[17]

The state has never opposed the widespread public ownership of guns because these weapons have rarely been deployed against the state. In this, the United States is an anomaly. It has a heavily armed population and yet maintains remarkable political stability—because, as Hofstadter writes in *American Violence*, "our violence lacks both an ideological and geographical center; it lacks cohesion; it has been too various, diffuse, and spontaneous to be forged into a single, sustained, inveterate hatred shared by entire social classes." He adds that Americans also have "a remarkable lack of memory where violence is concerned and have left most of our excesses a part of our buried history." Hofstadter notes that "most of our violence has taken the form of action by one group of citizens against another group, rather than by citizens against the state. The sheer size of the country, the mixed ethnic, religious, and racial composition of the people, and the diffuseness of power under our federal system have all tended to blunt or minimize citizen-versus-state conflicts and to throw citizen-versus-citizen conflicts into high relief."[18]

We are not a people with a revolutionary or an insurrectionary tradition. The War of Independence, while it borrowed the rhetoric of revolution, replaced a foreign oligarchy with a native, slaveholding oligarchy. The founding fathers were conservative. The primacy of private property, especially slaves, was paramount to the nation's founders.[19]

The framers of the Constitution established a series of mechanisms to thwart the popular will, from the electoral college to the appointment of senators, buttressed by the disenfranchisement of African Americans, women, Native Americans, and the landless. George Washington, probably the wealthiest man in the country when the war was over—much of his money was earned by speculating on seized Indian land—shared exclusive economic and political power with his fellow aristocrats. This distrust of popular rule among the elite runs in a straight line from *The Federalist Papers* and the Constitutional Convention of 1787 to the 2000 presidential election, where the Democratic candidate, Al Gore, received over half a million more popular votes than the Republican George W. Bush.

The few armed rebellions—such as the 1786 and 1787 Shays' Rebellion and the 1921 armed uprising at Blair Mountain—were swiftly and brutally put down by a combination of armed vigilante groups and government troops. More importantly, these rebellions were concerned with specific local grievances rather than broad political and ideological disputes. "Since our violence did not typically begin with anyone's desire to subvert the state, it did not typically end by undermining the legitimacy of authority," Hofstadter writes.[20] The federal structure, as Hofstadter notes, has effectively diverted violence away from symbols of national power to regional or state authority. The miners at Blair Mountain picked up weapons for the right to organize unions in West Virginia. African Americans, enraged by police violence in Oakland, Chicago, Philadelphia, and other cities in the 1960s, created groups such as the Black Panthers primarily for self-defense, although the party later evolved into a quasi-revolutionary movement.[21] The universal, radical ideologies and utopian visions that sparked revolutions in Russia and Germany after World War I are alien to our intellectual tradition.

"Most American violence," Hofstadter observes,

> has been initiated with a "conservative" bias. It has been unleashed against abolitionists, Catholics, radicals, workers and labor organizers, Negroes, Orientals, and other ethnic or racial or ideological minorities, and has been used ostensibly to protect the American, the Southern, the white Protestant, or simply the established middle-class way of life and morals. A high proportion of our violent actions has thus come from the top dogs or the middle dogs. Such has been the character of most mob and vigilante movements. This may help to explain why so little of it has been used against state authority, and why in turn it has been so easily and indulgently forgotten.[22]

Thomas Paine is America's single great revolutionary theorist. We have produced a slew of admirable anarchists (Alexander Berkman, Emma Goldman, Dorothy Day, and Noam Chomsky), and radical leaders have arisen out of oppressed groups (Sitting Bull, Frederick Douglass, Elizabeth Cady Stanton, Fannie Lou Hamer, Martin Luther King Jr., Malcolm X, Cornel West, and bell hooks). But we do not have a tradition of revolutionists. This makes Paine unique.

Paine's brilliance as a writer—his essay *Common Sense* is one of the finest pieces of rhetorical writing in the English language—was matched by his understanding of British imperial power. No revolutionist can challenge power if he or she does not grasp how power works. Of Paine's many contributions to the American Revolution, this understanding ranks as one of the most important.

Many American leaders, including Benjamin Franklin, were hoping to work out an accommodation with the British crown to keep America a British colony—just as many now believe they can work through traditional mechanisms of power, including electoral politics and the judicial system, to reform corporate power. Paine, partly because he did

not come to America from England until he was thirty-seven, understood that the British monarchy—not unlike our corporate state—had
no interest in accommodation.

It became Paine's job to explain to his American audience the reality
of British power and what effective resistance to this power would entail. Paine knew that the British government, which wielded the global
imperial power that America wields today, was blinded by its hubris and
military prowess. It had lost the ability to listen and as a result had lost
the ability to make rational choices—as the inhabitants of New York
would discover when British warships and mercenary troops during the
revolution mercilessly bombarded and occupied the city. The British
foolishly believed that their superior military force alone would decide
the conflict, the same mistake the United States made in Iraq and Afghanistan and earlier in Vietnam.

Paine created a new, revolutionary political vocabulary. *Common
Sense, Rights of Man,* and *The Age of Reason* were the most widely read
political tracts of the eighteenth century.[23] *Common Sense* went through
twenty-five editions and reached hundreds of thousands of readers in
1776 alone.[24] It was the first political essay in Enlightenment Europe to
call for a separation between *"civil society"* and *"the state,"* terms that
political philosophers as far back as Aristotle (*koinonìa politikè*) and
Cicero (*societas civilis*) had considered interchangeable.[25] Civil society,
Paine argued in defiance, must always act as a counterweight against the
state in a democracy. Power, he warned, even in a democracy, carries
within it the seeds of tyranny.

Paine, as George Orwell and James Baldwin did later, used his pen
as a weapon. He detested the flowery and ornate writing of his age, epit-
omized by academics and philosophers such as Edmund Burke, whose
turgid prose he called "Bastilles of the word."[26] His lucid, crystallite writing was deeply feared by the monarchies in Europe, as well as the Jacobins in France, who imprisoned Paine and planned to execute him for
denouncing the Reign of Terror. He fearlessly spoke undeniable truths.
And he did so in a language that was accessible. He called his readers to
act upon these truths. "My motive and object in all my political works,
beginning with *Common Sense,*" Paine remembered in 1806, " . . . have

been to rescue man from tyranny and false systems and false principles of government, and enable him to be free."[27] Chronically short of
money, Paine pressed his publishers to print cheap editions so the poor
and working classes could afford them.[28] And he famously donated the
profits of *Common Sense* and his popular *Crisis* essays to help fund the
revolutionary war effort.[29]

"Where liberty is, there is my country," Benjamin Franklin once said
to Paine. "Where liberty is not, there is my country," Paine replied. For
Paine, the role of a citizen extended beyond national borders. The fight
of those living under any system of tyranny was his fight. "When it shall
be said in any country in the world, 'My poor are happy; neither ignorance nor distress is to be found among them; my jails are empty of
prisoners, my streets of beggars; the aged are not in want, the taxes are
not oppressive; the rational world is my friend, because I am a friend of
happiness—when these things can be said," wrote Paine, "then may that
country boast of its constitution and its government."[30]

One of the most important keys to radical social change, as historian
J.G.A. Pocock points out, is a change in the nature of language itself,
in the emergence of both new words and new meanings for old words.
"Language," he wrote, "is both a product of history and possesses a history of its own."[31] The call for revolution advanced by Paine, like those
from writers such as Jean-Jacques Rousseau, were issued in the new language of secular rationalism rather than the older language of religion.
But Paine, unlike Rousseau, wrote in the everyday language of working
people. Grounding his writing in their common experiences, he was
the first political writer to extend debate beyond university halls, government office buildings, and elite clubs and salons to the streets and
the taverns. Paine knew liberty was intimately connected with language.
And he knew that those who seek to monopolize power always use inaccessible and specialized jargon to exclude the average citizen. Paine
broke these chains.

Paine's clarity will have to be replicated today. We too will have to
form a new language. We will have to articulate our reality through the
ideas of socialism rather than capitalism in an age of diminishing resources. And we will have to do this in a form that is accessible. Foner

cites Paine's ability to reach the general population as one of his most
significant achievements:

> Paine was one of the creators of this secular language of revolution, a
> language in which timeless discontents, millennial aspirations and pop-
> ular traditions were expressed in a strikingly new vocabulary. The very
> slogans and rallying cries we associate with the revolutions of the late
> eighteenth century come from Paine's writings: the "rights of man," the
> "age of reason," the "age of revolution" and the "times that try men's
> souls." Paine helped to transform the meaning of the key words of po-
> litical discourse. In *Common Sense* he was among the first writers to use
> "republic" in a positive rather than derogatory sense; in *The Rights of
> Man* he abandoned the old classical definition of "democracy," as a state
> where each citizen participated directly in government, and created its
> far broader, far more favorable modern meaning. Even the word "rev-
> olution" was transformed in his writing, from a term derived from the
> motion of planets and implying a cyclical view of history to one signify-
> ing vast and irreversible social and political change.[32]

Paine also understood that despotic regimes—and here the corporate state serves as a contemporary example—make war on reason and
rational thought. They circumscribe free speech and free assembly. They
marginalize and silence critics. They seek to subjugate all institutions to
despotism—or in our case, corporate power. They use propaganda to
rob people of the language to describe their daily reality and discredit
those who seek radical change. The goal is to render a population politically alienated. Those who live under despotic regimes, Paine noted,
are denied the ability to communicate and discuss in a national forum
their most basic concerns and grievances. And this suppression, Paine
understood, has consequences. "Let men communicate their thoughts
with freedom," Paine's attorney Thomas Erskine said, quoting Paine,
in Paine's 1792 trial in Britain for seditious libel, "and their indigna-
tion fly off like a fire spread on the surface; like gunpowder scattered,
they kindle, they communicate; but the explosion is neither loud nor
dangerous—keep them under restraint, it is subterranean fire, whose

agitation is unseen till it bursts into earthquake or volcano."[33] Finally, Paine understood that war is always the preferred activity of despotic states, for, as he would write in *The Rights of Man*, war is essentially "the art of conquering at home."

Paine paid for his honesty. When he returned to England, where he wrote *The Rights of Man*, he was relentlessly persecuted by the state, as he would later be persecuted in France and in America upon his final return. John Keane, in his biography *Tom Paine: A Political Life*, describes some of what Paine endured as a radical in late-eighteenth-century England:

> Government spies tailed him constantly on London's streets, sending back a stream of reports to the Home Secretary's office. Those parts of the press that functioned as government mouthpieces pelted him with abuse. "It is earnestly recommended to Mad Tom," snarled the *Times*, "that he should embark for France, and there be naturalized into the regular confusion of democracy." Broadsheets containing "intercepted correspondence from Satan to Citizen Paine" pictured him as a three-hearted, fire-breathing monster, named "Tom Stich." Open letters, often identically worded but signed with different pen names, were circulated through taverns and alehouses. "Brother Weavers and Artificers," thundered "a gentleman" to the inhabitants of Manchester and Salford, "Do not let us be humbugged by Mr. Paine, who tells us a great many Truths in his book, in order to shove off his Lies." Dozens of sermons and satires directed at Paine were published, many of them written anonymously for commoners by upper-class foes masquerading as commoners.[34]

Paine's power, like Orwell's and Baldwin's, lay in his refusal to be anyone's propagandist. He told people, even people who supported him, what they often did not want to hear. He may have embraced the American Revolution, as he embraced the French Revolution, but he was a fierce abolitionist and a foe of the use of terror as a political tool, a stance for which he was eventually imprisoned in revolutionary France. He asked the American revolutionaries "with what consistency, or decency," they could "complain so loudly of attempts to enslave them, while they hold so many hundred thousands in slavery."[35] He denounced in the National Convention in France—where he was one of two foreigners allowed to be elected and sit as a delegate—the calls in the chamber to execute the king, Louis XVI. "He that would make his own liberty secure must guard even his enemy from oppression," Paine said. "For if he violates this duty he establishes a precedent that will reach to himself."[36] Unchecked legislatures, he warned, could be as despotic as unchecked monarchs. His warning was prophetic.

On July 24, 1794, the revolutionary government ordered that Paine, held in the Luxembourg prison, be executed. The next morning a turnkey, walking down the corridor that held cells, chalked the doors of those to be taken to the guillotine the next morning. The turnkey chalked the number 4 on the inside of Paine's cell door, which was left open during the day for ventilation. It was only when another turnkey later in the day closed the door to Paine's cell that Paine and his cellmates were inadvertently spared. That evening the armed squad that came to collect the condemned passed by Paine's door, the number 4 now facing the inside of the cell. They dragged out screaming prisoners in nearby cells, but left behind Paine, who was suffering from a high fever, and the others waiting breathless in his cell.[37]

Paine's placidity and calm, even in the face of death, made him one of the most beloved prisoners in the Luxembourg. When George-Jacques Danton and his supporters were brought into the prison for execution, Paine called out to him. The other prisoners watched as the Luxembourg's most renowned prisoner and "the giant of the Revolution" clasped hands. Danton told Paine: "That which you did for the happiness and liberty of your country, I tried in vain to do for mine." Danton, after a moment, added: "I have been less fortunate."[38]

A fellow prisoner described Paine's countenance:

His cheerful philosophy under certain expectation of death, his sensibility of heart, his brilliant powers of conversation, and his sportive vein of wit rendered him a very general favourite with his companions of misfortune, who found a refuge from evil in the charms of society. He was the confidant of the unhappy, the counselor of the perplexed; and to his sympathizing friendship many a devoted victim in the hour of death confided the last cares of humanity, and the last wishes of tenderness.[39]

Paine hated the pomp and arrogance of power and privilege. He retained throughout his life a fierce loyalty to the working class in which he was raised. "High sounding names like '*My Lord,*'" he wrote, "served only to 'overawe the superstitious vulgar,' and make them 'admire in the great, the vices they would honestly condemn in themselves.'"[40] He ridiculed the divine right of kings and popes. The British monarchy, which traced itself back seven centuries to William the Conqueror, had been founded, he wrote, by "a French bastard landing with armed banditti and establishing himself king of England against the consent of the natives."[41] And he detested the superstition and power of religious dogma, equating Christian belief with Greek mythology. "All national institutions of churches, whether Jewish, Christian or Turkish, appear to me no other than human inventions, set up to terrify and enslave mankind, and monopolize power and profit," he wrote. Paine posited that the self-professed virtuous people would smash the windows of the actual Christian God if God ever lived on earth.[42]

With his unrelenting commitment to truth and justice and eternal rebelliousness, Paine would later be vilified by the leaders of the new American republic, who had no interest in the egalitarian society he championed. Paine attacked former revolutionaries, such as George Washington in the United States and Maximilien de Robespierre in France, who abused power in the name of "the people." He was driven out of England by the government of William Pitt and then ousted, after nearly a year in prison, from revolutionary France as well. By that time he was an old man, and even his former champions, in well-orchestrated smear campaigns, routinely denounced him for his religious and political radicalism. The popular press in America dismissed him as "that lying, drunken, brutal infidel."[43]

But Paine never veered from the proposition that liberty means the liberty to speak the truth even if that truth is unpopular. He did not seek anyone's adulation. And by the end of his life, like most rebels who have held fast to the vision that took hold of them, he was an outcast. He died, largely forgotten, in New York City in June 1809. Six people went to his funeral. Two of them were black.[44]

Any revolutionary movement that builds a mass following will have to contend with the kind of state-orchestrated vilification and vigilante violence that plagued Paine's life. Vitriol and violence will be unleashed, with the tacit approval of the state, on all who resist, even nonviolently. These reactionary movements, while defining themselves as the guardians of patriotism and the Christian faith, will draw on the deep reserves of racial hostility. The hidden agenda of right-wing militias, the Tea Party, the lunatic fringe of the Republican Party, the National Rifle Association, and the survivalist cults is to ensure that guns will keep the home and family from being overrun by the crazed black hordes that will escape from their colonies in our urban slums. The mother of Adam Lanza, who carried out the Newtown massacre after first killing her, was a survivalist; she had stockpiled weapons in her home for impending social and economic collapse. Scratch the surface of the survivalist cult in the United States and you expose terrified white supremacists.

This inchoate terror of black violence in retribution for white, vigilante violence and state-sanctioned violence is articulated in *The Turner Diaries,* a novel by William Luther Pierce that he published pseudonymously under the name Andrew Macdonald. The book inspired Timothy McVeigh to bomb the federal building in Oklahoma City. And it is given brilliant expression in Robert Crumb's savage exploration of white nightmares in his comic "When the Niggers Take Over America!"

"Again I say that each and every Negro, during the last 300 years, possesses from that heritage a greater burden of hate for America than they themselves know," Richard Wright noted in his journal in 1945.

Perhaps it is well that Negroes try to be as unintellectual as possible, for if they ever started really thinking about what happened to them they'd go wild. And perhaps that is the secret of whites who want to believe that Negroes really have no memory; for if they thought that Negroes remembered they would start out to shoot them all in sheer self-defense.[45]

The breakdown of American society will trigger a popular backlash, which we glimpsed in the Occupy movement, but it will also energize the traditional armed vigilante groups that embrace a version of American fascism that fuses Christian and national symbols. The longer we remain in a state of political paralysis, dominated by a corporate elite that refuses to respond to the growing misery and governed by an ineffectual liberal elite, the more the rage of the white male underclass—whose economic status often replicates that of poor blacks—will find expression through violence. If it remains true to the American tradition, this violence will not be directed at the power elite but will single out minorities, dissidents, activists, radicals, and scapegoats.

The language of violence always presages violence. I have watched this take place in the wars I covered as a foreign correspondent in Latin America, the Middle East, Africa, and the Balkans. The impoverishment of a working class and the snuffing out of hope and opportunity always produce angry mobs ready to kill and be killed. A discredited liberal elite gets swept aside. Thugs and demagogues play to the passions of the crowd. I know each act of the drama. I have heard it in other tongues in other lands. I recognize the stock characters: the same buffoons, charlatans, and fools, the same confused, enraged crowds, and the same impotent and despised liberal class that deserves the hatred it engenders.

The unraveling of America mirrors the unraveling of Yugoslavia. The Balkan war was not caused by ancient ethnic hatreds. It was caused by the economic collapse of Yugoslavia. The petty criminals and goons who took power harnessed the rage and despair of the unemployed and the desperate. They singled out convenient scapegoats, from ethnic Croats to Muslims to Kosovar Albanians to Gypsies, and armed their own vigilantes. They set up movements that unleashed a feeding frenzy leading to war and self-immolation. There is little difference between the ludicrous would-be poet Radovan Karadžić, who was a figure of ridicule in Sarajevo before the war, and the moronic Glenn Beck or Sarah

Palin. There is little difference between the Oath Keepers and the Serbian militias. We can laugh at these people. They are often idiots and buffoons. But they are also dangerous.

Gabrielle Giffords, a member of the US House of Representatives, was shot in the head in January 2011 as she held a meeting in a supermarket parking lot in Arizona. Eighteen other people were wounded. Six of them died.[46] Sarah Palin's political action committee had previously targeted Giffords and other Democrats with crosshairs on an electoral map. When someone like Palin posts a map with crosshairs, saying, "Don't Retreat, Instead—RELOAD!" there are desperate, enraged people with weapons who act.[47] When Christian fascists stand in the pulpits of megachurches and denounce Barack Obama as the Antichrist, there are messianic believers who believe it.[48] When a Republican lawmaker shouts "Baby killer!" at Michigan Democrat Bart Stupak, there are violent extremists who see the mission of saving the unborn as a sacred duty.[49] They have little left to lose.

These movements are not yet full-blown fascist movements. They do not openly call for the extermination of ethnic or religious groups. They do not openly advocate violence. But as I was told by Fritz Stern, a scholar of fascism who has written about the origins of Nazism and who fled Nazi Germany as a young man, "in Germany there was a yearning for fascism before fascism was invented." It is the yearning that we now see. If we do not swiftly reincorporate the unemployed and the poor back into the economy, giving them jobs and relief from crippling debt, then the nascent racism and violence that are leaping up around the edges of American society will become a full-blown conflagration.

Left unchecked, the hatred for radical Islam will transform itself into a hatred for Muslims. The hatred for undocumented workers will become a hatred for Mexicans and Central Americans. The hatred for those not defined by this largely white movement as American patriots will become a hatred for African Americans. The hatred for liberals will morph into a hatred for all democratic institutions, from universities to government agencies to the press.

Beleaguered whites, battered by a stagnant and flagging economy, are retreating, especially in the South, into a mythical self-glorification built around the Confederacy. This retreat resembles the absurdist national and ethnic myths that characterized the former Yugoslavia when it unraveled. Serbian, Croatian, and Muslim ethnic groups, out of work and plagued by hyperinflation, built fantasies of a glorious past that became a substitute for history. The ethnic groups, worshiping their own mythic virtues and courage and wallowing in historical examples of their own victimhood, vomited up demagogues and murderers such as Radovan Karadžić and Slobodan Milošević. To restore this mythological past they sought to remove, through exclusion and finally violence, competing ethnicities. The embrace of non-reality-based belief systems made communication among ethnic groups impossible. They no longer spoke the same cultural or historical language. They believed in their private fantasy. And because they believed in fantasy, they had no common historical narrative built around verifiable truth and no way finally to communicate with anyone who did not share their self-delusion.

———

Tennessee celebrates July 13 as Nathan Bedford Forrest Day, the birthday of the Confederate general and first leader of the KKK. There are thirty-two historical markers commemorating Forrest in Tennessee alone.[50] There are three Confederate holidays in Alabama, including Robert E. Lee/Martin Luther King Day. Florida, Georgia, and Mississippi also officially acknowledge Lee's birthday.[51] Jefferson Davis's birthday is recognized in Alabama, and reenactments of Confederate victories in the Civil War crowd Southern calendars. Although the South has long been in thrall to its Confederate history, there has been a surge of public commemoration of the Confederacy in recent years, as I would discover on a trip through the South in 2013. Those commemorations reminded me of the idealized historical narratives celebrated by competing ethnic groups that swept through Yugoslavia before the war. The desperate, then and now, whose identities and self-worth are lost in collapsing economies, fashion new identities out of myth.

Flyers reading "Loyal White Knights of the Ku Klux Klan Wants You to Join!" appeared in residential mailboxes in Memphis when I was in that city on this trip. The Klan had also recently distributed pamphlets in a suburb of Atlanta.[52] Later, in Montgomery, Alabama, I walked along the banks of the Alabama River, which were largely deserted, in the late afternoon with Bryan Stevenson, an African American lawyer who has spent his life fighting for prisoners on death row. He and I moved slowly up the cobblestones from the expanse of the river into the center of city. We passed through a small, gloomy tunnel beneath some railway tracks, climbed a slight incline, and stood at the head of Commerce Street, which runs into Court Square, the heart of Alabama's capital. The walk was one of the most notorious in the antebellum South.

"This street was the most active slave-trading space in America for almost a decade," Stevenson said. Four slave depots stood nearby. "They would bring people off the boat. They would parade them up the street in chains. White plantation owners and local slave traders would get on the sidewalks. They'd watch them as they went up the street. Then they would follow behind up to the circle. And that is when they would have their slave auctions.

"Anybody they didn't sell that day they would keep in these slave depots," he continued.

We walked past a monument to the Confederate flag as we retraced the steps taken by tens of thousands of slaves who had been chained together in coffles of up to 100 or more men, women, and children, all herded by traders who carried guns and whips. Stevenson and I stood in Court Square, where the slaves had been sold. A bronze fountain with a statue of the Goddess of Liberty spewed jets of water in the plaza.

"Montgomery was notorious for not having rules that required slave traders to prove that the person had been formally enslaved," Stevenson explained. "You could kidnap free black people, bring them to Montgomery, and sell them. They also did not have rules that restricted the purchasing of partial families."

We fell silent. It was here in this square—a square adorned with a historical marker celebrating the presence in Montgomery of Jefferson Davis, the president of the Confederacy—that men and women fell to their knees weeping and beseeching slaveholders not to separate them from their husbands, wives, and children. It was here that girls and boys screamed as their fathers and mothers were taken from them.

"This whole street is rich with this history," he said. "But nobody wants to talk about this slavery stuff. Nobody."

Stevenson said he wants to start a campaign to erect monuments to that history on the sites of lynchings, slave auctions, and slave depots.

"When we start talking about it, people will be outraged," he said. "They will be provoked. They will be angry."

The Confederate memorials, plaques, and monuments we passed, Stevenson said, "have all appeared in the last couple of decades." A massive Confederate flag, placed by the "Sons of Confederate Veterans," was displayed on the highway into the city. Whites in Montgomery, which is half black, had recently reenacted the inauguration of Confederate president Jefferson Davis by parading through the streets in Confederate uniforms, holding Confederate flags, and surrounding a carriage that carried a man dressed up as Davis. They held the ceremony of the inauguration on the steps of the state capitol.

At the same time, Alabama sentences more people to death per capita than any other state. With no state-funded program to provide legal assistance to death-row prisoners, half of the condemned are represented by court-appointed lawyers whose compensation is capped at $1,000. Few of the condemned ever have an adequate defense. According to the Equal Justice Initiative, "In a state with a population that is 27% black, nearly half of Alabama's death row is black and 83% of the 757 people executed by Alabama since capital punishment began in the state have been black."[53]

Stevenson's career as a lawyer for death-row prisoners began with a collect call from Herbert Richardson, a death-row inmate at Holman State Prison. Richardson, a disturbed Vietnam combat veteran, had left an explosive device on the porch of an estranged girlfriend. It killed a young girl. His execution was to be held in thirty days. Stevenson, after a second phone call, filed for an emergency stay of execution, which the state rejected.

"He never really got representation until we jumped in," Stevenson said.

Stevenson went to the prison on the day of the execution, which was scheduled for midnight. He found his client surrounded by a half-dozen family members, including the woman who had married him the week before. Richardson repeatedly asked Stevenson to make sure his wife received the American flag he would be given as a veteran.

Although "it was time for the visit to end," Stevenson recalled, the visitation officer was "clearly emotionally unprepared to make these people leave." When the officer insisted, Stevenson said, Richardson's wife grabbed her husband. "[His wife] says, 'I'm not leaving.' Other people don't know what to do. They are holding on to him." The officer left, but her superiors sent her back in. "[The officer] has tears running down her face. She looks to me and says, 'Please, please help me.'"

Stevenson began to hum a hymn. The room went still. The family started singing the words. Stevenson went over to the wife and said, "We're going to have to let him go."

She did.

He then walked with Richardson to the execution chamber.

"Bryan, it has been so strange," the condemned man said. "All day long people have been saying to me, 'What can I do to help you?' I got up this morning, 'What can I get you for breakfast? What can I get you for lunch? What can I get you for dinner? Can I get you some stamps to mail your last letters? Do you need the phone? Do you need water? Do you need coffee? How can we help you?' More people have said what can they do to help me in the last fourteen hours of my life than they ever did [before]."

"You never got the help you needed," Stevenson told him. And he made Richardson a promise: "I will try and keep as many people out of this situation as possible."

Richardson had asked the guards to play "The Old Rugged Cross" before he died. As he was strapped into the electric chair and hooded, the hymn began to blare out from a cassette player. Then the warden pulled the switch.

"Do you think we should rape people who rape?" Stevenson asked as we stood in the square. "We don't rape rapists, because we think about the person who would have to commit the rape. Should we assault people who have committed assault? We can't imagine replicating a rape or an assault and hold[ing] on to our dignity, integrity, and civility. But because we think we have found a way to kill people that is civilized and decent, we are comfortable."

Stevenson turns frequently to the Bible. He quoted to me from the Gospel of John, where Jesus says of the woman who committed adultery: "He that is without sin among you, let him first cast a stone at her." He tells me an elderly black woman once called him a "stone catcher."

"There is no such thing as being a Christian and not being a stone catcher," he said. "But that is exhausting. You're not going to catch them all. And it hurts. If it doesn't make you sad to have to do that, then you don't understand what it means to be engaged in an act of faith. . . . But if you have the right relationship to it, it is less of a burden, finally, than a blessing. It makes you feel stronger."

The South, indeed much of the country, is becoming increasingly inhospitable to stone catchers.

———————

On a windy afternoon I took a taxi to a depressed section of North Memphis to visit an old clapboard house that was once owned by a German immigrant named Jacob Burkle. Oral history—and oral history is all anyone has in this case, since no written documents survive—holds that Burkle used his house as a stop on the Underground Railroad for escaped slaves in the decade before the Civil War. The house is now a small museum called Slave Haven. It has artifacts such as leg irons, iron collars, and broadsheets advertising the sale of men, women, and children. In the gray floor of the porch is a trapdoor that leads to a long crawl space and a jagged hole in a brick cellar wall where fugitives could have pushed themselves down into the basement. Escaped slaves were purportedly guided by Burkle at night down a tunnel or trench toward the nearby Mississippi River and turned over to sympathetic river traders who took them north to Cairo, Illinois, and on to freedom in Canada.

Burkle and his descendants had good reason to avoid written records and to keep their activities secret. Memphis, on the eve of the Civil War, was one of the biggest slave markets in the South. After the war, the city was an epicenter for Ku Klux Klan terror that included lynching, the nighttime burning of black churches and schools, and the killing of black leaders and their white supporters, atrocities that continued into the twentieth century. A vigilante gunman in Memphis assassinated Martin Luther King Jr. in 1968. If word had gotten out that Burkle used his home to help slaves escape, the structure would almost certainly have been burned and Burkle or his descendants, at the very least, driven out of the city. The story of Burkle's aid to slaves fleeing bondage became public knowledge only a couple of decades ago.

The modest public profile of the Burkle house stands in stunning contrast with the monument I visited in the center of Memphis to native son Nathan Bedford Forrest. Forrest, who is buried in Forrest Park under a statue of himself in his Confederate general's uniform and mounted on a horse, is one of the most odious figures in American history. A moody, barely literate, violent man—he was not averse to shooting his own troops if he deemed them to be cowards—he became one of the wealthiest men in the South before the war as a planter and slave trader.[54] As a Confederate general, he was noted for moronic aphorisms such as "War means fighting, and fighting means killing."[55]

Forrest was, even by the accounts of those who served under him, a butcher. But he was also a brilliant cavalry commander who could move large numbers of troops over long distances to mount disastrously effective surprise assaults on Union troops. The historian Shelby Foote said that the Civil War produced two geniuses—Forrest and Abraham Lincoln.[56] Forrest's penchant for warfare, however, was accompanied by a penchant for killing. He ordered a massacre at Fort Pillow in Henning, Tennessee, of some 300 black Union troops, although they had surrendered and put down their weapons, as well as the women and children who had sheltered in the fort.[57] Following the war, Forrest was the first leader, or "Grand Wizard," of the Ku Klux Klan, and on the huge plantation he owned outside of Memphis he took advantage of the new convict lease system, which would last thirty years, to use black convicts as laborers—slaves in all but name.[58]

Forrest, like many other white racists of the antebellum South, is one of many Confederate leaders who is enjoying a huge renaissance. When the Sons of Confederate Veterans and the Shelby County Historical Commission in 2012 put up a 1,000-pound granite marker at the entrance to the park that read FORREST PARK, the city, saying the groups had not obtained a permit, removed it with a crane. The dispute

over the park name that was then raging in the Memphis City Council exposed the deep divide in Memphis and throughout much of the South between those who laud the Confederacy and those who detest it, a split that runs like a wide fault down racial lines. Blacks, who have called for the park to be named after the crusading black journalist Ida B. Wells, whose newspaper was based in Memphis, have been rebuffed.

Wells was one of the nation's most courageous and important journalists. She moved to Memphis as a young woman to live with her aunt. Her investigations revealed that lynching was fundamentally a mechanism to rid white businessmen of black competitors. When Thomas Moss of Memphis, a black man who ran the People's Grocery Co., was murdered with his partners by a mob of whites and his store was looted and destroyed, Wells was incensed. "This is what opened my eyes to what lynching really was," she wrote. She noted "that the Southerner had never gotten over this resentment that the Negro was no longer his plaything, his servant, and his source of income" and said that whites were using charges of rape against black business owners to mask this resentment. The lynching of Moss, she wrote, was "an excuse to get rid of Negroes who were acquiring wealth and property and thus keep the race terrorized and 'keep the nigger down.'"[59]

White mobs destroyed Wells's newspaper, *Free Speech*, which railed against white vigilante violence, the inadequate black schools, segregation, discrimination, and a corrupt legal system that denied justice to blacks. Wells was forced to flee the city, becoming, as she wrote, "an exile from home for hinting at the truth."[60]

The split in Memphis between those who hold up authentic heroes—people who fought to protect, defend, and preserve life, such as Wells and Burkle—and those who memorialize slave traders and bigots such as Forrest characterizes the ethic of vigilante violence. Honoring figures like Forrest in Memphis while ignoring Wells is like erecting a statue to the Nazi death camp commander Amon Goeth in the Czech Republic town of Svitavy, the birthplace of Oskar Schindler, who rescued 1,200 Jews. This capturing of the past by American vigilantes, now well under way, will have disastrous consequences, as it did in Yugoslavia. Intolerance that leads to violence is being bred with the steady rise of ethnic nationalism over the past decade and the replacing of history with fabricated stories of lost glory. Violence becomes in this perverted belief system a cleansing agent, a way to restore a lost world.

There are ample historical accounts that disprove the myths espoused by the neo-Confederates, including books such as the volume *Race, Slavery, and the Civil War: The Tough Stuff of American History and Memory*, edited by James Oliver Horton and Amanda Kleintop, along with numerous original documents, including South Carolina's "Declaration of the Immediate Causes Which Induce and Justify the Secession of South Carolina from the Federal Union." In that document, issued four days after South Carolina seceded from the Union, the state sited the election of a new president "whose opinions and purposes are hostile to slavery" as justifying its secession.[61] But facts hold little sway with those who insist that the Civil War was not about slavery but about states' rights and the protection of traditional Christianity. These records are useless in puncturing the collective self-delusion, just as documentary evidence does nothing to blunt the self-delusion of Holocaust deniers. Those who retreat into fantasy cannot be engaged in rational discussion, for fantasy is all that is left of their tattered self-esteem. Attacks on their myths as untrue trigger not a discussion of facts and evidence but a ferocious emotional backlash. Such challenges of the myth threaten what is left of hope.

Achilles V. Clark, a sergeant with the 20th Tennessee Cavalry under Forrest during the 1864 massacre at Fort Pillow, wrote to his sister after the attack:

> The slaughter was awful. Words cannot describe the scene. The poor deluded negroes would run up to our men, fall upon their knees, and with uplifted hands scream for mercy but they were ordered to their feet and then shot down. . . . I, with several others, tried to stop the butchery, and at one time had partially succeeded, but General Forrest ordered them shot down like dogs and the carnage continued. Finally our men became sick of blood and the firing ceased.[62]

Clark was a Southern white soldier in the Confederate army. But his eyewitness account cannot influence those desperately seeking meaning and worth in an invented past.

"People pay for what they do, and, still more, for what they have allowed themselves to become," James Baldwin wrote. "The crucial thing, here, is that the sum of these individual abdications menaces life all over the world. For, in the generality, as social and moral and political and sexual entities, white Americans are probably the sickest and certainly the most dangerous people, of any color, to be found in the world today." Observing these Americans, he "was not struck by their wickedness," he said, "for that wickedness was but the spirit and the history of America. What struck me was the unbelievable dimension of their sorrow. I felt as though I had wandered into hell."[63]

VII / The Rebel Defiant

Under a government which imprisons any unjustly, the true place for a just man is also a prison.[1]

—HENRY DAVID THOREAU, CIVIL DISOBEDIENCE

A British police officer in a black Kevlar vest stood on the steps of the red-brick row house on Hans Crescent that housed the Ecuadorean embassy in London. Another officer was stationed on a narrow side street, facing the iconic department store Harrods, half a block away on Brompton Road. A third officer peered out the window of a neighboring high-rise building a few feet from the modest ground-floor suite occupied by the embassy. A white police communications van with a rooftop array of antennas was parked in front of the building. I was greeted when I entered the lobby by a fourth police officer, stationed immediately outside the door of the embassy suite.

By the time I arrived, the cost of this round-the-clock vigilance by the Metropolitan Police Service (MPS), or Scotland Yard, at the embassy, where Julian Assange, the founder of Wikileaks, took refuge on June 19, 2012, had exceeded $1 million.[2] The police presence and the communications van, which most likely intercepted all forms of electronic communications in and out of the embassy, were the visible tips of the claws poking above the surface of the vast, secret global security and surveillance monster that has cornered Assange and obliterated our privacy. An array of governmental and intelligence agencies from around the globe are working to destroy WikiLeaks and wrest Assange from the embassy so that he can be extradited to the United States, tried, and imprisoned.

I was buzzed into the modest Ecuadorean embassy suite. I passed through a metal detector. An embassy employee escorted me, after I had turned over my cell phone, to the back room. Assange was seated at a small table surrounded by leatherette chairs. The room was cluttered with cables and computer equipment. He had a full head of gray hair and gray stubble on his face. He was wearing a traditional white embroidered Ecuadorean shirt.

Britain had rejected an Ecuadorean request that Assange be granted safe passage to an airport. Because he could not get to the airport, he was trapped in an embassy room. Assange said it was like being in a "space station." It is hard to envision how he will ever walk out to freedom.

Assange, Chelsea Manning, and WikiLeaks, by making public in 2010 half a million internal documents from the Pentagon and the State Department—along with the 2007 video of US helicopter pilots gunning down Iraqi civilians, including children, and two Reuters journalists—exposed the empire's hypocrisy and indiscriminate violence, as well as its use of torture, lies, bribery, and crude tactics of intimidation.[3] WikiLeaks fulfilled the most important role of a press when it turned a floodlight on the inner workings of the powerful, and for this it has become empire's most coveted prey. All those around the globe with the computer skills and inclination to make public the secrets of empire, from Jeremy Hammond to Edward Snowden, are targeted.

Australian diplomatic cables obtained by the *Sydney Morning Herald* described the US campaign against Assange and WikiLeaks as "unprecedented both in its scale and nature."[4] The size of the operation was also hinted at in off-hand statements made during Manning's pretrial hearing and reported by journalist Alexa O'Brien. According to O'Brien, the US Justice Department considered paying the contractor ManTech of Fairfax, Virginia, $1 million to $2 million for a computer system that, from the tender, appears to have been designed to exclusively handle the Wikileaks prosecution documents.[5] The government line item is oblique. It refers only to "WikiLeaks Software and Hardware Maintenance." At least a dozen US governmental agencies, including the Pentagon, the FBI, the Army's Criminal Investigative Department, the Justice Department, the Office of the Director of National Intelligence, and the Diplomatic Security Service, are assigned to the WikiLeaks case, while the CIA and the Office of the Director of National Intelligence are assigned to track down WikiLeaks's supposed breaches of security. The global assault—which saw Australia, after pressure from Washington, threaten to revoke Assange's passport—is part of the terrifying metamorphosis of the "war on terror" into a war on civil liberties.

The dragnet has swept up any person or organization that fits the profile of those who can burrow into the archives of power and disseminate it to the public. It no longer matters if they have committed a crime. Aaron Swartz, an Internet activist, was arrested in January 2011 for downloading roughly 5 million academic articles and documents from JSTOR, an online clearinghouse for scholarly journals. Swartz was charged by federal prosecutors with two counts of wire fraud and eleven violations of the Computer Fraud and Abuse Act. The charges carried the threat of $1 million in fines and thirty-five years in prison. Swartz committed suicide.[6] Barrett Brown, a journalist who specializes in military and intelligence contractors and is associated with the group Anonymous, which has mounted cyberattacks on government agencies at the local and federal levels, was arrested in September 2012. He entered a guilty plea to three counts after the government dropped some of the worst charges. He was sentenced to 63 months in federal prison. Also arrested has been Jeremy Hammond, a political activist who provided WikiLeaks with 5.5 million emails between the security firm Strategic Forecasting (Stratfor) and its clients.[7] Brown and Hammond were both arrested after being entrapped by an informant named Hector Xavier Monsegur, known as Sabu. Assange told me that he believed Sabu also attempted to entrap WikiLeaks while under FBI supervision. Manning was also entrapped by an FBI informant, Adrian Lamo.

Monsegur, who by the government's calculations took part in computer hacker attacks on more than 250 public and private entities at a cost of up to $50 million in damages, was released from a Manhattan courtroom in May 2014 after Judge Loretta Preska, who had previously sentenced Hammond to ten years, saluted his "extraordinary cooperation" with the FBI. The government told the court that Monsegur had helped to identify and convict eight of his peers in the Anonymous and

LulzSec hacker collectives. Judge Preska sentenced him to time served—
he had spent seven months in prison in 2013—plus a year's supervised
release. This was in exchange for working for three years as a federal informant. He had been facing a maximum sentence of more than twenty-
six years.[8]

With their fluency in computers and experience as the first victims
of wholesale surveillance, WikiLeaks collaborators or supporters understood before the rest of us the reach of the security and surveillance
organs. Those associated with WikiLeaks are routinely stopped—often
at international airports—and attempts are made to recruit them as informants. Jérémie Zimmermann, Smári McCarthy, Jacob Appelbaum,
David House, and one of Assange's lawyers, Jennifer Robinson, have all
been approached or interrogated by state security. The tactics are often
heavy-handed. McCarthy, an Icelander and WikiLeaks activist, was detained and extensively questioned when he entered the United States.
Soon afterward, three men who identified themselves as being from the
FBI approached McCarthy in Washington, attempted to recruit him as
an informant, and gave him instructions on how to spy on WikiLeaks.

On August 23, 2011, Sigurdur Thordarson, a young Icelandic
WikiLeaks activist, emailed the American embassy in Reykjavik. The following day, eight FBI agents landed in Iceland on a private jet. The team
told the Icelandic government that it had discovered a plan by Anonymous to hack into Icelandic government computers and proposed to
help thwart it. But it was soon clear that the team had come with a different agenda. The Americans spent the next few days, in flagrant violation
of Icelandic sovereignty, interrogating Thordarson in various Reykjavik
hotel rooms. The Icelandic Ministry of the Interior, suspecting that the
US investigation was an attempt to frame Assange, expelled the team
from the country. The FBI took Thordarson to Washington, DC, for
four days of further interrogation. Thordarson appears to have decided
to cooperate with the FBI. It was reported in the Icelandic press that in
March 2012 he went to Denmark, where he received about $5,000 in
petty cash after handing over the stolen WikiLeaks files to the FBI.[9]

There have been secret search orders for information from Internet
service providers, including Twitter, Google, and Sonic, and information

about Assange and WikiLeaks has been seized from the company Dynadot, a domain name registrar and Web host.[10] Assange told me that his suitcase and computer were stolen on a flight from Sweden to Germany on September 27, 2010. He said that his bank cards were blocked and that Moneybookers, WikiLeaks's primary donation account, was shut down after being placed on a blacklist in Australia and a "watch list" in the United States.[11] Following denunciations of WikiLeaks by the US government, financial service companies, including Visa, Master-Card, PayPal, Bank of America, Western Union, and American Express, blacklisted the organization.[12] And he said that denial-of-service attacks on WikiLeaks's infrastructure have been frequent and massive.[13] All this has come with a well-orchestrated campaign of character assassination against Assange, including mischaracterizations of the sexual misconduct case brought against him by Swedish police.

Assange sought asylum in the Ecuadorean embassy after exhausting his fight to avoid extradition from the United Kingdom to Sweden over the sexual misconduct charges. He and his lawyers contend that an extradition to Sweden would mean an extradition to the United States. And even if Sweden refused to comply with US demands for Assange, kidnapping, or "extraordinary rendition," would remain an option for Washington. Kidnapping was given legal cover by a 1989 memorandum issued by the Justice Department stating that "the FBI may use its statutory authority to investigate and arrest individuals for violating United States law, even if the FBI's actions contravene customary international law," and that an "arrest that is inconsistent with international or foreign law does not violate the Fourth Amendment."[14]

This is a stunning example of the corporate state's Orwellian doublespeak. The persecution of Assange and WikiLeaks and the practice of extraordinary rendition embody the evisceration of the Fourth Amendment, which was designed to protect us from unreasonable searches and seizures and requires any warrant to be judicially sanctioned and supported by probable cause.

Take the case of two Swedes and a Briton who were seized by the United States in August 2012 somewhere in Africa—it is assumed to have been in Somalia—and held in one of our black sites. They suddenly reappeared—with the Briton stripped of his citizenship—in a Brooklyn courtroom in December 2012 and facing terrorism charges. Sweden, rather than object to the extradition of its two citizens, dropped the Swedish charges against the prisoners to permit the rendition to occur. The prisoners, the *Washington Post* reported, were secretly indicted by a federal grand jury two months after being seized.[15]

Assange, who said he worked most of the night and slept into the late afternoon, was pale, although he was using an ultraviolet light to make up for getting no sunlight. A treadmill was tilted up against a wall of his quarters. He had set it up so that he could run three to five miles a day. He practiced calisthenics and boxing with a personal trainer. He was lanky at six feet two inches tall and exuded a raw, nervous energy. He leapt, sometimes disconcertingly, from topic to topic, idea to idea, his words rushing to keep up with his cascading thoughts. He worked with a small staff and had a steady stream of visitors, including celebrities such as Lady Gaga. When the Ecuadorean ambassador, Ana Alban Mora, and Bianca Jagger showed up late one afternoon, Assange pulled down glasses and poured everyone whiskey from a stock of liquor he kept in a cabinet. Jagger wanted to know how to protect her website from hackers. Assange told her to "make a lot of backup copies."

Assange, who attempted to run for a seat in Australia's upper house of Parliament from his refuge, was communicating with his global network of associates and supporters up to seventeen hours a day through numerous cell phones and a collection of laptop computers. He encrypted his communications. He religiously shredded anything put down on paper. But it was a difficult existence. The frequent movements of the police cordon outside his window disrupted his sleep. And he missed his son, whom he had raised as a single father. He may also have a daughter, but he did not speak publicly about his children, refusing to disclose their ages or where they live. His family, he said, had received death threats. He had not seen his children since his legal troubles started.

As a child, he grew up without television and moved from city to city with his stepfather and mother in a theater group that at times involved puppets. In one play called *The Brain*, a plaster mold of Assange's head was cast for each play—he breathed though straws inserted up his nose—and then the plaster mold was smashed during the performance. He told me that he disliked actors because of their thirst for adulation and applause. He had more time for directors. He attended thirty-seven different schools as a child, he said, and went on to study math and physics at university.

Assange saw WikiLeaks's primary role as giving a voice to the victims of US wars and proxy wars by using leaked documents to tell their stories. The release of the Afghan and Iraq "War Logs," Assange said, disclosed the extent of civilian death and suffering as well as the plethora of lies told by the Pentagon and the state to conceal the human toll. He added that the logs also unmasked the bankruptcy of the traditional press and its obsequious service as war propagandists.

"There were 90,000 records in the Afghan War Logs," Assange said. "We had to look at different angles in the material to add up the number of civilians who have been killed. We studied the records. We ranked events different ways. I wondered if we could find out the largest number of civilians killed in a single event. It turned out that this occurred during Operation Medusa, led by Canadian forces in September 2006. The US-backed local government was quite corrupt. The Taliban was, in effect, the political opposition and had a lot of support. The locals rose up against the government. Most of the young men in the area, from a political perspective, were Taliban. There was a government crackdown that encountered strong resistance. ISAF [the NATO-led International Security Assistance Force] carried out a big sweep. It went house to house. Then an American soldier was killed. They called in an AC-130 gunship. This is a C-130 cargo plane refitted with cannons on the side. It circled overhead and rained down shells. The War Logs say 181 'enemy' were killed. The logs also say there were no wounded or captured. It was a significant massacre. This event, the day when the largest number of people were killed in Afghanistan, has never been properly investigated by the old media."

Operation Medusa, which was carried out twenty miles west of Kandahar, took the lives of four Canadian soldiers and involved some 2,000 NATO and Afghan troops. It was one of the largest military operations by the ISAF in the Kandahar region.

Assange searched for accounts by reporters who were on the scene. What he discovered appalled him. An embedded Canadian reporter, Graeme Smith of the *Toronto Globe and Mail*, used these words on a Canadian military website to describe his experiences during Operation Medusa: "one of the most intense experiences of my life." Smith wrote about traveling with a Canadian platoon that called themselves the "Nomads." "They'd even made up these little patches for their uniforms that said 'Nomads' on them," he remembered. "The Nomads took me in and they sort of made me one of them." He said he spent two weeks with the "Nomads," used a bucket to wash himself and his clothes, and slept in his flak jacket. Smith talked about being "under fire together" and said that "they gave me a little 'Nomads' patch that I attached to my flak jacket."

Assange's point is correct. In every conflict I covered as a war correspondent, the press of the nation at war was an enthusiastic part of the machine—cheerleaders for slaughter and tireless mythmakers for the nation and the military. The few renegades within the press who refuse to wave the flag and lionize the troops become pariahs in newsrooms and find themselves attacked—like Assange and Manning—by the state.

There is no free press without a willingness to defy law and expose the abuses and lies carried out by the powerful. The Pentagon Papers, released to the *New York Times* in 1971, as well as the *Times*' Pulitzer-winning 2005 exposure of the warrantless wiretapping of US citizens by the National Security Agency, made public information that had been classified as "top secret"—a classification more restricted than the lower-level "secret" designation of the documents released by WikiLeaks.[16] But as the traditional press atrophies with dizzying speed—crippled by Barack Obama's use of the Espionage Act seven times since 2009 to target whistle-blowers, including Edward Snowden—our last hope lies with rebels such as Manning, Assange, Hammond, and Snowden.[17]

WikiLeaks released after-action reports authored by US diplomats and the US military. The cables invariably put a pro-unit or pro-US spin on events. The reality is usually much worse. Those counted as dead enemy combatants are often civilians. Military units use after-action reports to justify or hide inappropriate behavior. And despite the heated rhetoric of the state about American lives being endangered by WikiLeaks exposures, there has been no evidence that any action of WikiLeaks has cost lives. Then-Secretary of Defense Robert Gates, in a 2010 letter to Senator Carl Levin, conceded this point: "The initial assessment in no way discounts the risk to national security. However, the review to date has not revealed any sensitive intelligence sources and methods compromised by the disclosure."[18]

The New York Times, The Guardian, El País, Le Monde, and *Der Spiegel* printed redacted copies of some of the WikiLeaks files, but they have underreported the prosecution of Manning and entrapment of Assange. Do these news organizations believe that if the state shuts down organizations such as WikiLeaks and imprisons Manning and Assange, traditional news outlets will be left alone? Can't they connect the dots between the prosecutions of government whistle-blowers under the Espionage Act, warrantless wiretapping, the monitoring of communications, and the persecution of Manning, Assange, and Snowden? Haven't they realized that this is a war by a global corporate elite not against an organization or an individual but against liberty, the freedom of the press, and democracy itself?

"The national security state can try to reduce our activity," Assange said. "It can close the noose a little tighter. But there are three forces working against it. The first is the massive surveillance required to protect its communication, including the nature of its cryptology. In the military, everyone now has an ID card with a little chip on it so you know who is logged into what. A system this vast is prone to deterioration and breakdown. Secondly, there is widespread knowledge not only of how to leak, but how to leak and not be caught, how to even avoid suspicion that you are leaking. The military and intelligence systems collect a vast amount of information and move it around quickly. This means you can also get it out quickly. There will always be people within the system that have an agenda to defy authority. Yes, there are general deterrents, such as when the DOJ [Department of Justice] prosecutes and indicts someone. They can discourage people from engaging in this behavior. But the opposite is also true. When that behavior is successful, it is an example. It encourages others. This is why they want to eliminate all who provide this encouragement.

"The medium-term perspective is very good," he declared. "The education of young people takes place on the Internet. You cannot hire anyone who is skilled in any field without them having been educated on the Internet. The military, the CIA, the FBI, all have no choice but to hire from a pool of people that have been educated on the Internet. This means they are hiring our moles in vast numbers. And this means that these organizations will see their capacity to control information diminish as more and more people with our values are hired."

The long term, however, may not be as sanguine. Assange wrote a book with three coauthors—Jacob Appelbaum, Andy Müller-Maguhn, and Jérémie Zimmermann—called *Cypherpunks: Freedom and the Future of the Internet*. It warns that we are "galloping into a new transnational dystopia." As Assange says in the book, "We are living under martial law as far as our communications are concerned. We just can't see the tanks—but they are there. To that degree, the internet, which was supposed to be a civilian space, has become a militarized space."[19] The Internet has become not only a tool to educate, they write, but the mechanism to cement into place a "Postmodern Surveillance Dystopia" that is supranational and dominated by global corporate power. This new system of global control will "merge global humanity into one giant grid of mass surveillance and mass control."[20]

It is only through encryption that we can protect ourselves, Assange and his coauthors argue, and it is only by breaking through the digital walls of secrecy erected by the power elite that we can expose power. What they fear, however, is the possibility that the corporate state will eventually effectively harness the power of the internet to shut down dissent.

"The internet, our greatest tool of emancipation," Assange writes, "has been transformed into the most dangerous facilitator of totalitarianism we have ever seen."[21]

And yet, Assange continues to resist. His gloomy vision of a future when all privacy will be eradicated is in stark contrast to the utopian rebellions in the past that promised a new heaven and a new earth. He is acutely aware that his chances of escaping from the clutches of the security apparatus he can see out the windows of the embassy are very slim. Washington almost certainly has a sealed grand jury indictment prepared against him.

Chelsea Manning, like Assange, did not have a stable childhood. Her difficulties with alcoholic parents, the questioning of her sexuality, and her small stature—she is slight and five feet two inches tall—all combined with her intelligence and mole-like retreat into computers to make her an object of frequent ridicule. She joined the Army in a bid to get enough money to go to college. The hypermasculine culture of the military, where hazing is frequent and some of the soldiers and Marines targeted for physical and verbal abuse in foreign deployment commit suicide, saw Manning mistreated from the moment she enlisted.

"He was a runt, so pick on him," remembers a soldier who spoke to *The Guardian* but did not want to give his name. "He's crazy, so pick on him. He's a faggot. Pick on him. The guy took it from every side. He couldn't please anyone. He was targeted by bullies. He was targeted by the drill sergeants. Basically he was targeted by anybody who was within arm's reach.

"There were three guys that had him up front and cornered, and they were picking on him and he was yelling and screaming back," remembered this soldier from Memphis. "And I'm yelling at the guys, 'Get the hell out of here, back off,' and everything. I start to pull Manning off. The other guys were taking care of the ones that were picking on him and stuff, and I got Manning off to the side there, and yeah, he'd pissed himself. That wasn't the only time he did that."[22]

I was in the small courtroom at Fort Meade in Maryland to hear the sentencing by Army Colonel Judge Denise Lind of then-Private First Class Bradley Manning to thirty-five years in prison. Manning's sentence once again confirmed the inversion of our moral and legal order, the capitulation of the press, and the misuse of the law to prevent any oversight or investigation of official abuses of power, including war crimes.

The sentencing of Manning marked the day when the state formally declared that all who name and expose its crimes will become political prisoners or will be forced, like Snowden, to flee into exile. State power, the sentence showed us, will be unaccountable. And those who do not accept unlimited state power—always the road to tyranny—will be persecuted.

Two burly guards who towered over Manning hustled her out of a military courtroom at Fort Meade after the two-minute sentencing. I listened to half a dozen of Manning's supporters shout: "We'll keep fighting for you, Bradley! You're our hero!"

Manning, if we had a functioning judiciary, would have been a witness for the prosecution against the war criminals she helped expose. She would not have been headed, bound and shackled, to the military prison at Fort Leavenworth, Kansas.

But the government effectively shut down Manning's defense team. The Army private was not permitted to argue that she had a moral and legal obligation under international law to defy military orders and to make public the war crimes she had uncovered. Because the documents that detailed the crimes, torture, and killing that Manning revealed were classified, they were barred from discussion in court, and so the fundamental issue of war crimes was effectively removed from the trial. Manning was forbidden to challenge the government's unverified assertion that she had harmed national security. Lead defense attorney David E. Coombs said during pretrial proceedings that the judge's refusal to permit information on the lack of actual damage from the leaks would "eliminate a viable defense, and cut defense off at the knees."[23] And that is what happened.

Manning was also barred from presenting to the court her motives for giving WikiLeaks hundreds of thousands of classified diplomatic cables, war logs from Afghanistan and Iraq, and videos. The issues of her motives and the potential harm to national security could be raised only at the time of sentencing, but by then it was too late.

Coombs opened the trial by pleading with the judge for leniency based on Manning's youth and sincerity. Coombs was permitted by Lind to present only circumstantial evidence concerning Manning's motives or state of mind. He could argue, for example, that Manning did not know al-Qaeda might see the information she leaked. Coombs was also permitted to argue, as he did, that Manning was selective in her leak, intending no harm to national interests. But these were minor concessions by the court to the defense. Manning's most impassioned pleas for freedom of information, expressed in email exchanges with the confidential government informant Lamo, were never permitted to be heard in court.[24]

These restrictions prevented Manning from appealing to the Nuremberg principles, a set of guidelines created by the International Law Commission of the United Nations after World War II to determine what constitutes a war crime. The principles make political leaders, commanders, and combatants responsible for war crimes, even if domestic or internal laws allow such actions. The Nuremberg principles are designed to protect those, like Manning, who expose these crimes. Under the Nuremberg principles, military orders do not offer an excuse for committing war crimes. And the Nuremberg principles would clearly exonerate Manning and condemn the pilots, shown in the "Collateral Murder" video, who fired on unarmed civilians in Baghdad, leaving twelve dead, including the two Reuters journalists.[25] "He [Manning] knew that the video depicted a 2007 attack," Coombs said of the "Collateral Murder" video. "He knew that it [the attack] resulted in the death of two journalists. And because it resulted in the death of two journalists, it had received worldwide attention. He knew that the organization Reuters had requested a copy of the video in FOIA [Freedom of Information Act] because it was their two journalists that were killed, and they wanted to have that copy in order to find out what had happened and to ensure that it didn't happen again. He knew that the United States had responded to that FOIA request almost two years later, indicating what they could find and, notably, not the video."

Coombs continued: "He knew that David Finkel, an author, had written a book called *The Good Soldiers,* and when he read through David Finkel's account and he talked about this incident that's depicted in the video, he saw that David Finkel's account and the actual video were verbatim, that David Finkel was quoting the Apache air crew. And so at that point he knew that David Finkel had a copy of the video. And when he decided to release this information, he believed that this information showed how [little] we valued human life in Iraq. He was troubled by that. And he believed that if the American public saw it, they too would be troubled and maybe things would change.

"He was twenty-two years old," Coombs said as he stood near the bench, speaking quietly to the judge at the close of his opening statement. "He was young. He was a little naive in believing that the information that he selected could actually make a difference. But he was good-intentioned in that he was selecting information that he hoped would make a difference.

"He wasn't selecting information because it was wanted by WikiLeaks," Coombs concluded. "He wasn't selecting information because of some 2009 most wanted list. He was selecting information because he believed that this information needed to be public. At the time that he released the information, he was concentrating on what the American public would think about that information, not whether or not the enemy would get access to it, and he had absolutely no actual knowledge of whether the enemy would gain access to it. Young, naive, but good-intentioned."

"I believed if the public, particularly the American public, could see this, it could spark a debate on the military and our foreign policy in general as it applied to Iraq and Afghanistan," Manning said on February 28, 2013, when she pleaded guilty to the lesser charges, her back to a few dozen of us, including Cornel West, who made it into the courtroom as she faced the judge. She said that she had hoped the release of the information to WikiLeaks "might cause society to reconsider the need to engage in counterterrorism while ignoring the situation of the people we engaged with every day."

But it has not. Our mechanical drones still circle the skies delivering death. Our attack jets still blast civilians. Our soldiers and Marines still pump bullets into mud-walled villages. Our artillery and missiles still raze homes. Our torturers still torture. Our politicians and generals still lie. And the soldier who tried to stop it all is serving a thirty-five-year prison sentence.

The Afghans, the Iraqis, the Yemenis, the Pakistanis, and the Somalis know what American military forces do. They do not need to read

WikiLeaks. It is we who remain ignorant. Our terror is delivered daily to the wretched of the earth with industrial weapons. But to us, it is invisible. We do not stand over the decapitated and eviscerated bodies left behind on city and village streets by our missiles, drones, and fighter jets. We do not listen to the wails and shrieks of parents embracing the shattered bodies of their children. We do not see the survivors of air attacks bury their mothers, fathers, brothers, and sisters. We are not conscious of the long night of collective humiliation, repression, and powerlessness that characterizes existence in Israel's occupied territories, Iraq, and Afghanistan. We do not see the boiling anger that war and injustice turn into a cauldron of hate over time. We are not aware of the very natural lust for revenge against those who carry out or symbolize this oppression. We see only the final pyrotechnics of terror, the shocking moment when the rage erupts into an inchoate fury and the murder of innocents. And willfully uninformed, we do not understand our own complicity. We self-righteously condemn the killers as subhuman savages who deserve more of the violence that created them. This is a recipe for endless terror.

Manning, by providing a window into the truth, opened up the possibility of redemption. She offered hope for a new relationship with the Muslim world, one based on compassion and honesty, on the rule of law, rather than on the cold brutality of industrial warfare. But by refusing to heed the truth that Manning laid before us, by ignoring the crimes committed daily in our name, we not only continue to swell the ranks of our enemies but put the lives of our citizens in greater and greater jeopardy.

Manning showed us through the documents she released to WikiLeaks what all Iraqis know. They have endured hundreds of rapes and murders, along with systematic torture by the military and police of the puppet government we installed. None of the atrocities from the leaked videos and documents were investigated. Manning provided the data showing that between 2004 and 2009 there were at least 109,032 "violent deaths" in Iraq, including those of 66,081 civilians, and that coalition troops were responsible for at least 195 unreported civilian deaths. In the "Collateral Murder" video, she allowed us to watch as a

US helicopter attacked unarmed civilians in Baghdad and as a US Army tank then crushed one of the wounded lying on the street. The actions of the US military in this one video alone, as law professor Marjorie Cohn has pointed out, violate Article 85 of the First Protocol to the Geneva Conventions, which prohibits the targeting of civilians; Common Article 3 of the Geneva Conventions, which requires that the wounded be treated; and Article 17 of the First Protocol, which permits civilians to rescue and care for the wounded without being harmed.[26]

David Coombs read a brief statement from the twenty-five-year-old Manning after the sentencing:

The decisions that I made in 2010 were made out of a concern for my country and the world that we live in. Since the tragic events of 9/11, our country has been at war. We've been at war with an enemy that chooses not to meet us on any traditional battlefield, and due to this fact we've had to alter our methods of combating the risks posed to us and our way of life.

I initially agreed with these methods and chose to volunteer to help defend my country. It was not until I was in Iraq and reading secret military reports on a daily basis that I started to question the morality of what we were doing. It was at this time I realized in our efforts to meet this risk posed to us by the enemy, we have forgotten our humanity. We consciously elected to devalue human life both in Iraq and Afghanistan.

When we engaged those that we perceived were the enemy, we sometimes killed innocent civilians. Whenever we killed innocent civilians, instead of accepting responsibility for our conduct, we elected to hide behind the veil of national security and classified information in order to avoid any public accountability.

In our zeal to kill the enemy, we internally debated the definition of torture. We held individuals at Guantánamo for years without due process. We inexplicably turned a blind eye to torture and executions by the Iraqi government. And we stomached countless other acts in the name of our war on terror.

Patriotism is often the cry extolled when morally questionable acts are advocated by those in power. When these cries of patriotism drown out any logically based dissension, it is usually the American soldier that is given the order to carry out some ill-conceived mission.

Our nation has had similar dark moments for the virtues of democracy—the Trail of Tears, the Dred Scott decision, McCarthyism, and the Japanese-American internment camps—to mention a few. I am confident that many of the actions since 9/11 will one day be viewed in a similar light.

As the late Howard Zinn once said, "There is not a flag large enough to cover the shame of killing innocent people."

I understand that my actions violated the law; I regret if my actions hurt anyone or harmed the United States. It was never my intent to hurt anyone. I only wanted to help people. When I chose to disclose classified information, I did so out of a love for my country and a sense of duty to others.

If you deny my request for a pardon, I will serve my time knowing that sometimes you have to pay a heavy price to live in a free society. I will gladly pay that price if it means we could have a country that is truly conceived in liberty and dedicated to the proposition that all women and men are created equal.[27]

———————

I sat in the front row of a New York federal court in November 2013 the day Jeremy Hammond was sentenced to ten years in prison for hacking into the computers of a private security firm that works on behalf of the government, including the Department of Homeland Security, the Marine Corps, the Defense Intelligence Agency, and corporations such as Dow Chemical and Raytheon.

Hammond, then age twenty-six, released to WikiLeaks, *Rolling Stone,* and other publications some 5 million emails in 2011 from the Texas-based company Strategic Forecasting Inc., or Stratfor. His four codefendants, convicted in Great Britain, were sentenced to less time *combined*—the longest sentence was 32 months—than the 120-month sentence meted out to Hammond. The 5 million email exchanges, once made public, exposed the private security firm's infiltration, monitoring, and surveillance of protesters and dissidents on behalf of corporations and the national security state. And perhaps most importantly, the information provided chilling evidence that antiterrorism laws are being routinely used by the state to criminalize nonviolent, democratic dissent and falsely link dissidents to international terrorist organizations. Hammond sought no financial gain. He got none.

The email exchanges Hammond provided to the public were entered as evidence in my lawsuit against Barack Obama over Section 1021(b)(2) of the National Defense Authorization Act. One of my coplaintiffs was Alexa O'Brien, a journalist and content strategist who cofounded the US Day of Rage, an organization created to reform the election process. Because of the Hammond leaks, we know that Stratfor officials attempted to falsely link her and her organization to Islamic radicals and websites as well as jihadist ideology, setting her up for detention under the new law. US District Judge Katherine Forrest ruled, in part because of the leak, that we did as plaintiffs have a credible fear, and she nullified the law, a ruling that the higher appellate court overturned when the Obama administration appealed her ruling.

Hammond's ten-year sentence was one of the longest in US history for hacking. It was the maximum the judge could impose under a plea agreement in the case. It was wildly disproportionate to the crime—an act of nonviolent civil disobedience that championed the public good by exposing abuses of power by the government and a security firm. But the excessive sentence was the point.

I met Hammond in Manhattan's Metropolitan Correctional Center about a week and a half before his sentencing. He was wearing an oversized brown prison jumpsuit that fell over his shoes. He had long brown hair and a wispy beard. He had been held for twenty months.

"People have a right to know what governments and corporations are doing behind closed doors," he said.

Judge Preska, who sentenced Hammond with the same venom she displayed in sentencing Syed Fahad Hashmi, is a member of the right-wing Federalist Society.[28] And the hack into Stratfor disclosed the email address and password for a business account of Preska's husband, Thomas Kavaler, a partner at the law firm Cahill Gordon & Reindel.

Some emails of the firm's corporate clients, including Merrill Lynch, also were exposed. The National Lawyers Guild, because the judge's husband was a victim of the hack, filed a recusal motion. Preska, as chief judge of the US District Court for the Southern District of New York and therefore the final authority, was able to deny it. Her refusal to recuse herself allowed her to oversee a trial in which she had allegedly a huge conflict of interest.

The judge, who herself was once employed at Cahill Gordon & Reindel, fulminated from the bench about Hammond's "total lack of respect for the law."[29] She read a laundry list of his arrests for acts of civil disobedience. She damned what she called his "unrepentant recidivism." She said: "These are not the actions of Martin Luther King, Nelson Mandela . . . or even Daniel Ellsberg"—an odd analogy given that Mandela founded the *armed* wing of the African National Congress, was considered a terrorist by South Africa's apartheid government and the US government, and was vilified, along with King and Ellsberg, by the US government. Preska said that there was a "desperate need to promote respect for the law" and a "need for adequate public deterrence." She read from transcripts of Hammond's conversations in Anonymous chat rooms in which he described the goal of hacking into Stratfor as "destroying the target, hoping for bankruptcy, collapse," and called for "maximum mayhem." She admonished him for releasing the unlisted phone number of a retired Arizona police official who allegedly received threatening phone calls afterward.

The judge, in addition to the ten-year sentence, imposed equally harsh measures for after Hammond's release from prison. She ordered that he be placed under three years of supervised control, be forbidden to use encryption or aliases online, and submit to random searches of his computer equipment, person, and home by police and any internal security agency without the necessity of a warrant. The judge said that Hammond was legally banned from having any contact with "electronic civil disobedience websites or organizations."

The sentence required the judge to demonstrate a callous disregard for transparency and our right to privacy. It required her to ignore the disturbing information Hammond released showing that the government and Stratfor had attempted to link nonviolent dissident groups, including some within Occupy, to terrorist organizations so that peaceful dissidents could be prosecuted as terrorists. It required her to accept the frightening fact that intelligence agencies now work on behalf of corporations as well as the state. She also had to sidestep the fact that Hammond made no financial gain from the leak.

Hammond's draconian sentence, like the draconian sentences of other whistle-blowers, will fan open defiance of the state. It will solidify the growing understanding that we must resort, if we want to effect real change, to unconventional and illegal tactics to thwart the mounting abuses by the corporate state. There is no hope, this sentencing showed, for redress from the judicial system, elected officials, or the executive branch.

Why should we respect a court system, or a governmental system, that does not respect us? Why should we abide by laws that protect only criminals like Wall Street thieves while leaving the rest of us exposed to abuse? Why should we continue to have faith in structures of power that deny us our most basic rights and civil liberties? Why should we be impoverished so that the profits of big banks, corporations, and hedge funds can swell?

Hammond, six feet tall and wiry, defined himself when we met in jail as "an anarchist communist." He said he had dedicated his life to destroying capitalism and the centralized power of the corporate state and that he embraced the classic tools of revolt, including mass protests, general strikes, and boycotts. And he saw hacking and leaking as critical tools of this resistance, to be used not only to reveal the truths about systems of corporate power but to "disrupt/destroy these systems entirely."

Like Assange and Manning, Jeremy Hammond had an unconventional childhood. He and his twin brother Jason were raised by their single father, Jack, in Glendale Heights, Illinois, a working-class suburb in western Chicago. His mother, Rose, left the family when the twins were three; while she provided some financial support, she left most of the child rearing to Jack. Hammond's father was an aspiring punk rock musician who dropped out of high school and earned about $35,000 a year giving guitar lessons.

Jeremy showed an early and precocious talent for computers, as well as politics. He responded to the war jingoism that enveloped the country after the 9/11 attacks by organizing school protests against the calls to invade Iraq. He founded an underground newspaper that was designed, as he wrote in the first editor's letter, to get students to "most of all think." "WAKE UP . . . Your mind is programmable—if you're not programming your mind, someone else will program it for you."[30]

"My first memories of American politics was when Bush stole the election in 2000," he told me, "and then how Bush used the wave of nationalism after 9/11 to launch unprovoked, preemptive wars against Afghanistan and Iraq. In high school, I was involved in publishing 'underground' newsletters criticizing the Patriot Act, the wars, and other Bush-era policies. I attended many antiwar protests in the city [Chicago] and was introduced to other local struggles and the larger anticorporate globalization movement. I began identifying as an anarchist, started to travel around the country to various mobilizations and conferences, and began getting arrested for various acts."

He said that his experience of street protest, especially against the wars in Afghanistan and Iraq, was seminal, for he saw that the state had little interest in heeding the voices of protesters and other public voices. "Instead, we were labeled as traitors, beaten and arrested."

Hammond was living at home in Chicago in 2010 under a curfew from 7:00 PM to 7:00 AM for a variety of acts of civil disobedience when Manning was arrested. Like Manning, he had shown an astonishing aptitude for science, math, and the language of computers from a very young age. He hacked into the computers at a local Apple store when he was sixteen and then showed the stunned sales staff how he had done it. When he hacked into the computer science department's website at the University of Illinois–Chicago as a freshman, the university responded to this prank by refusing to allow him to return for his sophomore year. He was an early backer of "cyber-liberation" and in 2004 started an "electronic-disobedience journal" he named *Hack This Zine.*

That same year, Hammond called on hackers in a speech at the DefCon convention in Las Vegas—the largest and best-known underground hacking conference—to use their skills to disrupt the upcoming Republican National Convention.[31] By the time of his arrest, Hammond was one of the shadowy stars of the hacktivist underground. He was also the FBI's number-one most wanted cybercriminal in the world. It was Manning's courage that prompted Hammond to commit his own act of cyber civil disobedience, although he knew the chances of being caught were high.

"I saw what Chelsea Manning did," he said when we spoke, seated at a metal table in a tiny room reserved for attorney-client visits. "Through her hacking, she became a contender, a world changer. She took tremendous risks to show the ugly truth about war. I asked myself, *If she could make that risk, shouldn't I make that risk?* Wasn't it wrong to sit comfortably by, working on the websites of Food Not Bombs, while I had the skills to do something similar? I too could make a difference. It was her courage that prompted me to act."

Hammond, with black tattoos on each forearm—one a gridlike "Glider" symbol that was proposed by computer programmer Eric S. Raymond as a symbol for the hacker subculture, and the other the *shi* hexagram from the I Ching, meaning "leading" or "army" or "troops"— is steeped in radical thought. He swiftly migrated politically as a young teenager from the liberal wing of the Democratic Party to the militancy of Black Bloc anarchists. He was an avid reader in high school of material put out by CrimethInc, an anarchist collective that publishes anarchist literature and manifestos, including *The Anarchist Cookbook*. Hammond is steeped in the work of old radicals, from Alexander Berkman and Emma Goldman to black revolutionaries such as George Jackson, Elaine Brown, and Assata Shakur. He admires the Weather Underground.

Hammond told me he made numerous trips while in Chicago to Forest Home Cemetery to visit the Haymarket Martyrs' Monument, which honors anarchists who took part in the labor wars, four of whom were hanged in 1887. On the sixteen-foot-high granite monument are the final words of one of the condemned men, August Spies: THE DAY WILL COME WHEN OUR SILENCE WILL BE MORE POWERFUL THAN THE VOICE YOU ARE THROTTLING TODAY. Emma Goldman is buried nearby.

Hammond became well known to the state for a variety of acts of civil disobedience over the last decade, ranging from painting antiwar graffiti on walls in Chicago to protesting at the 2004 Republican National Convention in New York, to hacking into the right-wing website Protest Warrior, for which he was sentenced to two years at Federal Correctional Institution (FCI) Greenville in Illinois.[32]

He told me that his goal was to build "leaderless collectives based on free association, consensus, mutual aid, self-sufficiency and harmony with the environment." It is essential, he said, that all of us work to cut our personal ties with capitalism and engage in resistance that includes "mass organizing of protests, strikes, and boycotts," as well as hacking and leaking, which are "effective tools to reveal ugly truths of the system or to disrupt/destroy these systems entirely."

Hammond spent months within the Occupy movement in Chicago. He embraced its "leaderless, nonhierarchical structures, such as general assemblies and consensus, and occupying public spaces." But he was critical of what he said was Occupy's "vague politics, which allowed it to include followers of Ron Paul and some in the Tea Party, as well as "reformist liberals and Democrats." Hammond said he was not interested in a movement that "only wanted a 'nicer' form of capitalism and favored legal reforms, not revolution." He said he did not support what he called a "dogmatic nonviolence doctrine" held by many in the Occupy movement, describing it as "needlessly limited and divisive." He rejected the idea of protesters carrying out acts of civil disobedience that they know will lead to arrest. "The point," he said, "is to carry out acts of resistance and not get caught." He condemned the "peace patrols"—units formed within the Occupy movement that sought to prohibit acts of vandalism and violence by other protesters, most often members of the Black Bloc—as "a secondary police force."

Furthermore, Hammond dismissed the call by many in Occupy not to antagonize the police, whom he characterized as "the boot boys of the one percent, paid to protect the rich and powerful." He said such a tactic of nonconfrontation with the police ignored the long history of repression by the police in attacking popular movements, as well as the "profiling and imprisonment of our comrades." He went on: "Because we were unprepared, or perhaps unwilling, to defend our occupations, police and mayors launched coordinated attacks driving us out of our own parks."

"I fully support and have participated in Black Bloc and other forms of militant direct action," he said. "I do not believe that the ruling powers listen to the people's peaceful protests. Black Bloc is an effective, fluid, and dynamic form of protest. It causes disruption outside of predictable/controllable mass demonstrations through unarrests, holding streets, barricades, and property destruction. Smashing corporate windows is not violence, especially when compared to the everyday economic violence of sweatshops and 'free trade.' Black Bloc seeks to hit them where it hurts, through economic damage. But more than smashing windows, they seek to break the spell of 'law and order' and the artificial limitations we impose on ourselves."

When he was sentenced, Hammond told the courtroom: "The acts of civil disobedience that I am being sentenced for today are in line with the principles of community and equality that have guided my life. I hacked into dozens of high-profile corporations and government institutions, understanding very clearly that what I was doing was against the law, and that my actions could land me back in federal prison. But I felt that I had an obligation to use my skills to expose and confront injustice—and to bring the truth to light.

"Could I have achieved the same goals through legal means?" he asked the court. "I have tried everything from voting petitions to peaceful protest and have found that those in power do not want the truth to be exposed. When we speak truth to power, we are ignored at best and brutally suppressed at worst. We are confronting a power structure that does not respect its own system of checks and balances, never mind the rights of its own citizens or the international community.

"I targeted law enforcement systems because of the racism and inequality with which the criminal law is enforced," he admitted in court. "I targeted the manufacturers and distributors of military and police equipment who profit from weaponry used to advance US political and economic interests abroad and to repress people at home. I targeted information security firms because they work in secret to protect government and corporate interests at the expense of individual rights, undermining and discrediting activists, journalists, and other truth seekers and spreading disinformation.

"Why the FBI would introduce us to the hacker [Sabu] who found the initial vulnerability and allow this hack to continue remains a mystery," Hammond said as he faced the judge. "As a result of the Stratfor hack, some of the dangers of the unregulated private intelligence industry are now known. It has been revealed through WikiLeaks and other journalists around the world that Stratfor maintained a worldwide network of informants that they used to engage in intrusive and possibly illegal surveillance activities on behalf of large multinational corporations."

At Sabu's urging, Hammond broke into other websites too. Hammond, at Sabu's request, provided information to hackers that enabled them to break into and deface official foreign government websites, including those of Turkey, Iran, and Brazil.

"I broke into numerous sites and handed over passwords and backdoors that enabled Sabu—and by extension his FBI handlers—to control these targets," Hammond said.

"I don't know how other information I provided to him may have been used, but I think the government's collection and use of this data needs to be investigated," he went on. "The government celebrates my conviction and imprisonment, hoping that it will close the door on the full story. I took responsibility for my actions, by pleading guilty, but when will the government be made to answer for its crimes?

"The hypocrisy of 'law and order' and the injustices caused by capitalism cannot be cured by institutional reform but through civil disobedience and direct action," Hammond told the court. "Yes, I broke the law, but I believe that sometimes laws must be broken in order to make room for change."

As Hammond was escorted out of the courtroom on the ninth floor of the federal courthouse at 500 Pearl Street after the sentencing, he shouted to roughly 100 people—including a class of prim West Point cadets attending in their blue uniforms—gathered there: "Long live Anonymous! Hurrah for anarchy!" In a statement he read in court, he thanked "Free Anons, the Anonymous Solidarity Network, [and] Anarchist Black Cross" for their roles in the fight against oppression.

"Being incarcerated has really opened my eyes to the reality of the criminal justice system," Hammond told me in the jail. "[It] is not a criminal justice system about public safety or rehabilitation, but reaping profits through mass incarceration. There are two kinds of justice—one for the rich and the powerful who get away with the big crimes, then [one] for everyone else, especially people of color and the impoverished. There is no such thing as a fair trial. In over 80 percent of the cases, people are pressured to plea out instead of exercising their right to trial, under the threat of lengthier sentences. I believe no satisfactory reforms are possible. We need to close all prisons and release everybody unconditionally."

After committing a series of minor infractions, as well as testing positive, along with other prisoners on his tier, for marijuana that had been smuggled into the prison, Hammond had already lost social visits for the next two years and "spent time in the box." He said prison involved "a lot of boredom." He was playing a lot of chess, teaching guitar, and helping other prisoners study for their GED.

He insisted that he did not see himself as different from other prisoners, especially poor prisoners of color, who were in for common crimes, especially drug-related crimes. He said that most prisoners are political prisoners, caged unjustly by a system of totalitarian capitalism that has snuffed out basic opportunities for democratic dissent and economic survival.

"The majority of people in prison did what they had to do to survive," he said. "Most were poor. They got caught up in the war on drugs, which is how you make money if you are poor. The real reason they get locked in prison for so long is so corporations can continue to make big profits. It is not about justice. I do not draw distinctions between us.

"Jail is essentially enduring harassment and dehumanizing conditions with frequent lockdowns and shakedowns," he said. "You have to constantly fight for respect from the guards, sometimes getting yourself thrown in the box. However, I will not change the way I live because I am locked up. I will continue to be defiant, agitating and organizing whenever possible."

He said resistance must be a way of life. "The truth," he said, "will always come out." He cautioned activists to be hypervigilant and aware that "one mistake can be permanent." Activists should "know and accept the worst possible repercussion" before carrying out an action and should be "aware of mass counterintelligence/surveillance operations targeting our movements." But, he added, "don't let paranoia or fear deter you from activism. Do the down thing!"

"In these times of secrecy and abuse of power there is only one solution—transparency," wrote Sarah Harrison, the British journalist who accompanied Snowden to Russia and who has also gone into self-imposed exile in Berlin. "If our governments are so compromised that they will not tell us the truth, then we must step forward to grasp it. Provided with the unequivocal proof of primary source documents people can fight back. If our governments will not give this information to us, then we must take it for ourselves.

"When whistleblowers come forward we need to fight for them, so others will be encouraged," she went on. "When they are gagged, we must be their voice. When they are hunted, we must be their shield. When they are locked away, we must free them. Giving us the truth is not a crime. This is our data, our information, our history. We must fight to own it. Courage is contagious."[33]

———

I walked down Sloane Street in London after I left Assange in the Ecuadorean embassy. Red double-decker buses and automobiles inched along the thoroughfare. I passed boutiques with window displays of Prada, Armani, and Gucci. The global superrich, seeking a tax haven, have colonized this section of London. The area has the highest household income in the United Kingdom. "Much of London's housing wealth now lies in the hands of a global elite for whom the city represents not a home but a tax haven attached to an exclusive resort town," a *Financial Times* editorial bemoaned.[34] Shoppers who seemed blissfully unaware of the tragedy unfolding a few blocks away crowded the sidewalk.

I stopped in front of the four white columns that led into the brick-turreted Cadogan Hotel. The Cadogan is where Oscar Wilde was arrested, in room 118, on April 6, 1895, before being charged with "committing acts of gross indecency with other male persons." John Betjeman imagined the shock of that arrest, which ruined Wilde's life, in his 1937 poem "The Arrest of Oscar Wilde at the Cadogan Hotel":

> *A thump, and a murmur of voices—*
> *("Oh why must they make such a din?")*
> *As the door of the bedroom swung open*
> *And TWO PLAIN CLOTHES POLICEMEN came in:*
>
> *"Mr. Woilde, we 'ave come for tew take yew*
> *Where felons and criminals dwell:*
> *We must ask yew tew leave with us quoietly*
> *For this is the Cadogan Hotel."* [35]

The world has been turned upside down. The pestilence of corporate totalitarianism is spreading over the earth. The criminals have seized power. It is not only Assange, Hammond, Abu-Jamal, Manning, and Hashmi they want. It is all who dare to defy the destructive fury of the global corporate state. The persecution of these rebels is the harbinger of what is to come: the rise of a bitter world where criminals in tailored suits and gangsters in beribboned military uniforms—propped up by a vast internal and external security apparatus, a compliant press, and a morally bankrupt political elite—hunt down and cage all who resist.

VIII / Sublime Madness

The duty of a revolutionary is to always struggle, no matter what, to struggle to extinction.[1]

— AUGUSTE BLANQUI, "LA CRITIQUE SOCIALE"

It might be a basic characteristic of existence that those who would know it completely would perish, in which case the strength of a spirit should be measured according to how much of the "truth" one could still barely endure.[2]

— FRIEDERICH NIETZSCHE, "BEYOND GOOD AND EVIL"

The man who waged the first significant war in North America against hydraulic fracturing, commonly known as "fracking," was an eccentric, messianic Christian preacher named Wiebo Ludwig. Ludwig, with his small Christian community in the Canadian province of Alberta, sabotaged at least one wellhead by pouring cement down its shaft, and he blew up several others. The Canadian authorities, along with the oil and gas barons, have demonized Ludwig as an ecoterrorist—an odd charge given that they are the ones responsible for systematically destroying the environment and the planet.[3]

The anti-fracking movement, especially in rural communities in Colorado, Pennsylvania, and upstate New York, is one of the most potent grassroots insurgencies in North America. The movement has been able to block the natural gas industry's plans to exploit shale gas in New York State. And it is a huge stumbling block for the industry in many other parts of the United States and Canada. If the anti-fracking movement has a founding father, it is Wiebo Ludwig.

Ludwig swiftly understood that environmental laws are not designed to protect the environment. The laws are designed, at best, to regulate the environment's continued exploitation. It was futile, he argued, to spend energy attempting to improve or adjust these regulations. We might be able to slow or delay environmental degradation, but we would not stop it.

Ludwig exposed the absurdity of attempting to build an environmental movement that had as its goal the more efficient oversight and regulation of the oil and gas industry. He realized that lobbying those in power, testifying in hearings, writing letters of protest, contacting celebrities to attract press attention, and organizing petition drives to get the government to intervene was useless. Corporations, he understood, determined and often wrote the laws that were ostensibly designed to regulate their activity. Environmental laws were, he found, a circular joke on the public. And the Big Green environmental groups that worked within these legal parameters were largely ineffectual and often complicit in the destruction of the ecosystems they claimed they wanted to protect. Resistance, he argued, would have to be militant and it would have to be local. It could not play by the rules imposed by the corporate state.

As Thomas Linzey, the executive director of the Community Environmental Legal Defense Fund, which has helped organize dozens of communities to impose local bans on oil and gas extraction, pointed out, "Forty years after the major environmental laws were adopted in the US, and forty years after trying to regulate the damage caused by corporations to the natural environment and our communities, by almost every major environmental statistic, things are worse now than they were before."[4]

Calgary, Alberta, is a boomtown. Glittering skyscrapers, monuments to the obscene profits amassed by a fossil fuel industry that is exploiting the tar sands and the vast oil and natural gas fields, have transformed Calgary, declaring the city's new identity as a mecca for money, dirty politics, greed, and industry jobs. The city is as soulless and sterile as Houston. The death of the planet, for a few, is very good business.

"Wiebo felt that our society was in a spiritual crisis, rather than an environmental or an economic crisis," David York told me. York's film

Wiebo's War is a portrayal of Ludwig and his fight with the oil and gas industry.[5] "He felt that our addiction to fossil fuels, rampant consumerism and materialism, addictions, breakdown of family units, were all symptoms of a society that has lost its root connection to God. Further, he felt that we are in a kind of end times state, where the forces of good are in a terrible struggle with the forces of evil. He wasn't so crass as to put a timetable on it, but in his view, 'any fool can see the times.'"

That one of our era's most effective figures of resistance against the oil and gas industry was a messianic Christian is perhaps not coincidental. He was propelled forward by a vision. I do not share Ludwig's Christian fundamentalism—his community was a rigid patriarchy—but I do share his belief that when human law comes into conflict with what is moral, human law must be defied. Ludwig grasped the moral decadence of the consumer society, its unchecked hedonism, worship of money, and deadening cult of the self. He retreated in 1985 with his small band of followers into the remoteness of northern Alberta. His community, called Trickle Creek, was equipped with its own biodiesel refinery, windmill, and solar panels—which permitted it to produce its own power—as well as a greenhouse and a mill.[6] Its members, who grew their own food, severed themselves from the contaminants of consumer culture. But like the struggle of Axel Heyst, the protagonist in Joseph Conrad's novel *Victory*, Ludwig's flight from evil resulted in evil coming to him.

Ludwig's farm was atop one of the largest oil and gas reserves in the world. Landowners in Alberta own only the top six inches of soil. The mineral rights below it belong to the state. The province can lease these rights without the knowledge or acquiescence of the owner. Beneath Ludwig's farm lay a fossil fuel known as sour gas, a neurotoxin that, if released from within the earth, even in small amounts, can poison livestock, water tables, and people.

"Wherever a man goes, men will pursue and paw him with their dirty institutions," wrote Henry David Thoreau.[7] This is what happened to Ludwig.

The oil and gas companies began a massive drilling effort in the early 1990s. At first, like many other reformers and activists, Ludwig used legal and political channels to push back against the companies, which were putting down wells on the edge of his 160-acre farm. He spent the first five years attending hearings with civil regulators, writing letters—he even wrote to Jane Fonda—and appealing in vain to elected officials, government agencies, the press, environmentalists, and First Nations groups. His family—he had eleven children—posted a sign in 1990 that decried "the ruthless interruption and cessation" of privacy; "the relentless greedy grabbing of Creational resources"; "the caloused [sic] disregard for the sanctity of the Lord's Day"; the legislation of land and mineral ownership policy "that does violence to the God-given 'right to property.'"[8] Ludwig then presented the offending oil company, Ranchmen's, with a bill for the sign.

"He was primarily motivated by his love for his family and a strong sense of justice," said Andrew Nikiforuk, the author of a book on Ludwig called *Saboteurs: Wiebo Ludwig's War Against Big Oil,* whom I met in Calgary. He told me, "It did not seem right to him that the oil industry could park a drilling well for sour gas in view of his family's communal dining room. 'Is a man not even master in his own house, let alone his own land, on matters like these?'

"His war against industry illustrated the cost of our addiction to hydrocarbons: our materialistic way of life is based on the destruction of groundwater, the devaluing of rural property, the invasion of rural communities, the poisoning of skies with carcinogens, the fragmentation of landscapes," Nikiforuk said. "Urban people do not understand the sacrifices now being imposed on rural people."

Ludwig's first acts of sabotage, as Nikiforuk's book and York's film document, were minor. He laid down nails poking up out of boards on roads to puncture the tires on the industry's trucks. He smashed solar panels. He blocked roads by downing trees. He disabled vehicles and drilling equipment. But after two leaks of hydrogen sulfide sour gas from nearby wells—which forced everyone on the farm to evacuate and were followed by numerous farm animals giving birth to deformed or stillborn offspring, as well as five human miscarriages or stillbirths within Ludwig's community—and after the destruction of two of his water wells, he declared open war on the oil and gas industry. He began to blow up oil and gas facilities. He said he had to fight back to "protect his children."

The Canadian Mounted Police, accompanied by private security agents hired by the oil companies, spent millions to investigate and halt the sabotage. Ludwig's farm was occupied by police five times and searched for incriminating evidence. The police and Encana Corporation infiltrated Ludwig's tight community with an agent provocateur who, to prove he could be trusted, blew up a well owned by what was then Alberta Energy Corporation (now Encana). Ludwig was blamed for the explosion. The oil company also brought in a "terrorism expert" from Toronto to speak at local town hall gatherings—York filmed one of the talks—and the expert warned residents of the rising "terrorism" of religious cults led by fanatic, charismatic leaders.

Ludwig was undeterred. "People are talking here that maybe someone should be shooting guys in pinstripe suits to get them to stop," he said.

Ludwig, whose intimate knowledge of the Albertan terrain allowed him to outfox hundreds of police officers, was never caught in an act of sabotage, but he probably had a hand in damage to hundreds of remote well sites estimated at $12 million. The federal government in Ottawa, in desperation, considered sending in the army. Ludwig was finally arrested in 2000 on five counts of property damage and possession of explosives and imprisoned for nineteen months. He spent his time in prison reading a treatise in Dutch—he was fluent—on the nature of hell.

He referred to the biblical tale of David and Goliath and quoted Sun Tzu's *The Art of War* to justify his struggle against colossal corporate power, saying, "The war is won before it is fought." Ludwig believed that if you fought for righteousness, you would always be assured of spiritual victory, even if you were defeated in the eyes of the world. "It's not size," he said. "It's whether a man is right or not. The fight is won on principle." In his home he kept a poster of activist and journalist Ken Saro-Wiwa, a Nigerian hanged in 1995 after he campaigned against Shell Oil's exploitation of his country. The poster read: "The environment is man's first right. Without a clean environment man cannot exist to claim other rights be they political, social or economic."

Ludwig once invited visiting civil servants who worked for oil and gas regulators to dinner. He fed them homemade cheeses, preserves, jams, and wild cranberry wine. The pièce de résistance, which Ludwig unveiled with his usual flair, was the skull of a horse killed by sour gas. "It's just a symbol of all the death we've had around here," he informed his startled guests. On another occasion, he dumped noxious sour crude on the carpet in the office of local regulators to see if it "bothered" them.

The sabotage did not end with Ludwig's death in 2012. There are periodic reports of ongoing sabotage along the path of the XL pipeline and in the Alberta oil fields. "I'd also say that sabotage in the oil patch is one of the oil and gas industry's dirty little secrets," York said. "It is widespread, and to many landowners it is a natural consequence of the industry's attitudes and behavior to those whose land they are occupying. The industry doesn't make a big fuss because they don't want to encourage the response."

But violence begets violence. And the more facilities Ludwig blew up, the harsher became the intrusion of the state.

"Meeting industrial violence against livestock and families with more industrial violence against oil and gas installations is not the answer," said Nikiforuk. "It is an act of frustration as well as a reflection of the captured state of regulators. And it submits an entire community to a reign of industry- and state-sanctioned terror. A second war broke out in the bush in the 2000s during an intense period of hydraulic fracking. Six bombings occurred at Encana well sites in northern British Columbia just fifty kilometers from Ludwig's farm. The government sent in 250 officers to investigate. They treated rural citizens like members of the Taliban. The campaign ended as mysteriously as it began and had all the earmarks of Ludwig. It did not change industry practices."

Ludwig's gravest mistake was his decision, or the decision of someone in his small community, to shoot at two trucks carrying rowdy teenagers. The sons and daughters of oil and gas workers roared through the group's compound at about 4:00 AM on June 20, 1999. Karman Willis, a sixteen-year-old girl, was fatally shot by someone on the farm, and a second teenager survived a wound. York in his film shows Ludwig family members repeating like automatons that they thought they were under attack because the backfiring of the vehicles sounded like gunshots. No one on the farm took responsibility for the shooting. No one was charged. But after the killing of the girl, most of those in the area refused to associate with Ludwig and his community. Local businesses put up signs that read: NO SERVICE FOR LUDWIGS.

Ludwig, before he died at age seventy after refusing chemotherapy for esophageal cancer, denounced violence. With his family, he had read Jacques Ellul's 1969 book *Violence: Reflections from a Christian Perspective*. Ellul, like Ludwig's Dutch father, had been part of the resistance against the Nazis in World War II. "What constantly marked the life of Jesus was not nonviolence but in every situation the choice not to use power," Ellul writes in *What I Believe*. "This is infinitely different."[9]

"The Christian should participate in social and political efforts in order to have an influence in the world," Ellul argues in *The Presence of the Kingdom*,

> not with the hope of making a paradise (of the earth), but simply to make it more tolerable—not to diminish the opposition between this world and the Kingdom of God, but simply to modify the opposition between the disorder of this world and the order of preservation that God wants it to have—not to bring in the Kingdom of God, but so that the Gospel might be proclaimed in order that all men might truly hear the good news.[10]

"We feel weak in all the things we are fighting," Ludwig reflected. "I think the match is very unequal. But it's all right. Instead of griping about it, we might as well give ourselves to it."[11]

The battle with the corporate state will take place not only in city streets and plazas but in the nation's heartland. Ranchers, farmers, and enraged citizens—often after seeing their land seized by eminent domain and their water supplies placed under mortal threat—have united with activists to oppose fracking and the building of the Keystone XL tar sand pipeline. The Tar Sands Blockade (TSB), which is working to stop the northern leg of the Keystone XL from being built, is an example of this grassroots movement. The centers of resistance it has set up in Texas and Oklahoma and on tribal lands along the proposed route of this six-state, 1,700-mile proposed pipeline are fast becoming flashpoints.[12]

The XL pipeline, which would cost $7 billion and whose southern portion is complete, is a symbol of the dying order. If the northern section is built, it will pump 830,000 barrels a day of unrefined tar sand fluid from tar sand mine fields in Canada to the Texas Gulf Coast.[13] Tar sand oil is not conventional crude oil. It is a synthetic slurry that, because tar sand oil is solid in its natural state, cannot flow without being laced with toxic chemicals and gas condensates. Tar sands are boiled and diluted with these chemicals before being blasted down a pipeline at high pressure. Water sources are instantly contaminated if there is a rupture.[14]

The pipeline, if built, would cross nearly 2,000 US waterways, including the Ogallala Aquifer, source of one-third of US farmland irrigation water. And it is not a matter of if, but when, it would spill. TransCanada's Keystone I pipeline, built in 2010, spilled fourteen times in its first twelve months of operation.[15] Because the extraction process emits such a large quantity of greenhouse gases, the pipeline has been called the fuse to the largest carbon bomb on the planet. The climate scientist James Hansen warns that successful completion of the pipeline, along with the exploitation of Canadian tar sands it would facilitate, would mean "game over for the climate."[16]

Keystone XL is part of the final phase of extreme exploitation by the corporate state. The corporations intend to squeeze the last vestiges of profit from an ecosystem careening toward collapse. Most of the oil that can be reached through drilling from traditional rigs is depleted. In response, the fossil fuel industry has developed new technologies to go after dirtier, less efficient forms of energy. These technologies bring with them a dramatically heightened cost to ecosystems. They accelerate the warming of the planet and contaminate vital water sources. Deepwater Arctic drilling, tar sand extraction, hydraulic fracturing (or hydrofracking), and drilling horizontally, given the cost of extraction and the effects on the environment, amount to ecological suicide.

The pipeline has attracted construction crews and rebels alike. Surviving on canned food and bottled water, protesters carried out tree-sits in September 2012 to block the path of the pipeline near Winnsboro,

Texas. Others chained themselves to logging equipment, locked themselves in trucks carrying pipe to construction sites, and hung banners at equipment staging areas.[17] Doug Grant, a former Exxon employee, was arrested outside Winnsboro when he bound himself to clear-cutting machinery. Shannon Bebe and Benjamin Franklin, after handcuffing themselves to equipment being used to cut down trees, were tasered, pepper-sprayed, and physically assaulted by local police, reportedly at the request of TransCanada officials.[18] The actor Daryl Hannah and a seventy-eight-year-old East Texas great-grandmother and farmer, Eleanor Fairchild, were arrested on October 4, 2012, while blocking Trans-Canada bulldozers on Fairchild's property. The Fairchild farm, like other properties seized by TransCanada, was taken under Texas eminent domain laws on behalf of a foreign corporation. At the same time, private security companies employed by TransCanada, along with local law enforcement, aggressively detained and restricted reporters, including a *New York Times* reporter and photographer, who were attempting to cover the protests. Most of the journalists were on private property with the permission of the landowners.[19]

I reached climate activist Tom Weis nearly 1,000 miles from the southern blockade, in Colorado. Weis was pedaling up and down the Front Range, hand-delivering copies of an open letter that activists had sent to the president. Weis had been joined in his protests and rallies by indigenous leaders, including Tom Poor Bear, vice president of Oglala Lakota Nation, and in Denver by members of the Occupy Denver community.

In 2011 Weis had ridden his bright-yellow "rocket trike"—"a recumbent tricycle wrapped in a lightweight aerodynamic shell"—for ten weeks and 2,150 miles along the proposed Keystone XL pipeline route.[20] "Keystone XL is being built as an export pipeline for Canada to sell its dirty oil to foreign markets," he said when we spoke by phone. "This is not about energy security; it's about securing TransCanada's profits." Weis cited the conclusion of a report by the Global Labor Institute at Cornell University that the jobs estimates put forward by TransCanada are unsubstantiated and that the project could actually destroy more jobs than it creates.[21]

Local resistance along the proposed pipeline has grown, especially as the project has begun to be put in place. And there have been reports of sabotage along the pipeline route. "Activists dump salt into the gas tanks, slash the tires of construction equipment, and disable equipment," said a pipeline activist based in Houston who did not want to give her name. "The companies don't want to talk about it because they fear the sabotage will grow if it is publicized. We can't talk about it openly because we will be arrested."

If completed—the House of Representatives passed a Senate bill that authorized construction of the northern leg of the pipeline in February 2015—the 485-mile southern leg, from Cushing, Oklahoma, to Nederland, Texas, would slice through major waterways that include the Neches, Red, Angelina, and Sabine Rivers as well as the Carrizo-Wilcox Aquifer, which provides drinking water for some 10 million Texans.

The invasive extraction of tar sands and shale deposits and the deep-sea drilling in the Arctic, Alaska, and the Gulf of Mexico and on the Eastern Seaboard have been sold to the US public as a route to energy independence, a way to create tens of thousands of new jobs, and a boost to the sagging economy, but this is another corporate lie. The process of extracting shale oil through hydraulic fracking requires millions of gallons of chemically treated water that leaves behind poisoned aquifers and huge impoundment ponds of toxic waste. Extracting oil shale, or kerogen, for melting requires expending tremendous amounts of energy for a marginal return. It also involves vast open-pit mining operations and pumping underground that melts the oil with steam jets. Tar sand extraction, because it emits significantly more greenhouse gases than conventional oil drilling, will accelerate global warming.

Weis said that he saw the struggle to halt the Keystone XL pipeline as a symbolic crossroads for the country and the planet. One path leads, he said, toward decay, and the other toward renewal.

"There comes a time when we must make a stand for the future of our children, and for all life on Earth," he said. "That time is here. That time is now."

———

Reinhold Niebuhr wrote that those who defy the forces of injustice and repression are possessed by "a sublime madness" in the soul "which disregards immediate appearances and emphasizes profound and ultimate unities." Niebuhr noted that "nothing but madness will do battle with malignant power and 'spiritual wickedness in high places.'"[22] This sublime madness, as Niebuhr understood, is dangerous, but it is vital. Without it, "truth is obscured." And Niebuhr also knew that traditional liberalism is a useless force in moments of extremity. Liberalism, Niebuhr wrote in *The New Republic,* "lacks the spirit of enthusiasm, not to say, fanaticism, which is so necessary to move the world out of its beaten tracks. [It] is too intellectual and too little emotional to be an efficient force in history."[23]

The prophets in the Hebrew Bible had this sublime madness. The words of the Hebrew prophets, as Abraham Heschel notes, were "a scream in the night. While the world is at ease and asleep, the prophet feels the blast from heaven."[24] Because he sees and faces an unpleasant reality, the prophet is "compelled to proclaim the very opposite of what his heart expected."[25]

It is impossible to defy "radical evil"—a phrase originally coined by Immanuel Kant to describe those who surrender their freedom and morality to an extreme form of self-adulation and later adopted by Hannah Arendt to describe totalitarianism—without "sublime madness." Sublime madness demands self-sacrifice and entails the very real possibility of death. Not that the rebel possessed of sublime madness wants to die, for the fight against radical evil is the ultimate affirmation of life. The rebel understands the terrible power of the forces arrayed against all rebels, and how far these forces, once threatened, will go to silence rebels, and yet is so possessed that he or she is unable to conform.

The rebel, dismissed as impractical and zealous, is chronically misunderstood. Those cursed with timidity, fear, or blindness and those who are slaves to opportunism call for moderation and patience. They distort the language of religion, spirituality, compromise, generosity, and compassion to justify cooperation with systems of power that are bent on our destruction. The rebel is deaf to these critiques. The rebel hears only his or her inner voice, which demands steadfast defiance.

Self-promotion, positions of influence, the adulation of the public, and the awards and prominent positions that come with bowing before authority mean nothing to the rebel, who understands that virtue is not rewarded. The rebel expects nothing and gets nothing. But for the rebel, to refuse to struggle, to refuse to rebel, is to commit spiritual and moral suicide.

"You do not become a 'dissident' just because you decide one day to take up this most unusual career," Vaclav Havel said when he stood up to the Communist regime in Czechoslovakia.

> You are thrown into it by your personal sense of responsibility, combined with a complex set of external circumstances. You are cast out of the existing structures and placed in a position of conflict with them. It begins as an attempt to do your work well, and ends with being branded an enemy of society. . . . The dissident does not operate in the realm of genuine power at all. He is not seeking power. He has no desire for office and does not gather votes. He does not attempt to charm the public. He offers nothing and promises nothing. He can offer, if anything, only his own skin—and he offers it solely because he has no other way of affirming the truth he stands for. His actions simply articulate his dignity as a citizen, regardless of the cost.[26]

The rebel, possessed of "sublime madness," speaks words that resonate only with those who can see through the facade. The rebel functions as a prophet. He or she has what Leo Tolstoy described as the three characteristics of prophecy: "First, it is entirely opposed to the general ideas of the people in the midst of whom it is uttered; second, all who hear it feel its truth; and thirdly, above all, it urges men to realize what it foretells."[27]

The message of the rebel is disturbing because of the consequences of the truth he or she speaks. To accept that Barack Obama is, as Cornel West says, "a black mascot for Wall Street" means having to challenge some frightening monoliths of power and give up the comfortable illusion that the Democratic Party or liberal institutions or a single elected official can be instruments for genuine reform. To accept that nearly all forms of electronic communication are captured and stored by the government is to give up the illusion of freedom.

The rebel, by disseminating this truth, forces us to embrace a new radicalism. The rebel shows us that there is no hope for correction or reversal by appealing to power. The rebel makes it clear that it is only by overthrowing traditional systems of power that we can be liberated.

The denunciation of the rebel is a matter of self-preservation for the liberal class. For once the callous heart of the corporate state is exposed, so is the callous heart of its liberal apologists. And the rebel, who has few friends, is the constant target of the liberal establishment.

Socrates, for this reason, is reported by some ancient accounts to have stood mute when he was being tried for sedition and condemned to death. Plato, however, has Socrates defend himself in the *Apology*. Socrates' judges could not grasp the inner compulsion—the sublime madness—that drove Socrates to risk his life for the truth. They failed to grasp the central Socratic paradox: that it is better to suffer wrong than to do wrong. Socrates' call for individuals to eschew the claims of society and the state on the citizen—like the rebellions of Assange, Abu-Jamal, Manning, and Snowden—was a form of civic heresy. His demand that we do what is right for its own sake—not for the sake of the *polis* or others, and not because we adhere to a particular moral or religious code—made no sense to those confined by law. Because he saw the political system in Athens as ignorant and morally bankrupt, he said that it was impossible for a good person to participate in the charade of justice it perpetrated. And for speaking this truth, for challenging the legitimacy of a decadent system, he was sentenced to die, charged with corrupting the morals of Athenian youth.

Socrates tells Callicles in the *Gorgias* in *The Dialogues of Plato* that, if he is put on trial, this is the reason why he will be bereft of an effective defense:

> I'll be judged like a doctor tried before a jury of children on charges brought by a pastry-cook. "Children, the defendant here has done many bad things to you. He corrupts the youngest among you by cutting and burning, he reduces them to perplexity by drying them out and stewing

them, prescribing the most bitter potions, compelling hunger and thirst; nor does he entertain you, as I do, with all kinds of delicious treats." What do you think a doctor caught up in this evil could say? If he told the truth, if he said, "Children, I did do all these things, and for your health," how great do you think the outcry from such judges would be? A pretty big one?[28]

Socrates goes on:

I know that if I am brought into court, it will be the same with me. I will not be able to tell them of the pleasure I provided, the things they consider kindness and benefits; and I envy neither those who provide them nor those for whom they are provided. If someone accuses me of corrupting the youth by reducing them to perplexity, or of abusing their elders with sharp and pointed speech, in public or private, I won't be able to tell the truth, which is, "I say all these things justly, Gentlemen and Judges, and do so for your benefit." Nor will I be able to say anything else. The result, no doubt, will be that I'll take whatever comes.[29]

Martin Luther King Jr.'s life was marked by this Socratic paradox. Christian theology calls the Socratic defiance of radical evil "bearing the cross." And Christian theology warns that all those who are successful in their defiance pay a bitter price. "When I took up the cross," King said less than a year before he was killed, "I recognized its meaning. . . . The cross is something that you bear, and ultimately that you die on."[30] Or as King told a church congregation in Atlanta:

I choose to identify with the underprivileged. I choose to identify with the poor. I choose to give my life for the hungry. I choose to give my life for those who have been left out of the sunlight of opportunity. I choose to live for and with those who find themselves seeing life as a long and desolate corridor with no exit sign. This is the way I am going. If it means suffering a little bit, I'm going that way. If it means sacrificing, I'm going that way. If it means dying for them, I'm going that way, because I heard a voice saying, "Do something for others."[31]

The moral life, celebrated only in the afterglow of history and often not celebrated at all, is lonely, frightening, and hard. The crowd condemns you. The state brands you a traitor. You struggle with your own fears and doubts. The words you speak are often not understood. And you are never certain if your words and actions, in the end, will make any difference. The rebel knows the odds. To defy radical evil does not mean to be irrational. It is to have a sober clarity about the power of evil and one's insignificance and yet to rebel anyway. To face radical evil is to accept self-sacrifice.

Herman Melville's Captain Ahab and John Milton's Satan in *Paradise Lost,* like Marek Edelman, shared these qualities of "sublime madness." They understood the strength of divine power, which they saw as malevolent, yet pitted themselves against it. It is those possessed by sublime madness who keep alive another way of being. W. H. Auden captured the solitude and even futility of such a life at the end of his poem "September 1, 1939."

> *Defenceless under the night*
> *Our world in stupor lies;*
> *Yet, dotted everywhere,*
> *Ironic points of light*
> *Flash out wherever the Just*
> *Exchange their messages:*
> *May I, composed like them*
> *Of Eros and of dust,*
> *Beleaguered by the same*
> *Negation and despair,*
> *Show an affirming flame.*[32]

I traveled to the Swiss village of Begnins outside Geneva shortly after the fall of the Berlin Wall in November 1989 to see Axel von dem Bussche. He was a former Wehrmacht major, holder of the Knight's Cross of the Iron Cross for extreme battlefield bravery, three times wounded in

World War II, and one of the last surviving members of the inner circle of German army officers who attempted to assassinate Adolf Hitler.

Resistance to Nazism was painfully rare, even as Germany was losing the war. The slightest whisper of dissent could mean death, as evidenced by the execution of the five Munich University students and their philosophy professor who were members of the White Rose resistance movement. The White Rose distributed thousands of anti-Nazi leaflets before they were arrested by the Gestapo and guillotined. The text of their sixth and final set of leaflets was smuggled out of Germany by the resistance leader Helmuth James Graf von Moltke, who was hanged by the Nazis in January 1945. Copies of the leaflets were dropped over Germany by Allied planes in 1943.

The White Rose has been lionized by postwar Germans—one of its members, Alexander Schmorell, was made a saint by the Russian Orthodox Church, and squares and schools in Germany are named for the resisters—but in a BBC interview, Liselotte Fürst-Ramdohr, a member of the group who was arrested but released by the Nazis, said that the resisters had little support among the public during the war. "At the time, they'd have had us all executed," said Fürst-Ramdohr, who hid leaflets for the group and helped make the stencils they used to paint slogans on walls.[33]

History has vindicated resistance groups such as the White Rose and plotters such as von dem Bussche. But they were desperately alone while they defied the law, their oaths of allegiance, and public opinion. Von dem Bussche said that even after the war he was spat upon as he walked down city streets in Germany. Rebellion, when it begins, is not legal, safe, comfortable, or popular.

"Somebody, after all, had to make a start," one of the White Rose members, Sophie Scholl, said on February 22, 1943, at her trial in a Nazi court. "What we wrote and said is also believed by many others. They just don't dare express themselves as we did."[34]

Von dem Bussche, who died in 1993, took part as a twenty-year-old lieutenant in the invasions of Belgium; Luxembourg, France—where a French sniper shot off his right thumb and he was wounded in the shoulder—and Poland. He was stationed after the invasion of Poland

in the town of Dubno in the western Ukraine. His military unit was ordered to secure an abandoned air base. The young officer watched as the SS escorted some 2,000 Jews to the airfield.

"The Jews were trucked in from the surrounding countryside, stripped and forced by the black-uniformed officers toward long, deep trenches," von dem Bussche told me. "They were shot in their heads by an SS officer with a machine pistol, and then the next row was made to lie down and shot in their heads. It is not an easy memory to live with, especially as I considered myself, as an officer of the German army, to be an accessory to these murders."

It was then that he decided to defy Hitler. But it would not be until 1943, when it was clear that the Germans were losing the war, that he and a small group of other officers led by Colonel Claus von Stauffenberg began to plot to assassinate the Nazi leader. The conspirators did not defy the Nazis on behalf of the Jews, von dem Bussche conceded, but to save the country from defeat, dismemberment, and catastrophe.

"One motive, along with just stopping the killing, was the most valid—to stop the Russians east of Poland," he said of the plotters. "If we had managed to keep the Russians out, Europe would have been spared the division and pain of the last forty-four years."

In 1943 von dem Bussche was a captain. He was asked to model the army's new winter coat for Hitler at the Wolfsschanze, the Nazi leader's headquarters in East Prussia. He and von Stauffenberg managed to obtain fuses and plastic explosives from the British (so that they could avoid the noise made by German fuses, which hissed when lit). Von dem Bussche also had two hand grenades. He planned to physically seize Hitler and ignite the grenades in a suicide mission intended to kill the Führer and perhaps other high-ranking Nazi officials in the room. The code name for the operation was "Overcoat."

Von dem Bussche said that von Stauffenberg told him, "I am committing high treason with all my might and means," but added that under natural law the plotters had a duty to use violence to defend the innocent from the horrific crimes of the state.

Von dem Bussche was summoned to Hitler's headquarters in November 1943. He waited for three days about ten miles away, rarely leaving his room. He woke up every morning and wondered, he said, if he would be alive in the evening, and "if my nerve would hold." But the train carrying the winter uniforms was bombed by Allied warplanes, and von dem Bussche was sent back to the Russian front, where he lost a leg in the bitter fighting.

Von dem Bussche, six feet five inches tall with cobalt-blue eyes and a voice that rumbled like a freight train, refused to describe what he or the other plotters did as heroism. He detested words like "honor" and "glory" being applied to warfare. He had no time for those who romanticized combat. He had no option as a human being but to resist, he said, and acted, as Edelman did, to save his "self-esteem."

"There was no hero stuff involved, none at all," he said. "I thought this was an adequate means to balance out what I had seen. I felt that this was justifiable homicide and was the only means to stop mass murder inside and outside Germany." His was the tenth thwarted attempt on Hitler's life. There would be one more.

On July 20, 1944, von Stauffenberg carried two small bombs in a briefcase to a meeting with Hitler. He struggled before the meeting to arm the bombs with pliers, a difficult task as he had lost his right hand and had only three fingers on his left hand after being wounded in North Africa. He managed to arm only one bomb. After placing the briefcase with the bomb under the table near Hitler, he left the room. Von Stauffenberg was outside at the time of the explosion, which killed four people—including Hitler's security double—but only slightly wounded Hitler, who was shielded by a table leg. Nazi propaganda chief Joseph Goebbels announced over the radio that Hitler had survived. Hitler spoke to the nation not long afterward. Von Stauffenberg and other conspirators were captured and executed by a firing squad.

Von dem Bussche, recovering from the loss of his leg in a Waffen-SS hospital outside Berlin, anxiously followed the news of the assassination attempt on the radio. He listened to Hitler's angry tirade against the "traitors" who had attempted to kill him. He knew it would not be long before the SS appeared at his bedside. He spent the night eating page after page of his address book, which had the names of every major conspirator who was being hunted, was under arrest, or was dead. The

British explosive material from his aborted suicide bombing was in a suitcase under his bed. He asked another officer to carry the suitcase out of the hospital and toss it into a lake. He was repeatedly interrogated over the next few days, but because none of the other plotters had implicated him, even under torture, he managed to elude their fate.

He did not succeed, at least not in killing Hitler and overthrowing the Nazis. He felt that as an army officer, even with his involvement in the assassination plots, he remained part of the murderous apparatus that had unleashed indefensible suffering and death. He worried that he had not done enough. The brutality and senselessness of the war haunted him. The German public's enthusiastic collusion with the Nazi regime tormented him. And the ghosts of the dead, including those he admired, never left him. He understood, as we must, that to do nothing in a time of radical evil is to be complicit.

"I should have taken off my uniform in the Ukraine," he told me on the last afternoon of my visit, "and joined the line of Jews to be shot."

————

Those with sublime madness accept the possibility of their own death as the price paid for defending life. This curious mixture of gloom and hope, of defiance and resignation, of absurdity and meaning, is born of the rebel's awareness of the enormity of the forces that must be defeated and the remote chances for success. "Hope is definitely not the same thing as optimism," Havel wrote. "It is not the conviction that something will turn out well, but the certainty that something makes sense, regardless of how it turns out."[35]

Optimism, especially the naive optimism fed to us by the corporate state, engenders self-delusion and passivity and is the opposite of hope. Rebels who are self-aware, who are possessed of sublime madness, are also often plagued by a gnawing despair. When the movie producer Abby Mann, who wanted to film Martin Luther King's life story, asked King facetiously, "How does the movie end?" King responded, "It ends with me getting killed." As Mann recalled, "I looked at him. He was smiling, but he wasn't joking."[36]

Social and economic life will again have to be rationed and shared. The lusts of capitalism will have to be curtailed or destroyed. And there will have to be a recovery of reverence for the sacred, the bedrock of premodern society, so we can see each other and the earth not as objects to exploit but as living beings to be revered and protected. This recovery will require a very different vision for human society.

William Shakespeare lamented the loss of the medieval Catholic rituals eradicated by the Reformation. When Shakespeare was a boy, the critic Harold Goddard pointed out, he experienced the religious pageants, morality plays, church festivals, cycle plays, feast and saint's days, displays of relics, bawdy May Day celebrations, and tales of miracles. The Puritans, the ideological vanguard of the technological order, made war on the Elizabethan and Jacobean theaters for celebrating these premodern practices.

The London authorities in 1596 prohibited the public presentation of plays within city limits. The theaters had to relocate to the south side of the River Thames. The Puritans, in power under Cromwell in 1642, closed the London theaters and in 1644 tore down Shakespeare's Globe Theater. Within four years, all theaters in and around London had been destroyed. The Puritans understood, in a way that is perhaps lost to us today, that Shakespeare was attacking the cold ethic of modernity and capitalism.

Shakespeare portrays the tension between the dying ethic of the premodern and the modern, a theme that would be explored by William Faulkner in American fiction. Shakespeare, like Faulkner, saw the rise of the modern as dangerous. The premodern reserved a place in the cosmos for human imagination, what the poet John Milton called "things invisible to mortal sight."[37] The new, modern Machiavellian ethic of self-promotion, manipulation, bureaucracy, and deceit—personified by Iago, Richard III, and Lady Macbeth—deforms human beings and society. Shakespeare lived during a moment when the modern world—whose technology allowed it to acquire weapons of such unrivaled force that it could conquer whole empires, including the Americas and later China—instilled this new secular religion through violence. He feared its demonic power.

Prospero in Shakespeare's *The Tempest* is master of a magical island where he has absolute power. He keeps the primitive Caliban and the spirit Ariel as his slaves. Shakespeare reminds us that the power unleashed in the wilderness can prompt us to good, if we honor the sacred, but to monstrous evil if we do not. There are few constraints in the wilderness, a theme that would later be explored by the novelist Joseph Conrad. The imagination triumphs in *The Tempest* because those who are bound to their senses and lusts are subjugated and Ariel is freed from enslavement. But in the Spanish, French, and British colonies in the Americas, as Shakespeare had seen, the lust for power and wealth, embodied by the evil dukes of the world, led to an orgy of looting, subjugation, and genocide.

"Imagination," as Shakespeare scholar Harold Goddard writes,

is neither the language of nature nor the language of man, but both at once, the medium of communion between the two—as if the birds, unable to understand the speech of man, and man, unable to understand the songs of birds, yet longing to communicate, were to agree on a tongue made up of sounds they both could comprehend—the voice of running water perhaps or the wind in the trees. Imagination is the *elemental speech* in all senses, the first and the last, of primitive man and of the poets.[38]

In the presence of the natural world, all of the great visionaries have heard it speak to them. It spoke to Shakespeare, as it spoke to Emily Dickinson and Walt Whitman. This communion blurs the lines between the self and the world. It is what Percy Shelley meant when he wrote that poetry "lifts the veil from the hidden beauty of the world and makes familiar things as if they were not familiar."[39] Too often this wisdom comes too late, as it does when Othello stands contrite and broken over the dead Desdemona, or when Lear lifts up his murdered daughter, Cordelia. This wisdom makes grace and transformation possible.

In the kind of visions that were experienced by Black Elk and revered by Native Americans, the kind that inspire artists and rebels, the visionary encounters the strange, unexplainable, mysterious forces that define life. And visionary language speaks, as poets and rebels do, only in abstractions and allegory. It is the language of sublime madness. "'The Lord at Delphi,' says Heraclitus, 'neither speaks nor conceals, but gives a sign,'" writes Goddard.

> Dreams have the same Delphic characteristic. So does poetry. To our age anything Delphic is anathema. We want the definite. As certainly as ours is a time of the expert and the technician, we are living under a dynasty of the intellect, and the aim of the intellect is not to wonder and love and grow wise about life, but to control it. The subservience of so much of our science to invention is the proof of this. We want the facts for the practical use we can make of them.[40]

Black Elk expressed the power and importance of the reality of human existence that lies beyond articulation. "Also, as I lay there thinking of my vision, I could see it all again and feel the meaning with a part of me like a strange power glowing in my body," he said, "but when the part of me that talks would try to make words for the meaning, it would be like fog and get away from me."[41]

Chants, work songs, spirituals, the blues, poetry, dance, and art converged under slavery to nourish and sustain the imagination. "For the art—the blues, the spirituals, the jazz, the dance—was what we had in place of freedom," Ralph Ellison wrote.[42] It was sublime madness that permitted African Americans such as Harriet Tubman, Frederick Douglass, and Fannie Lou Hamer to resist during slavery and Jim Crow. It was sublime madness that sustained the defiance of Sitting Bull and Black Elk as their land was seized, their people were slaughtered, and their cultures and means of existence were decimated. The oppressed—for they know their fate—would be the first to admit that, on a rational level, it is absurd to think that it is only through the imagination that they survive—but they also know that it is true. It was sublime madness that allowed the survivors in the Nazi death camps to hold on to the sacred. Jewish inmates in Auschwitz reportedly put God on trial for the Holocaust. They condemned God to death. A rabbi stood after the guilty verdict to lead the evening prayers.

African Americans and Native Americans, for centuries, had little control over their destinies. Forces of bigotry and violence kept them subjugated. The suffering of the oppressed was tangible, and death was a constant companion. And it was only their imagination, as William Faulkner notes at the end of *The Sound and the Fury,* that permitted them—unlike the novel's white Compson family, which self-destructed—to "endure."[43]

The theologian James H. Cone, who stresses the importance of Niebuhr's "sublime madness" for all those who resist oppression, captures this in his book *The Cross and the Lynching Tree.* Cone says that for oppressed blacks, the cross is a "paradoxical religious symbol because it *inverts* the world's value system with the news that hope comes by way of defeat, that suffering and death do not have the last word, that the last shall be first and the first last." Cone continues:

> That God could "make a way out of no way" in Jesus' cross was truly absurd to the intellect, yet profoundly real in the souls of black folk. Enslaved blacks who first heard the gospel message seized on the power of the cross. Christ crucified manifested God's loving and liberating presence *in* the contradictions of black life—that transcendent presence in the lives of black Christians that empowered them to believe that *ultimately,* in God's eschatological future, they would not be defeated by the "troubles of this world," no matter how great and painful their suffering. Believing this paradox, this absurd claim of faith, was only possible through God's "amazing grace" and the gift of faith, grounded in humility and repentance. There was no place for the proud and the mighty, for people who think that God called them to rule over others. The cross was God's critique of power—white power—with powerless love, snatching victory out of defeat.[44]

Primo Levi, in his memoir *Survival in Auschwitz,* writes of teaching Italian to another inmate, Jean Samuel, in exchange for lessons in French. Levi recited to Samuel, from memory, fragments of Canto XXVI of Dante's "The Inferno." It is the story of Ulysses' doomed, final voyage. Levi writes that as he recited the lines it was "as if I also was hearing it for the first time: like the blast of a trumpet, like the voice of God. For a moment I forgot who I am and where I am."[45]

> *And three times round she went in roaring smother*
> *With all the waters; at the fourth the poop*
> *Rose, and the prow went down, as pleased Another.*
> *And over our head the hollow seas closed up.*

"He has received the message," Levi writes of his friend and what they shared in Dante, "he has felt that it has to do with him, that it has to do with all men who toil, and with us in particular." Levi goes on: "It is vitally necessary and urgent that he listen, that he understand . . . before it is too late; tomorrow he or I might be dead, or we might never see each other again."[46]

It was sublime madness that let bluesman Ishman Bracey in Hinds County, Mississippi, sing: "I've been down so long, Lawd, down don't worry me." And yet, in the mists of this despair also lies the absurdity and certainty of justice:

> *I feel my hell a-risin', a-risin' every day;*
> *I feel my hell a-risin', a-risin' every day;*
> *Someday it'll burst this levee and wash the whole*
>   *wide world away.*[47]

King Lear, who after suffering and affliction is finally able to see, warns us that unbridled human passion and unchecked hubris spell the suicide of the species. "It will come," Albany says in *King Lear*. "Humanity must perforce prey on itself / Like monsters of the deep."[48]

The human imagination, as Emma Goldman pointed out, has the power to make ideas felt. Goldman noted that when Andrew Undershaft, a character in George Bernard Shaw's play *Major Barbara*, says that poverty is "the worst of crimes" and "all the other crimes are virtues beside it," his impassioned declaration elucidates the cruelty of class warfare more effectively than Shaw's socialist tracts.[49] It was the poems of Federico García Lorca that sustained the republicans fighting the fascists in Spain. Covering the war in El Salvador, I saw that the rebel units often traveled with musicians and theater troupes.

Culture, real culture, is radical and transformative. Culture can express what lies deep within us and give words to our reality. Making us feel as well as see, culture allows us to empathize with those who are different or oppressed. Even as it reveals what is happening around us, it honors mystery. It saves us from ourselves. "The role of the artist, then, precisely, is to illuminate that darkness, blaze roads through the vast forest," Baldwin writes, "so that we will not, in all our doing, lose sight of its purpose, which is, after all, to make the world a more human dwelling place."[50]

"Ultimately, the artist and the revolutionary function as they function, and pay whatever dues they must pay behind it because they are both possessed by a vision, and they do not so much follow this vision as find themselves driven by it," writes Baldwin. "Otherwise, they could never endure, much less embrace, the lives they are compelled to lead."[51]

Rebellion requires an emotional intelligence. It requires empathy and love. It requires self-sacrifice. It requires the honoring of the sacred. It requires an understanding that, as with the heroes in classical Greece, one cannot finally overcome fate or *fortuna,* but that we must resist regardless.

"Ours is a time that would have sent the Greeks to their oracles," Goddard writes. "We fail at our own peril to consult our own."[52]

"The people noticed that Crazy Horse was queerer than ever," Black Elk says in *Black Elk Speaks,* remembering the great Oglala Lakota warrior in the final days of the wars of Western expansion.

He hardly ever stayed in the camp. People would find him out alone in the cold, and they would ask him to come home with them. He would not come, but sometimes he would tell the people what to do. People wondered if he ate anything at all. Once my father found him out alone like that, and he said to my father: "Uncle, you have noticed me the way I act. But do not worry; there are caves and holes for me to live in, and out here the spirits may help me. I am making plans for the good of my people."[53]

I do not know if we can build a better society. I do not even know if we will survive as a species. But I do know that these corporate forces have us by the throat. And they have my children by the throat. I do not fight fascists because I will win. I fight fascists because they are fascists.[54] And this is a fight that in the face of the overwhelming forces against us requires that we follow those possessed by sublime madness, that we become stone catchers and find in acts of rebellion the sparks of life, an intrinsic meaning that lies outside the possibility of success. We must grasp the harshness of reality at the same time as we refuse to allow this reality to paralyze us. People of all creeds and people of no creeds must make an absurd leap of faith to believe, despite all the empirical evidence around us, that the good draws to it the good.[55] The fight for life goes somewhere—the Buddhists call it karma—and in these acts we make possible a better world, even if we cannot see one emerging around us.

ACKNOWLEDGMENTS

Eunice is my most important critic and editor. She challenges and amplifies ideas, clarifies and corrects passages, restructures whole sections, and fixes sentences that drift into obscurity. All ideas are filtered, often first in conversation, through her. This book, like so many of my books, is dependent on her intellectual and artistic brilliance and her considerable skill as a critic, editor, and writer. That theater rather than writing is her profession makes her literary talent all the more impressive and intimidating. I dedicate this book to her not only because I adore her, not only because our love is the most wondrous thing in my life, but because, as with so many books before this one, it is in many ways her book. She has enriched and deepened this work, as she has my life and the lives of our children.

There is material in the book that made up some of the columns I wrote for the online magazine Truthdig, along with articles I wrote for *The Nation, Smithsonian,* and *The Walrus* magazines. The Truthdig columns were edited by Thomas Caswell. I worked at the *New York Times* with some of the finest copyeditors in the newspaper industry, but few of them come close to Tom. Copyediting is an art, one I fear is dying, and I am deeply grateful that each week Tom applies his decades of expertise and experience at the *Los Angeles Times* to my columns. There are more times than I can count that he has saved me from myself.

This book could not have been written without the generous support of the Lannan Foundation, the Nation Institute, and the NoVo Foundation, which provided a grant to Truthdig to fund my weekly columns.

Carl Bromley at Nation Books is one of the finest editors in publishing. He loves books. He astutely edited and shaped this book, as he did my three previous books. He blesses the writers who work with him with his literacy, passion, integrity, and generosity. Daniel LoPreto and

Benjamin Pokross, along with Alessandra Bastagli, who replaced Carl Bromley as the editor at Nation Books as I neared completion, invested considerable time on the manuscript. They provided astute and important critiques, editing, and suggestions that greatly improved the book. I appreciate their hard work. Patrick and Andy Lannan, along with Jo Chapman, at the Lannan Foundation have for years provided crucial support. It would be very difficult to do my work without them. Jeannette Quinton and Boris Rorer were instrumental in fact-checking and research. I am very grateful for their meticulous work and friendship. Todd Clayton also worked with his usual rigor and exacting accuracy on the book. He has been a joy to have as part of our family for the last two years as he finished his degree at Union Theological Seminary in New York.

I am privileged to work with Robert Scheer, the editor of Truthdig, whose dazzling skill as a writer and editor is matched by his wisdom, boundless generosity, and profound integrity. He is what we all want to become. Zuade Kaufmann, who matches Bob in her commitment to great journalism and commentary and who publishes Truthdig, has been a pillar to all of us who write for the site. I am fortunate to have them and the Truthdig site as my home. I would like to thank Ralph Nader, whom I speak with frequently, as well as Cornel West and James Cone, who, along with Noam Chomsky, are the intellectuals I admire most. Thanks also to my good friend Joe Sacco, who produces, year after year, brilliant, astonishing, and original work that never wavers from his clarion vision of what it means to be a truth teller, an artist, and a rebel.

Other friends and colleagues who have supported me in my work include Kevin Zeese; Dr. Margaret Flowers; Steve Kinzer; Peter Scheer, who holds together Truthdig; Narda Zacchino, whose talents as a writer and editor rival those of her husband Bob Scheer; Kasia Anderson; Donald Kaufman; Dwayne Booth, who ranks with Sacco as a cartoonist; Max Blumenthal; the Reverend Terry Burke; Paul Jay; Bonnie Kerness; Ojore Lutalo; Alexa O'Brien, my friend and coplaintiff who, along with the lawyers Carl Mayer and Bruce Afran, led our suit against Section 1021(b)(2) of the National Defense Authorization Act in federal court;

Ann and Walter Pincus; Jennifer and Peter Buffett; John Timpane; Marty Brest; Roy Singham; Peter Hershberg; Richard Wolff; Maria-Christina Keller; Lauren B. Davis; June Ballinger; Michael Goldstein; Gerald Stern; Anne Marie Macari; Tom Artin; the Reverend Michael Granzen; the Reverend Karen Hernandez; Joe and Heidi Hough; Mark Kurlansky; my former Shakespeare professor Margaret Maurer; my mentor and former religion professor the Reverend Coleman Brown, who has critiqued and edited many of my books and whom we lost as this book was being finished; Irene Brown; Sam Hynes, who proves there are scholars who are also great writers; Sonali Kolhatkar; Francine Prose; Russell Banks; Celia Chazelle; Toby Sanders; Esther Kaplan; and John Ralston Saul. Dorothea von Molke and Cliff Simms, who run one of the finest bookstores in the country and donated over 700 books to the prison library in New Jersey where I teach, are valued neighbors. I would finally like to thank the students in my classes at East Jersey State Prison. They inspire me with their fierce commitment to the life of the mind, their brilliance, and their deep integrity. I look forward every week to our classes. The crime of mass incarceration means their families, as well as the wider society, are deprived of their talents, their wisdom, and their contributions. This is an injustice we must fight.

Lisa Bankoff of International Creative Management handled the contracts, as usual, for the book. We have been together since my first book. I look forward to a long continuation of our partnership.

My four children, Thomas, Noëlle, Konrad, and Marina, along with Eunice, comprise my precious universe, the one that keeps me whole. Konrad and Marina, my youngest, make for a noisy and chaotic household, one that is not always optimal for the prolonged silence coveted by a writer, but they infuse our lives with irreplaceable joy, wonder, and beauty. I write and struggle for them. I worry about the world they will inherit. I fear I have never done enough.

NOTES

INTRODUCTION

1. Herbert Marcuse, "Repressive Tolerance," in *A Critique of Pure Tolerance* by Robert Paul Wolff, Barrington Moore Jr., and Herbert Marcuse (Boston: Beacon Press, 1965), 95–137, 137.

2. Francesco Guicciardini, *Maxims and Reflections of a Renaissance Statesman (Ricordi)* [1528], trans. Mario Domandi (Philadelphia: University of Pennsylvania Press, 1965), Series C-1, 39.

3. Karl Marx, *The Civil War in France* [1871], in *The First International and After* (New York: Verso Books, 2010), 226–228.

4. Crane Brinton, *The Anatomy of Revolution* (New York: Vintage Books, 1965), 34.

5. Ibid., 56.

6. Karl Marx, *The Manifesto of the Communist Party* [1848], authorized English translation, edited and annotated by Friedrich Engels (New York: International Publishers, 1968), 9–21.

7. Brinton, *The Anatomy of Revolution,* 101.

8. Ibid., 89–90.

9. James C. Davies, "Toward a Theory of Revolution," *American Sociological Review* 27, no. 1 (1962): 5–19, reprinted in *When Men Revolt and Why,* ed. James Chowning Davies (New Brunswick, NJ: Transaction Publishers, 1997), 133, 135.

10. Ibid., 133–134.

11. Ibid., 140.

12. Ibid.

13. Ibid., 141.

14. Leon Trotsky, *History of the Russian Revolution* (Chicago: Haymarket Books, 2008), 353.

15. Michael Greenstone and Adam Looney, "The Uncomfortable Truth About American Wages," *New York Times,* October 22, 2012.

16. Barbara Ehrenreich explores this false promise in her book *Bright-Sided: How Positive Thinking Is Undermining America* (New York: Henry Holt/Metropolitan Books, 2009).

17. Rami Zurayk, "Use Your Loaf: Why Food Prices Were Crucial to the Arab Spring," *The Guardian,* July 16, 2011.

18. Ibid.

19. Liz Alderman, "More Children in Greece Are Going Hungry," *New York Times,* April 17, 2013.

20. Carmen DeNavas-Walt, Bernadette D. Proctor, and Jessica C. Smith, "Income, Poverty, and Health Insurance Coverage in the United States: 2012," *Current Population Reports* P60-245 (Washington, DC: US Census Bureau, September 2013), http://www.census.gov/prod/2013pubs/p60-245 .pdf (accessed June 14, 2014).

21. According to the summary for Elise Gould, Hilary Wething, Natalie Sabadish, and Nicholas Finio, *What Families Need to Get By: The 2013 Update of EPI's Family Budget Calculator* (Washington, DC: Economic Policy Institute, 2013, http://www.epi.org/publication/ib368-basic-family-budgets/, accessed December 15, 2014): "The basic family budget for a two-parent, two-child family ranges from $48,166 (Marshall County, Miss.) to $94,676 (New York City). In the median family budget area, Topeka, Kan., a two-parent, two-child family needs $63,364 to secure an adequate but modest living standard. This is well above the 2012 poverty threshold of $23,283 for this family type."

22. DeNavas-Walt, Proctor, and Smith, "Income, Poverty, and Health Insurance Coverage in the United States: 2012," 15.

23. National Center for Law and Economic Justice, "Poverty in the United States: A Snapshot," http://www.nclej.org/poverty-in-the-us.php.

24. J. R. Porter et al., "Food Security and Food Production Systems," in *Climate Change 2014: Impacts, Adaptation, and Vulnerability,* Part A, *Global and Sectoral Aspects: Contribution of Working Group II to the Fifth Assessment Report of the Intergovernmental Panel on Climate Change* (New York: Cambridge University Press, 2014), 2–4.

25. Vladimir Lenin, *"Left-Wing" Communism: An Infantile Disorder* (Chippendale, Australia: Resistance Books, 1999), 83 (emphasis in the original).

26. The historians and political philosophers who have examined the phenomenon of revolutionary waves include Robert Roswell Palmer, Crane Brinton, Hannah Arendt, Eric Hoffer, Jacques Godechot, and Antonio Gramsci.

27. Walter Benjamin, "Goethe's *Elective Affinities*," in *Walter Benjamin: Selected Writings, 1913–1926,* vol. 1 (Cambridge, MA: Belknap Press of Harvard University Press, 1996).

28. Ibid.

29. Friedrich Engels arrived in England in October 1842 to work for his family's cotton business in Manchester, where he witnessed the deplorable conditions in the mills. He drew on what he saw to write *The Condition of the Working Class in England in 1844* and became a contributor to the Chartist newspaper *Northern Star.*

30. Adam B. Ulam, *The Bolsheviks: The Intellectual and Political History of the Triumph of Communism in Russia* (Cambridge, MA: Harvard University Press, 1998), 39–41.

31. Adam B. Ulam, *Ideologies and Illusions: Revolutionary Thought from Herzen to Solzhenitsyn* (Cambridge, MA: Harvard University Press, 1976), 12.

32. Auguste Blanqui, "Contre le Progrès" ["Against Progress," 1869 manuscript], published in Auguste Blanqui, *Instructions pour une prise d'armes: L'Éternité par les astres et autres textes* (*Instructions for Taking Up Arms: Eternity According to the Stars and Others Texts*), ed. Miguel Abensour and Valentin Pelosse (Paris: Éditions de la Tête de Feuille, 1972), 103–105; cited in Daniel Bensaïd and Michael Löwy, "August Blanqui, Heretical Communist," *Radical Philosophy* 185 (May-June 2014).

33. Auguste Blanqui, "La Critique sociale" ("Social Criticism"), part III of Auguste Blanqui, *Textes choisis* (*Selected Texts*), preface and notes by V. P. Volguine (Paris: Éditions Sociale, 1971), 74; cited in Bensaïd and Löwy, "August Blanqui."

34. Ibid., 159.

35. Quoted in Gustave Geffroy, *L'Énfermé* (*Locked*), vol. II (Paris: Éditions G. Crès et Cle, 1926), 19–20; cited in Bensaïd and Löwy, "August Blanqui."

36. Karl Marx, *The Revolutions of 1848: Political Writings*, vol. 1, ed. David Fernbach (London: Verso Books, 2010), 24.

37. Paul Avrich, *Anarchist Portraits* (Princeton, NJ: Princeton University Press, 1988), 217–219.

38. Nicholas Kulish, "As Scorn for Vote Grows, Protests Surge Around the Globe," *New York Times*, September 27, 2011.

39. Sheldon S. Wolin, *Democracy Incorporated: Managed Democracy and the Specter of Inverted Totalitarianism* (Princeton, NJ: Princeton University Press, 2010), xviii (emphasis in original).

40. Hannah Arendt, *Eichmann in Jerusalem: A Report on the Banality of Evil* (New York: Penguin, 2006), 289.

41. Wolin, *Democracy Incorporated,* xviii.

42. Michel de Montaigne, *The Complete Essays of Michel de Montaigne* (New York: Digireads, 2004), 78.

43. Seumas Milne, "Venezuela Shows That Protest Can Be a Defence of Privilege," *The Guardian,* April 9, 2014.

44. Gabriel García Márquez and Subcomandante Marcos, "A Zapatista Reading List," *The Nation,* July 2, 2001.

CHAPTER I

1. Norman Cohn, *The Pursuit of the Millennium: Revolutionary Messianism in Medieval and Reformation Europe and Its Bearing on Modern Totalitarian Movements* (New York: Harper & Row, 1961), 74.

2. "Hurricane Sandy's Rising Costs" (editorial), *New York Times,* November 27, 2012.

3. Eric S. Blake, Todd B. Kimberlain, Robert J. Berg, John P. Cangialosi, and John L. Beven II, "Tropical Cyclone Report: Hurricane Sandy, AL182012, 22–29 October 2012," National Hurricane Center, February 12, 2013, http://www.nhc.noaa.gov/data/tcr/AL182012_Sandy.pdf.

4. Richard D. Knabb, Jamie R. Rhome, and Daniel P. Brown, "Tropical Cyclone Report: Hurricane Katrina, 23–30 August 2005," National Hurricane Center, December 20, 2005, http://www.nhc.noaa.gov/pdf/TCR-AL12 2005_Katrina.pdf.

5. Connor Adams Sheets, "Hurricane Sandy Anniversary 2014: NYC Victims Still Waiting for Home Repair Funding Two Years After Storm Hit New York," *International Business Times,* October 28, 2014; Hilary Russ, "New York, New Jersey Put $71 Billion Price Tag on Sandy," Reuters, November 26, 2012.

6. Russ, "New York, New Jersey Put $71 Billion Price Tag on Sandy."

7. "De-coding the Black Death," BBC News, October 3, 2001, http://news.bbc.co.uk/2/hi/health/1576875.stm.

8. Climate Vulnerability Forum, *Climate Vulnerability Monitor: A Guide to the Cold Calculus of a Hot Planet,* 2nd ed., http://www.thecvf.org/web/publications-data/climate-vulnerability-monitor/2012-monitor/.

9. Koko Warner, Charles Ehrhart, Alex de Sherbinin, Susana Adamo, and Tricia Chai-Onn, "In Search of Shelter: Mapping the Effects of Climate Change on Human Migration and Displacement," Center for International Earth Science Information Network, Earth Institute of Columbia University,

May 2009, http://ciesin.columbia.edu/documents/clim-migr-report-june09 _media.pdf.

10. Andre Delbanco, *Melville: His World and Work* (New York: Vintage, 2006), 6–7.

11. Carl Van Doren, *The American Novel* (New York: Macmillan, 1921).

12. D. H. Lawrence, *Studies in Classic American Literature* [1923], vol. 2 (New York: Penguin, 1990).

13. E. M. Forster, *Aspects of the Novel* (New York: Mariner Books, 1955), 138; Lewis Mumford, "The Significance of Herman Melville," *The New Republic*, October 10, 1928, http://www.newrepublic.com/article/114098 /significance-herman-melville-lewis-mumford-stacks.

14. Nathaniel Philbrick, "The Road to Melville," *Vanity Fair*, November 2011, http://www.vanityfair.com/culture/features/2011/11/moby-dick-201111.

15. Edward Said, "Islam and the West Are Inadequate Banners," *The Observer*, September 16, 2001, http://www.theguardian.com/world/2001/sep /16/september11.terrorism3.

16. C.L.R. James, *Mariners, Renegades, and Castaways: The Story of Herman Melville and the World We Live In* (Hanover, NH: University Press of New England, 2001).

17. Greg Grandin, *The Empire of Necessity: Slavery, Freedom, and Necessity in the New World* (New York: Henry Holt/Metropolitan Books, 2014); Morris Berman, *Why America Failed: The Roots of Imperial Decline* (New York: John Wiley & Sons, 2011).

18. Nathaniel Philbrick, *Why Read* Moby-Dick? (New York: Viking, 2011), 6.

19. International Programme on the State of the Ocean, "Greater, Faster, Closer: Latest Review of Science Reveals Ocean in Critical State from Cumulative Impacts" (press release), October 3, 2013, http://www.stateofthe ocean.org/pdfs/IPSO-PR-2013-FINAL.pdf.

20. Seth Borenstein, "Study: Species Disappearing Far Faster Than Before," Associated Press, May 29, 2014.

21. Binyamin Appelbaum, "Citing Growth, Fed Again Cuts Monthly Bond Purchases, *New York Times*, January 29, 2014.

22. "Bloomberg Billionaires: Today's Ranking of the World's Richest People," Bloomberg.com, April 22, 2014, http://www.bloomberg.com /billionaires/2014-04-22/cya.

23. Thomas Piketty, *Capital in the Twenty-First Century* (Cambridge, MA: Belknap Press of Harvard University Press, 2014).

24. Clive Hamilton, *Requiem for a Species: Why We Resist the Truth About Climate Change* (London: Earthscan, 2010), xiv.

25. National Oceanic and Atmospheric Administration (NOAA), National Climatic Data Center, "Climatological Rankings," http://www.ncdc.noaa.gov/temp-and-precip/climatological-rankings/index.php?periods%5B%5D=12&parameter=tavg&state=110&div=0&month=12&year=2009#ranks-form; see also World Meteorological Organization (WMO), "WMO Annual Climate Statement Highlights Extreme Events," press release 985, March 24, 2014, http://www.wmo.int/pages/mediacentre/press_releases/pr_985_en.html.

26. Joseph A. Tainter, *The Collapse of Complex Societies* (Cambridge: Cambridge University Press, 1988); Charles L. Redman, *Human Impact on Ancient Environments* (Tucson: University of Arizona Press, 1999); Ronald Wright, *A Short History of Progress* (New York: Carroll & Graf, 2005).

27. Reinhold Niebuhr, *Beyond Tragedy: Essays on the Christian Interpretation of History* (New York: Scribner's, 1965), 39.

28. Louis-Ferdinand Céline, *Castle to Castle* (New York: Dell Publishing, 1968), 184.

29. Margaret Atwood, *Oryx and Crake* (New York: Anchor Books, 2003), 120.

30. Daniel J. Boorstin, *The Image: A Guide to Pseudo-Events in America* (New York: Vintage, 1987), 37.

31. Anthony Everitt, *Cicero: The Life and Times of Rome's Greatest Politician* (New York, Random House, 2001), 319.

32. Mikhail Bulgakov, *The Master and Margarita* (New York: Vintage, 1985), 231.

33. Ibid., 227.

34. Ibid.

35. Ibid., 299–300.

36. Karl Schlögel, *Moscow, 1937* (Malden, MA: Polity Press, 2013), 26.

37. Joseph Roth, *Hotel Savoy* (Woodstock, NY: Overlook Press, 1986), 9.

38. Ibid., 108.

39. J. M. Coetzee, "Emperor of Nostalgia," *New York Review of Books,* February 28, 2002.

40. Herman Melville, *Moby-Dick* (New York: W. W. Norton & Co., 1976), 417.

41. Ibid., 211.

42. Ibid., 164.

43. Ibid., 166–167.

44. Ibid., 164–165.

45. Ibid., 167.

46. Ibid., 69.

47. Nathaniel Philbrick, *In the Heart of the Sea: The Tragedy of the Whale-ship* Essex (New York: Penguin Books, 2000), 65.

48. Herman Melville, *Moby-Dick* (New York: W. W. Norton & Co., 1976), 417.

49. Philbrick, *In the Heart of the Sea,* 56–57.

50. Melville, *Moby-Dick,* 519.

51. Ibid., 186.

52. Ibid., 113.

53. Ibid., 169.

54. Ibid., 561.

55. Walter Benjamin, "Capitalism as Religion" [written in 1921], reprinted in *Selected Writings,* vol. 1, *1913–1926* (Cambridge, MA: Harvard University Press, 1996), 288.

56. Ibid.

57. Ibid., 288–289.

CHAPTER II

1. Paul Celan, "Death Fugue," *Mohn und Gedächtnis,* © 1952, Deutsche Verlags-Anstalt, München, in der Verlagsgruppe Random House GmbH.

2. Federal Bureau of Prisons inmate locator, available at: http://www.bop.gov/inmateloc/.

3. Douglas Jehl, "70 Die in Attack at Egypt Temple," *New York Times,* November 18, 1997.

4. "Chris Hedges Interviews Lynne Stewart Following Release from Prison—Truthdig" (video), February 6, 2014, https://www.youtube.com/watch?v=-etkEPHA3zI.

5. Ibid.

6. US Supreme Court, *Certiorari, Hedges v. Obama,* April 28, 2014.

7. Open Congress, "HR1540—National Defense Authorization Act for Fiscal Year 2012," http://www.opencongress.org/bill/hr1540-112/show.

8. *Hedges v. Obama,* Opinion and Order, September 12, 2012, 12–13; on *Korematsu v. United States,* see ACLU, "ACLU History: A Dark Moment in History: Japanese Internment Camps," September 1, 2010, https://www.aclu.org/national-security/aclu-history-dark-moment-history-japanese-internment-camps.

9. John O. Koehler, *Stasi: The Untold Story of the East German Secret Police* (Boulder, CO: Westview Press, 1999), 8.

10. Ibid., 8–9.

11. Hannah Arendt, *The Origins of Totalitarianism* [1951] (New York: Houghton Mifflin, 1994), 426.

12. Ibid., 245.

13. "Esclusiva Panorama: Datagate, anche il Papa è stato intercettato" ("Exclusive Panorama: Datagate, Even the Pope Was Intercepted"), *Panorama*, October 30, 2013, http://news.panorama.it/cronaca/urbi-et-orbi/papa-francesco-datagate.

14. Jacob Appelbaum, Holger Stark, Marcel Rosenbach, and Jörg Schindler, "Berlin Complains: Did US Tap Chancellor Merkel's Mobile Phone?" *Spiegel International*, October 23, 2013, http://www.spiegel.de/international/world/merkel-calls-obama-over-suspicions-us-tapped-her-mobile-phone-a-929642.html; Ewen MacAskill and Julian Borger, "New NSA Leaks Show How US Is Bugging Its European Allies," *The Guardian*, June 30, 2013.

15. Scott Shane, "No Morsel Too Minuscule for All-Consuming NSA," *New York Times*, November 2, 2013.

16. "NSA Documents Show United States Spied Brazilian Oil Giant," *Fantástico*, August 9, 2013, http://g1.globo.com/fantastico/noticia/2013/09/nsa-documents-show-united-states-spied-brazilian-oil-giant.html; James Risen and Laura Poitras, "Spying by NSA Ally Entangled US Law Firm," *New York Times*, February 15, 2014.

17. Ewen MacAskill and Lenore Taylor, "NSA: Australia and US Used Climate Change Conference to Spy on Indonesia," *The Guardian*, November 2, 2013.

18. John Keane, *Tom Paine: A Political Life* (New York: Grove Press, 1995), 302.

19. Brian Fung, "Darrell Issa: James Clapper Lied to Congress About NSA and Should Be Fired," *Washington Post*, January 27, 2014.

20. "Al Gore: Snowden 'Revealed Evidence' of Crimes Against US Constitution," *The Guardian*, November 6, 2013.

21. Charlie Savage, "Judge Questions Legality of NSA Phone Records," *New York Times*, December 16, 2013; see also Adam Liptak, "Judge Upholds NSA's Bulk Collection of Data on Calls," *New York Times*, December 27, 2013.

22. "Judge Rules NSA Phone Tracking Legal," Associated Press, December 27, 2013.

23. Barton Gellman, "NSA Broke Privacy Rules Thousands of Times per Year, Audit Finds," *Washington Post,* August 13, 2013.

24. Barton Gellman and Ashkan Soltani, "NSA Infiltrates Links to Yahoo, Google Data Centers Worldwide, Snowden Documents Say," *Washington Post,* October 30, 2013.

25. Nicole Perlroth, Jeff Larson, and Scott Shane, "NSA Able to Foil Basic Safeguards of Privacy on Web," *New York Times,* September 5, 2013.

26. Scott Shane and Jonathan Weisman, "Earlier Denials Put Intelligence Chief in Awkward Position," *New York Times,* June 11, 2013.

27. Charlie Savage and Scott Shane, "Secret Court Rebuked NSA on Surveillance," *New York Times,* August 21, 2013.

28. Charlie Savage, "Judge Questions Legality of NSA Phone Records," *New York Times,* December 16, 2013.

29. "Edward Snowden, Whistle-Blower" (editorial), *New York Times,* January 1, 2014; see also David E. Sanger and Charlie Savage, "Obama Is Urged to Sharply Curb NSA Data Mining," *New York Times,* December 18, 2013.

30. "Ex-Official for NSA Accepts Deal in Leak Case," Reuters, June 10, 2011.

31. "NSA Whistleblower Edward Snowden: 'I Don't Want to Live in a Society That Does These Sort of Things'" (video), *The Guardian,* June 9, 2013.

32. Lewis Carroll, *Lewis Carroll: Complete Illustrated Works,* ed. Edward Guiliano (Avenel, NJ: Crown, 1982), 434.

33. F. Scott Fitzgerald, *The Short Stories of F. Scott Fitzgerald* (New York: Scribner, 1989), 318.

34. Aristotle, *Politics* (Chicago: University of Chicago Press, 2013), Book V.

35. F. Scott Fitzgerald, *The Great Gatsby* (Ware, Hertfordshire, UK: Wordsworth Editions, 1993), 114.

36. Aristotle, *Politics of Aristotle,* ed. Justin D. Kaplan (New York: Simon & Schuster, 1983), 331.

37. Karl Marx, "The German Ideology," in *Karl Marx: A Reader,* ed. John Elster (Cambridge: Cambridge University Press, 1986), 302.

38. Joseph Stiglitz, "Of the 1%, by the 1%, for the 1%," *Vanity Fair,* May 2011.

39. David Cay Johnston, "9 Things the Rich Don't Want You to Know About Taxes," *Willamette Week,* April 13, 2011, http://www.wweek.com /portland/article-17350-permalink.html.

40. Brandon Roberts, Deborah Povich, and Mark Mather, "Low-Income Working Families: The Growing Economic Gap" (policy brief), The Working

Poor Families Project, Winter 2012–2013, http://www.workingpoorfamilies
.org/wp-content/uploads/2013/01/Winter-2012_2013-WPFP-Data-Brief
.pdf; see also US Census Bureau, "2013 Highlights," https://www.census.gov
/hhes/www/poverty/about/overview/index.html.

41. Craig K. Elwell, "Inflation and the Real Minimum Wage: A Fact
Sheet," Congressional Research Service, January 8, 2014, http://fas.org/sgp
/crs/misc/R42973.pdf.

42. Wendell Berry, "Compromise, Hell," Orion, November-December
2004, http://www.orionmagazine.org/index.php/articles/article/147/.

43. National Alliance on Mental Illness, "Mental Illness: Facts and Numbers," http://www.nami.org/factsheets/mentalillness_factsheet.pdf.

44. "LB Collective Labour Incidents Map," China Labour Bulletin, www
.numble.com/PHP/mysql/clbmape.html (accessed June 24, 2014).

45. "Searching for the Union: The Workers' Movement in China 2011–
2013," China Labour Bulletin, February 20, 2014, www.clb.org.hk/en/content
/searching-union-workers'-movement-china-2011-13-0 (accessed June 24,
2014).

46. "Striking Chinese Workers Are Headache for Nike, IBM, Secret Weapon for Beijing," Bloomberg News, May 6, 2014, www.bloomberg.com/news
/2014-05-06/china-workers-power-sets-off-strikes-for-nike-wal-mart.html.

47. "Defeat Will Only Make Us Stronger: Workers Look Back at the Yue
Yuen Shoe Factory Strike," China Labour Bulletin, May 22, 2014, www.clb
.org.hk/en/content/defeat-will-only-make-us-stronger-workers-look-back
-yue-yuen-shoe-factory-strike (accessed June 24, 2014).

48. Teresa Cheng, "48,000 Chinese Strikers Say, Adidas, Nike, Timber-
land: You Fix It!" Labor Notes, April 23, 2014, www.labornotes.org/2014/04
/48000-chinese-strikers-say-adidas-nike-timberland-you-fix-it (accessed
June 24, 2014).

49. Bloomberg News, "Striking Chinese Workers Are Headache for Nike,
IBM, Secret Weapon for Beijing."

CHAPTER III

1. Alexander Herzen, From the Other Shore: The Russian People and Socialism (Westport, CT: Hyperion Press, 1981), 124.

2. Alexander Berkman, "The Idea Is the Thing," Anarchy Archives,
http://dwardmac.pitzer.edu/anarchist_archives/bright/berkman/iish/idea
/ideathing.html.

3. Steven Pinker, "The Evolutionary Social Psychology of Off-Record Indirect Speech Acts," *Intercultural Pragmatics* 4, no. 4 (2007): 437–461, http://scholar.harvard.edu/files/pinker/files/evolutionary_social_psychology_of_off-record_indirect_speech_acts.pdf.

4. Edward Sapir, "The Status of Linguistics as a Science," *Language* 5, no. 4 (December 1929): 207–214, 210.

5. Antonio Gramsci, *Prison Notebooks*, vol. 2 (New York: Columbia University Press, 1996), 32–33.

6. John Ralston Saul, *Voltaire's Bastards: The Dictatorship of Reason in the West* (New York: Vintage, 1992), 22, 29.

7. Ibid., 116.

8. Stefan Zweig, *Chess Story* (New York: New York Review Book Classics, 2005), 13.

9. Hannah Arendt, *Eichmann in Jerusalem: A Report on the Banality of Evil* (New York: Penguin Books, 2006), 49.

10. Enlace Zapatista, "Between Light and Shadow," May 2014, http://enlacezapatista.ezln.org.mx/2014/05/27/between-light-and-shadow/.

11. Subcomandante Insurgente Marcos, "A History About Herons and Eagles in the Lacandon Jungle" (letter to John Berger), May 12, 1995, http://flag.blackened.net/revolt/mexico/ezln/marcos_heron_eagle_may95.html.

12. Enlace Zapatista, "Between Light and Shadow."

13. "Zapatistas Call Attention to Violence Targeting Their Communities," Free Speech Radio News, May 29, 2014, http://fsrn.org/2014/05/zapatistas-call-attention-to-violence-targeting-their-communities/.

14. Enlace Zapatista, "Between Light and Shadow."

15. "The Zapatista Uprising 1994–2004: A Look at How an Indigenous Rebel Group from Chiapas Took on Mexico and Corporate Globalization," Democracy Now, January 2, 2004.

16. Enlace Zapatista, "Between Light and Shadow," May 2014.

17. Ibid.

18. Ibid.

19. E. Roy Weintraub, "Neoclassical Economics," in *The Concise Encyclopedia of Economics*, 2007, available at Library of Economics and Liberty website, http://www.econlib.org/library/Enc1/NeoclassicalEconomics.html.

20. Adam B. Ulam, *The Bolsheviks: The Intellectual and Political History of the Triumph of Communism in Russia* (Cambridge, MA: Harvard University Press, 1998), 313.

21. Peter Kropotkin, *Anarchism: A Collection of Revolutionary Writings* (Mineola, NY: Courier/Dover Publications, 2012), 80.

22. Paul Avrich, *Anarchist Portraits* (Princeton, NJ: Princeton University Press, 1988).

23. Emma Goldman, "Minorities Versus Majorities," in *Anarchism and Other Essays* (New York: Dover Publications, 1969), 77.

24. According to the Bureau of Labor Statistics, "in 2013, the union membership rate—the percent of wage and salary workers who were members of unions—was 11.3 percent." US Department of Labor, Bureau of Labor Statistics, "Economic News Release: Union Members Summary," January 24, 2014, http://www.bls.gov/news.release/union2.nr0.htm.

25. "Trial Judge to Appeals Court: Review Me" (editorial), *New York Times,* July 16, 2012.

26. Michelle Alexander, *The New Jim Crow: Mass Incarceration in the Age of Colorblindness* (New York: New Press, 2010).

27. Jennifer Schuessler, "Drug Policy as Race Policy: Best Seller Galvanizes the Debate," *New York Times,* March 6, 2012.

28. Hanqing Chen, "What Militarization Has Done to Our Police Departments," *Mother Jones,* August 21, 2014.

29. Maria J. Stephan and Erica Chenoweth, "Why Civil Resistance Works: The Strategic Logic of Nonviolent Conflict," *International Security* 33, no. 1 (Summer 2008): 7–44.

30. Ibid., 11–12.

31. Heather C. McGhee and Amy Traub, "State of the American Dream: Economic Policy and the Future of the Middle Class," Demos, June 6, 2013, http://www.demos.org/publication/state-american-dream-economic -policy-and-future-middle-class.

32. Berkman, "The Idea Is the Thing."

33. Thomas C. Schelling, "Some Questions on Civilian Defense," in *Civilian Resistance as a National Defense: Nonviolent Action Against Aggression,* ed. Adam Roberts (Harrisburg, PA: Stackpole, 1967), 351–353.

34. Berkman, "The Idea Is the Thing."

35. Ibid.

CHAPTER IV

1. Thomas Paine, *Rights of Man and Common Sense* (New York: Everyman's Library, 1994), 196.

2. Peter Parker and Joyce Mokhesi-Parker, *In the Shadow of Sharpeville: Apartheid and Criminal Justice* (New York: New York University Press, 1998), 19.

3. Ronnie Kasrils, *Armed and Dangerous: My Undercover Struggle Against Apartheid* (Oxford: Heinemann Educational Publishers, 1993).

4. Ibid., 22.

5. Ibid., 23.

6. "There are excellent grounds for believing that Lenin's radicalism flowered after Alexander's death, and largely as a result of reading his martyred brother's books," writes Adam Ulam in *The Bolsheviks: The Intellectual and Political History of the Triumph of Communism in Russia* (Cambridge, MA: Harvard University Press, 1998), 10.

7. Albert Camus, *The Rebel* (New York: Vintage, 1984), 304.

8. Sean K. Anderson and Steven Sloan, *Historical Dictionary of Terrorism* (Lanham, MD: Scarecrow Press, 2009), 685.

9. "One Year On, Marikana Is Emblematic of South Africa's Woes" (editorial), *The Independent*, August 16, 2013, http://www.independent.co.uk /voices/editorials/one-year-on-marikana-is-emblematic-of-south-africas -woes-8770862.html.

10. Camus, *The Rebel*, 249.

11. South African Institute of Race Relations (IRR), "South African Survey, 2011/2012," http://irr.org.za/reports-and-publications/south-africa -survey/south-africa-survey-2012.

12. Vaclav Havel, "The Power of the Powerless," in *The Power of the Powerless: Citizens Against the State in Central-Eastern Europe*, ed. John Keane (Abingdon, Oxon, UK: Routledge, 2010), 13.

13. Ibid., 21.

14. Ibid. (emphasis in original).

15. Human Rights Watch, "China's Rights Defenders," http://www.hrw .org/Chinas-rights-defenders.

16. Tania Branigan, "US Calls on China to Release Liu Xiaobo," *The Guardian*, December 10, 2013.

17. Starhawk, Lisa Fithian, and Lauren Ross, "An Open Letter to the Occupy Movement," Tikkun Daily, November 10, 2011, http://www.tikkun .org/tikkundaily/2011/11/10/an-open-letter-to-the-occupy-movement/.

18. Ibid.

19. Nelson Mandela, *Conversations with Myself* (Toronto: Random House, 2011), 233.

20. Hanna Krall, *Shielding the Flame: An Intimate Conversation with Dr. Marek Edelman, the Last Surviving Leader of the Warsaw Ghetto Uprising,* trans. Joanna Stasinska and Lawrence Weschler (New York: Henry Holt, 1986), 8.

21. Ibid., 37.

22. Ibid., 48.

23. Ibid., 42.

24. Ibid., 50.

25. Ibid., 9.

26. Ibid., 9–10.

27. Ibid., xii.

28. Ibid., 85.

29. Ibid., 38.

30. Ibid., 10.

CHAPTER V

1. "August Wilson on Blackness," *Moyers & Company,* October 20, 1988, http://billmoyers.com/content/august-wilson/.

2. Richard Wright, *Black Boy* (New York: HarperCollins, 2005), 302.

3. Amnesty International, "United States of America: A Life in the Balance: The Case of Mumia Abu-Jamal," AI Index AMR 51/01/00, February 17, 2000, http://www.amnesty.org/en/library/asset/AMR51/001/2000/en /0987a185-dfd3-11dd-8e17-69926d493233/amr510012000en.pdf.

4. *Mumia: Long Distance Revolutionary: A Journey with Mumia Abu-Jamal* (2012), directed by Stephen Vittoria.

5. "Mumia Abu-Jamal Sues Pennsylvania over New Convicts Gag Law," Associated Press, November 10, 2014.

6. Criminal Justice USA, "10 Stats You Should Know About Our Prison System," May 17, 2011, http://www.criminaljusticeusa.com/blog/2011/10 -stats-you-should-know-about-our-prison-system/.

7. Erica Goode, "Incarceration Rates for Blacks Have Fallen Sharply, Report Shows," *New York Times,* February 27, 2013.

8. Adam B. Ulam, *Ideologies and Illusions: Revolutionary Thought from Herzen to Solzhenitsyn* (Cambridge, MA: Harvard University Press, 1976), 12.

9. Legislative Analyst's Office of the California State Legislature, "The Federal Crime Bill: What Will It Mean for California?" (policy brief), September 27, 1994, http://www.lao.ca.gov/1994/pb092794.html.

10. US Department of Justice, "Violent Crime Control and Law Enforcement Act of 1994: Fact Sheet," October 24, 1994, https://www.ncjrs.gov/txtfiles/billfs.txt.

11. "Bill Clinton Was Incredibly Destructive to Black People," Prison Culture, April 24, 2012, http://www.usprisonculture.com/blog/2012/04/24/bill-clinton-was-incredibly-destructive-for-black-people; see also Violent Crime Control and Law Enforcement Act of 1994, 103rd Congress (1993–1994), HR 3355, available at: http://www.gpo.gov/fdsys/pkg/BILLS-103hr3355enr/pdf/BILLS-103hr3355enr.pdf.

12. Justice Policy Institute, "Too Little Too Late: President Clinton's Prison Legacy," February 2001, http://www.justicepolicy.org/uploads/justicepolicy/documents/too_little_too_late.pdf.

13. Tracey Kyckelhahn, "State Corrections Expenditures, FY 1982–2010," US Department of Justice, Bureau of Justice Statistics, NCJ 239672, December 2012, revised April 30, 2014, http://www.bjs.gov/content/pub/pdf/scefy8210.pdf.

14. Mumia Abu-Jamal, *All Things Censored* (New York: Seven Stories Press, 2001), 195.

15. Mumia Abu-Jamal, *Faith of Our Fathers: An Examination of the Spiritual Life of African and African-American People* (Trenton, NJ: Africa World Press, 2004), xi–xii.

16. Marie Gottschalk, *Caught: The Prison State and the Lockdown of American Politics* (Princeton, NJ: Princeton University Press, 2015), 1.

17. Ibid., 4–5.

18. Mary Bosworth, ed., *Encyclopedia of Prisons and Correctional Facilities* (London: Sage Publications, 2004), 273.

19. Ibid., 707.

20. Harry Camisa and Jim Franklin, *Inside Out: Fifty Years Behind the Walls of New Jersey's Trenton State Prison* (Adelphia, NJ: Windsor Press and Publishing, 2003), 195; Bosworth, *Encyclopedia of Prisons and Correctional Facilities,* 708.

21. Bosworth, *Encyclopedia of Prisons and Correctional Facilities,* 570.

22. Ibid., 16.

23. Massachusetts Department of Correction, Office of Investigative Services, "Security Threat Group Monthly Report," March 2012, http://www.mass.gov/eopss/docs/doc/march2012.pdf.

24. Center for Constitutional Rights, "CMUs: The Federal Prison System's Experiment in Social Isolation," http://ccrjustice.org/cmu-factsheet.

25. Rachael Kamel and Bonnie Kerness, "The Prison Inside the Prison: Control Units, Supermax Prisons, and Devices of Torture," American Friends Service Committee, Justice Visions Briefing Paper, 2003, http://www.afsc.org/sites/afsc.civicactions.net/files/documents/PrisonInside ThePrison.pdf.

26. Alfred McCoy, *A Question of Torture: CIA Interrogation, from the Cold War to the War on Terror* (New York: Macmillan, 2007), 6.

27. Ibid., 8.

28. Bonnie Kerness, ed., "Torture in United States Prisons: Evidence of Human Rights Violations," 2nd ed., American Friends Service Committee, 2011, https://afsc.org/sites/afsc.civicactions.net/files/documents/torture_in _us_prisons.pdf.

29. Ibid., 15–16.

30. Centers for Disease Control and Prevention (CDC), "Viral Hepatitis Specific Settings: Correctional Facilities and Viral Hepatitis," http://www .cdc.gov/hepatitis/Settings/Corrections.htm; Dara Masoud, Dato Chorgoliani, and Pierpaolo de Colombani, "TB Prevention and Control Care in Prisons," http://www.euro.who.int/__data/assets/pdf_file/0005/249197 /Prisons-and-Health,-8-TB-prevention-and-control-care-in-prisons.pdf?ua =1; AIDS.gov, "HIV/AIDS and Incarceration," http://www.aids.gov/federal -resources/policies/incarceration/.

31. Council of State Governments, Justice Center, "Medicaid and Financing Health Care for Individuals Involved with the Criminal Justice System," December 2013, http://csgjusticecenter.org/wp-content/uploads/2013/12 /ACA-Medicaid-Expansion-Policy-Brief.pdf.

32. Matthew R. Durose, Alexia D. Cooper, and Howard N. Snyder, "Recidivism of Prisoners Released in 30 States in 2005: Patterns from 2005 to 2010," US Department of Justice, Bureau of Justice Statistics, Office of Justice Programs, April 22, 2014, http://www.bjs.gov/index.cfm?ty=pbdetail &iid=4986.

33. Staughton Lynd, *Lucasville: The Untold Story of a Prison Uprising* (Oakland, CA: PM Press, 2004), 153.

34. Ibid.

35. Jeanne Theoharis, "The Legal Black Hole in Lower Manhattan: The Unfairness of the Trial of Muslim Activist Fahad Hashmi," *Slate*, April 27, 2010; see also Jeanne Theoharis, "My Student, the 'Terrorist,'" *Chronicle of Higher Education*, April 3, 2011, http://chronicle.com/article/My-Student -the-Terrorist/126937/.

36. Theoharis, "The Legal Black Hole in Lower Manhattan"; Theoharis, "My Student, the 'Terrorist.'"

37. Sami Al-Arian, a former computer engineering professor at the University of South Florida and a leading Palestinian activist, was indicted on terrorism charges in February 2003. In 2005 he endured a six-month trial in Florida with three codefendants in which the government's case collapsed. The Justice Department spent an estimated $50 million and several years investigating and prosecuting Al-Arian. The government called eighty witnesses and subjected the jury to hundreds of hours of trivial phone transcriptions and recordings made over a ten-year period that the jury eventually dismissed as "gossip." Out of the ninety-four charges made against the four defendants, there were no convictions. Of the seventeen charges against Al-Arian—including "conspiracy to murder and maim persons abroad"—the jury acquitted him of eight and was hung on the rest. The jurors disagreed on the remaining charges, with ten of the twelve jurors favoring his full acquittal. Two others in the case, Ghassan Ballut and Sameeh Hammoudeh, were acquitted of all charges.

Following the acquittal—a disaster for the government, especially because then-Attorney General John Ashcroft had announced the indictment—prosecutors threatened to retry Al-Arian. The Palestinian professor, under duress, accepted a plea bargain agreement that would spare him a second trial, saying in his agreement that he had helped people associated with Palestinian Islamic Jihad with immigration matters. It was a tepid charge given the high profile of the case. The US Attorney's Office for the Middle District of Florida and the counterterrorism section of the Justice Department agreed to recommend to the judge the minimum sentence of forty-six months. But US District Judge James S. Moody sentenced Dr. Al-Arian to the maximum fifty-seven months. In referring to Al-Arian's contention that he had only raised money for Palestinian Islamic Jihad's charity for widows and orphans, the judge said acidly to the professor that "your only connection to orphans and widows is that you create them."

The government kept him in jail for five years after he refused to testify before a secret grand jury in Virginia investigating Islamic organizations in the United States in a separate case. Al-Arien's lawyers said that his plea agreements had exempted him from any further testimony.

Al-Arien was jailed and then held under house arrest in northern Virginia from 2008 until 2014. In 2014, US District Judge Anthony J. Trenga signed the order dismissing the indictment against Al-Arian. All charges were dropped.

38. Jeffrey A. Sluka, ed., *Death Squad: The Anthropology of State Terror* (Philadelphia: University of Pennsylvania Press, 1999), 7–30.

39. Theoharis, "The Legal Black Hole in Lower Manhattan"; Theoharis, "My Student, the 'Terrorist.'"

40. Kareem Fahim, "Restrictive Terms of Prisoner's Confinement Add Fuel to Debate," *New York Times,* February 4, 2009.

41. Theoharis, "My Student, the 'Terrorist.'"

42. Fahim, "Restrictive Terms of Prisoner's Confinement Add Fuel to Debate."

43. Amnesty International, "Entombed: Isolation in the US Prison System," 2014, 3.

44. Christopher S. Stewart, "Little Gitmo," *New York,* July 10, 2011; see also Amnesty International, "Entombed."

45. Franz Kafka, *Franz Kafka: The Complete Short Stories* (New York: Schocken Books, 1995).

46. Jesse McKinley and Abby Goodnough, "Cities Begin Cracking Down on 'Occupy' Protests," *New York Times,* October 27, 2011.

47. In February 2011, protesters gathered in the state capital of Madison to protest the 2011 Wisconsin Act 10, also known as the "Wisconsin budget repair bill," which would have stripped state employees of their collective bargaining rights and forced them to pay a larger share of their health care and pension costs. As many as 100,000 state workers, including teachers, firefighters, and police, protested the anti-union measure, and some occupied the state capitol building from February 20 until March 3.

48. Jon Swaine, "NYPD Officer Embroiled in Assault Trial Sued by Another Occupy Campaigner," *The Guardian,* April 4, 2014.

49. Ibid.

50. "Occupy Arrests Near 8,000 as Wall Street Eludes Prosecution," Huffington Post, May 23, 2013, http://www.huffingtonpost.com/2013/05/23/occupy-wall-street-arrests_n_3326640.html.

51. Jon Swaine, "Pussy Riot Members Visit Occupy Activist Cecily McMillan in Prison," *The Guardian,* May 9, 2014.

52. "Freedom, Leniency, and Pardon Cecily McMillan NOW!" (petition), change.org, http://www.change.org/p/freedom-leniency-and-pardon-cecily-mcmillan-now.

53. E. V. Debs, "Statement to the Court Upon Being Convicted of Violating the Sedition Act," September 18, 1918, https://www.marxists.org/archive/debs/works/1918/court.htm.

CHAPTER VI

1. James Baldwin, *James Baldwin: Collected Essays*, ed. Toni Morrison (New York: Library of America, 1998), 202.

2. Graduate Institute of International Studies, *Small Arms Survey 2007: Guns and the City* (New York: Cambridge University Press, 2007).

3. Heather Loney, "Canada's 2012 Homicide Rate at Lowest Level in Nearly 50 Years: StatsCan," *Global News*, December 19, 2013.

4. "Gen. Smith's Counsel Admits Main Charges; Orders Were Given to Make Samar a 'Howling Wilderness.' Commander Wanted Everybody Killed Capable of Bearing Arms and Specified All Over Ten Years of Age," *New York Times*, April 26, 1902.

5. D. H. Lawrence, *Studies in Classic American Literature*, vol. 2 (New York: Penguin, 1990), 65.

6. Richard Hofstadter and Michael Wallace, eds., *American Violence: A Documentary History* (New York: Alfred A. Knopf, 1970), 16; see also PBS, "The Ku Klux Klan in the 1920s," *American Experience*, http://www.pbs.org/wgbh/americanexperience/features/general-article/flood-klan/.

7. Scott Martelle, *Blood Passion: The Ludlow Massacre and Class War in the American West* (New Brunswick, NJ: Rutgers University Press, 2008), 172–175.

8. Philip Taft and Philip Ross, "American Labor Violence: Its Causes, Character, and Outcome," in *The History of Violence in America: A Report to the National Commission on the Causes and Prevention of Violence*, ed. Hugh Davis Graham and Ted Robert Gurr (Frederick A. Praeger, 1969), 270, cf. 360; see also Philip Taft's essay "Violence in American Labor Disputes," *Annals of the American Academy of Political and Social Science* (March 1966): 128.

9. Robert Shogan, *The Battle of Blair Mountain: The Story of America's Largest Labor Uprising* (New York: Basic Books, 2006), 4; Lon Savage, *Thunder in the Mountains: The West Virginia Mine War 1920–21* (Pittsburgh: University of Pittsburgh Press, 1990), 147–148.

10. Richard Rorty, *Achieving Our Country: Leftist Thought in Twentieth-Century America* (Cambridge, MA: Harvard University Press, 1998), 90.

11. Hofstadter and Wallace, *American Violence*, 35.

12. Melvyn Stokes, *D. W. Griffith's* The Birth of a Nation: *A History of the Most Controversial Motion Picture of All Time* (Oxford: Oxford University Press, 2008), 111.

13. Ibid., 234–235. For Nancy Maclean, see her book *Behind the Mask of Chivalry: The Making of the Second Ku Klux Klan* (New York: Oxford University Press, 1994), 197; for Lawrence Reddick, see "Educational Programs for the Improvement of Race Relations: Motion Pictures, Radio, the Press, and Libraries," *Journal of Negro Education* 13, no. 3 (Summer 1944): 367–389; for James Baldwin, see *Baldwin: Collected Essays*, 511.

14. Michael Freitag, "Goetz Released After Spending 8 Months in Jail," *New York Times*, September 21, 1989.

15. The Brady Campaign to Prevent Gun Violence averaged the most recent three years of data from death certificates (2008–2010) and estimates of emergency room admissions (2009–2011); available at CDC, "Injury Prevention and Control: Data and Statistics (WISQARS™)," http://www.cdc.gov/injury/wisqars/index.html (accessed December 28, 2012).

16. Craig R. Whitney, "Arms and the Men: *The Second Amendment* and *This Nonviolent Stuff'll Get You Killed*" (book review), *New York Times*, June 19, 2014.

17. Joseph Straw, "School Shootings Happen Every 10 Days Since Sandy Hook, Gun Control Groups Find," *New York Daily News*, February 12, 2014.

18. Hofstadter and Wallace, *American Violence*, 3, 10.

19. The historian Gerald Horne documents the role of private property in the founding of the country in his book *The Counter-Revolution of 1776* (New York: New York University Press, 2014).

20. Hofstadter and Wallace, *American Violence*, 10.

21. Jennifer B. Smith, *An International History of the Black Panther Party* (New York: Routledge, 1999), 35.

22. Hofstadter and Wallace, *American Violence*, 11.

23. John Keane, *Tom Paine: A Political Life* (New York: Grove Press, 1995), x.

24. Eric Foner, *Tom Paine and Revolutionary America* (New York: Oxford University Press, 1976), 79.

25. Keane, *Tom Paine*, 116–117.

26. Ibid., xi.

27. Foner, *Tom Paine and Revolutionary America*, 75.

28. Elsie Begler, *Thomas Paine: Common Sense for the Modern Era* (San Diego: San Diego State University Press, 2007), 159.

29. Ibid., 99.

30. Keane, *Tom Paine*, xiii.

31. J.G.A. Pocock, *Politics, Language, and Time* (New York: Atheneum, 1971), 12, 38, 105, and passim; cf. Walter J. Ong, *Rhetoric, Romance, and*

Technology (Ithaca, NY: Cornell University Press, 1971); cited in Foner, *Tom Paine and Revolutionary America,* xv.

32. Foner, *Tom Paine and Revolutionary America,* xv.

33. Keane, *Tom Paine,* 347–348.

34. Keane, *Tom Paine,* 337.

35. Thomas Paine, "African Slavery in America," March 18, 1775, Constitution Society, http://www.constitution.org/tp/afri.htm.

36. Keane, *Tom Paine,* 362.

37. Ibid., 413–414.

38. Thomas Carlyle, *The French Revolution: A History,* vol. 3 [1837] (London, 1888), 217; cited in Keane, *Tom Paine,* 408.

39. Ibid., 409.

40. Foner, *Tom Paine and Revolutionary America,* 72.

41. Keane, *Tom Paine,* 115.

42. Ibid., 394, 395.

43. Ibid., 457.

44. Moncure Daniel Conway, *The Life of Thomas Paine* [1892], vol. 2 (New York: G. P. Putnam's, 1908), 417–418.

45. Journals of Richard Wright, 1945–1947, entries for January 7, 28, and 29, 1945, Richard Wright Papers, Beinecke Rare Book and Manuscript Library, Yale University.

46. Federal Bureau of Investigation, "Jarod Lee Loughner Pleads Guilty to Federal Charges in Tucson Shooting," August 7, 2012, http://www.fbi .gov/phoenix/press-releases/2012/jared-lee-loughner-pleads-guilty-to -federal-charges-in-tucson-shooting.

47. Michael Cooper, "Accusations Fly Between Parties over Threats and Vandalism," *New York Times,* March 25, 2010.

48. Matthew Avery Sutton, "Why the Antichrist Matters in Politics," *New York Times,* September 25, 2011.

49. Carl Hulse, "Texas Lawmaker Admits 'Baby Killer' Remark," *New York Times,* March 22, 2010.

50. James W. Loewen, *Lies Across America: What Our Historic Sites Get Wrong* (New York: Simon & Schuster, 2007), 237.

51. Hunter Schwarz, "Georgia Will Celebrate Two Confederate Holidays Next Year," *Washington Post,* August 7, 2014.

52. "Ku Klux Klan Recruitment Fliers Prompt Investigation by Ga. Authorities," CBS News, January 23, 2013, http://www.cbsnews.com/news /ku-klux-klan-recruitment-fliers-prompt-investigation-by-ga-authorities/.

53. Equal Justice Initiative, "Death Penalty in Alabama," http://www.eji
.org/files/02.03.11%20Death%20Penalty%20in%20Alabama%20Fact%20
Sheet.pdf.

54. "Death of General Forrest," *New York Times,* October 30, 1877.

55. Brian Steel Wills, *A Battle from the Start: The Life of Nathan Bedford Forrest* (New York: HarperCollins, 1992), 173.

56. William C. Carter, *Conversations with Shelby Foote* (Jackson: University Press of Mississippi, 1989), 173.

57. Shelby Foote, *The Civil War: A Narrative,* vol. 3, *Red River to Appomattox* (New York: Vintage Books, 1986), 108–111.

58. Ibid., 478.

59. Alfreda M. Duster, ed., *Crusade for Justice: The Autobiography of Ida B. Wells* (Chicago: University of Chicago Press, 1972), 64.

60. Ibid., 62–63.

61. James Oliver Horton and Amanda Kleintop, eds., *Race, Slavery, and the Civil War: The Tough Stuff of American History and Memory* (Richmond: Virginia Sesquicentennial of the Civil War Commission, 2011); "Confederate States of America: Declaration of the Immediate Causes Which Induce and Justify the Secession of South Carolina from the Federal Union," The Avalon Project, Yale Law School Library, http://avalon.law
.yale.edu/19th_century/csa_scarsec.asp.

62. Eddy W. Davidson and Daniel Foxx, *Nathan Bedford Forrest: In Search of an Enigma* (Gretna, LA: Pelican Publishing Co., 2007), 246.

63. Baldwin, *Collected Essays,* 386.

CHAPTER VII

1. Henry David Thoreau, *Civil Disobedience,* in *Thoreau: Political Writings,* ed. Nancy L. Rosenblum (Cambridge: Cambridge University Press, 1996), 10.

2. "Statement of the Government of the Republic of Ecuador on the Asylum Request of Julian Assange," May 10, 2013, http://cancilleria.gob.ec
/statement-of-the-government-of-the-republic-of-ecuador-on-the-asylum
-request-of-julian-assange/?lang=en; "Julian Assange Police Guard Cost Nears £3m," BBC News, February 15, 2013, http://www.bbc.com/news/uk
-21480648.

3. "WikiLeaks Fast Facts," CNN Library, April 23, 2014, http://www
.cnn.com/2013/06/03/world/wikileaks-fast-facts/.

4. Philip Dorling, "US Targets WikiLeaks Like No Other Organisation," *Sydney Morning Herald*, December 3, 2011, http://www.smh.com.au/technology/technology-news/us-targets-wikileaks-like-no-other-organisation-20111202-1obeo.html.

5. Alexa O'Brien, "Witness: US v. Pfc. Manning, Mark Johnson, Man-Tech International Contractor, Reports to Special Agent David Shaver, CCIU," December 19, 2011, http://www.alexaobrien.com/secondsight/wikileaks/bradley_manning/witness_profiles_us_v_pfc_bradley_manning/agents/witness_us_v_pfc_manning_mark_johnson_mantech_contractor_reports_to_cciu_special_agent_david_shaver.html.

6. Elizabeth Day, "Aaron Swartz: Hacker, Genius . . . Martyr?" *The Guardian*, June 1, 2013.

7. Ed Pilkington, "Jailed Anonymous Hacker Jeremy Hammond: 'My Days of Hacking Are Done,'" *The Guardian*, November 15, 2013.

8. Ed Pilkington, "LulzSec Hacker 'Sabu' Released After 'Extraordinary' FBI Cooperation: Authorities Credit Hector Xavier Monsegur with Helping Them Cripple Anonymous in Lenient Sentence of Time Served," *The Guardian*, May 27, 2014.

9. David Kushner, "The WikiLeaks Mole," *Rolling Stone*, January 6, 2014, http://www.rollingstone.com/politics/news/the-wikileaks-mole-20140106; Kevin Poulsen, "WikiLeaks Volunteer Was a Paid Informant for the FBI," *Wired*, June 27, 2013, http://www.wired.com/2013/06/wikileaks-mole/all/.

10. Alexa O'Brien, "Newly Published Secret Grand Jury Orders and Other Docs Shed Light on US Investigation of WikiLeaks Now Entering 5th Year," February 17, 2014, http://www.alexaobrien.com/secondsight/wikileaks/grand_jury/newly_published_secret_grand_jury_orders_and_related_material_shed_light_on_the_continuing_us_investigation_of_wikileaks_now_entering_its_fifth_year.html.

11. David Leigh and Rob Evans, "WikiLeaks Says Funding Has Been Blocked After Government Blacklisting: Founder Julian Assange Hits Out at Decision by Moneybookers, Which Collects the Whistleblowing Website's Donations," *The Guardian*, October 14, 2010.

12. "WikiLeaks Readies Suit Against Credit Card Companies over 'Economic Blockade,'" *Democracy Now!*, July 6, 2011, http://www.democracynow.org/2011/7/6/wikileaks_sues_credit_card_companies_over; Alessandra Prentice and Adrian Croft, "WikiLeaks' Assange Blames US Right for Funding Block," Reuters, November 27, 2012.

13. Leigh and Evans, "WikiLeaks Says Funding Has Been Blocked After Government Blacklisting."

14. "Authority of the Federal Bureau of Investigation to Override International Law in Extraterritorial Law Enforcement Activities," June 21, 1989, http://www.justice.gov/sites/default/files/olc/opinions/1989/06/31/op-olc-v013-p0163.pdf.

15. Craig Whitlock, "Renditions Continue Under Obama, Despite Due-Process Concerns," Washington Post, January 1, 2013.

16. Anna Mulrine, "Pentagon Papers vs. WikiLeaks: Is Bradley Manning the New Daniel Ellsberg?" Christian Science Monitor, June 13, 2011.

17. Cora Currier, "Charting Obama's Crackdown on National Security Leaks," Propublica, July 30, 2013.

18. "Gates: No Sensitive Info in WikiLeaks Afghan Papers," Reuters, October 17, 2010.

19. Julian Assange, with Jacob Appelbaum, Andy Müller-Maguhn, and Jérémie Zimmermann, Cypherpunks: Freedom and the Future of the Internet (New York: OR Books, 2012), 33.

20. Ibid., 6.

21. Ibid., 1.

22. Teresa Smith et al., "Bradley Manning: 35 Years in Jail for an Outsider Who Had Trouble Fitting In" (video), The Guardian, August 21, 2013, http://www.theguardian.com/world/video/2011/may/27/bradley-manning-wikileaks-iraq-video.

23. Alexa O'Brien, "Transcript: US v. Pfc. Manning, Article 39(a) Session, 07/18/12," July 18, 2012, http://www.alexaobrien.com/secondsight/wikileaks/bradley_manning/transcripts/transcript_us_v_manning_article_39a_july_18_2012.html.

24. Chase Madar, "Bradley Manning's Informant: On Adrian Lamo," The Nation, June 5, 2013.

25. "Leaked US Video Shows Deaths of Reuters' Iraqi Staffers," Reuters, April 5, 2010.

26. Marjorie Cohn, "Bradley Manning's Legal Duty to Expose War Crimes," Truthout, June 3, 2013, http://www.truth-out.org/news/item/16731-bradley-mannings-legal-duty-to-expose-war-crimes.

27. Manning's statement is reprinted at Democracy Now, August 22, 2013, http://www.democracynow.org/2013/8/22/bradley_manning_sometimes_you_have_to.

28. Katherine Stewart, "Loretta Preska's Judicial Crusade to Establish Churches in School," The Guardian, July 6, 2012.

29. Kevin Gosztola, "Judge Rules No Evidence to Disqualify Her from Hearing Case of Alleged Stratfor Hacker Jeremy Hammond," Firedoglake, February 21, 2013, http://dissenter.firedoglake.com/2013/02/21/judge-refuses-to-recuse-herself-from-case-of-jeremy-hammond-who-allegedly-hacked-into-stratfor/.

30. Janet Reitman, "The Rise and Fall of Jeremy Hammond: Enemy of the State," *Rolling Stone*, December 7, 2012.

31. Jeremy Hammond, "Electronic Civil Disobedience and the Republican National Convention," https://www.youtube.com/watch?v=XvXk5xCM6PM.

32. Reitman, "The Rise and Fall of Jeremy Hammond."

33. "Statement by Sarah Harrison," November 6, 2013, WikiLeaks, https://wikileaks.org/Statement-by-Sarah-Harrison-on.html.

34. "How the Other Half Lives in London" (editorial), *Financial Times*, November 1, 2013, http://www.ft.com/intl/cms/s/0/a2bb7c7c-42fe-11e3-9d3c-00144feabdc0.html#axzz3JR4lLn00.

35. John Betjeman, *John Betjeman: Collected Poems* (London: John Murray, 1958), 16.

CHAPTER VIII

1. Auguste Blanqui, "La Critique sociale" ("Social Criticism"), part III of Auguste Blanqui, *Textes choisis* (*Selected Texts*), preface and notes by V. P. Volguine (Paris: Éditions Sociale, 1971), 74; cited in Daniel Bensaïd and Michael Löwy, "August Blanqui, Heretical Communist," *Radical Philosophy* 185 (May-June 2014).

2. Friedrich Nietzsche, *Beyond Good and Evil*, cited in Max Weber, *The Vocation Lectures* (Indianapolis: Hackett, 2004), ix.

3. Andrew Nikiforuk, *Saboteurs: Wiebo Ludwig's War Against Big Oil* (Toronto: Macfarlane, Walter & Ross, 2002).

4. Community Environmental Legal Defense Fund, "Firing Big Green," *The Community Rights Papers* 3, http://www.celdf.org/downloads/Community_Rights_Paper_3_Firing_Big_Green.pdf.

5. *Wiebo's War*, dir. David York (National Film Board of Canada, 2011).

6. Nikiforuk, *Saboteurs*, 3–4, 26.

7. Henry David Thoreau, *Walden: A Fully Annotated Edition* (New Haven, CT: Yale University Press, 2004), 166.

8. Nikiforuk, *Saboteurs*, 22–23.

9. Jacques Ellul, *What I Believe* (Grand Rapids, MI: Zondervan, 1989), 147.

10. Jacques Ellul, *The Presence of the Kingdom* (Philadelphia: Wesminster Press, 1951), 47.

11. Nikiforuk, *Saboteurs*, xiii.

12. See the TSB website at http://www.tarsandsblockade.org/.

13. Paul W. Parfomak, Robert Pirog, Linda Luther, and Adam Vann, *Keystone XL Pipeline Project: Key Issues*, Congressional Research Service, January 24, 2013, http://www.washingtonpost.com/r/2010-2019/Washington Post/2013/04/09/National-Politics/Graphics/CRSRptKeystoneXLPipeline ProjectKeyIssues.pdf.

14. John M. Broder and Dan Frosch, "US Delays Decision on Pipeline Until After Election," *New York Times*, November 10, 2011.

15. Dave Saldana, "Keystone PipeLIES Exposed: The Facts on Sticky Leaks, Billion Dollar Spills, and Dirty Air," Center for Media and Democracy, PR Watch, February 26, 2014, http://www.prwatch.org/news/2014 /02/12401/keystone-pipelies-exposed-sticky-oil-leaks-billion-dollar-spills -and-human-health; see also Parfomak et al., *Keystone XL Pipeline Project: Key Issues*, 29.

16. James Hansen, "Game Over for the Climate," *New York Times*, May 9, 2012.

17. Tar Sands Blockade, "5 Blockaders Arrested for Stopping Keystone XL Machinery," September 19, 2012, http://www.tarsandsblockade.org /4th-action/.

18. Candice Bernd, "Texas Tar Sands Tree-Sit Launches to Halt Keystone XL Indefinitely," Truthout, September 26, 2012, http://truth-out.org/news /item/11797-texas-tar-sands-tree-sit-launches-to-halt-keystone-xl -indefinitely.

19. Daryl Hannah, "Why I'm Standing Up to TransCanada's Keystone XL Pipeline in East Texas," *The Guardian*, October 17, 2012.

20. Ride for Renewables, "Rocket Trike," http://www.rideforrenewables .com/the-rocket-trike/.

21. Lara Skinner and Sean Sweeney, with Ian Goodman and Brigid Rowan, "Pipe Dreams? Jobs Gained, Jobs Lost by the Construction of the Keystone XL," Cornell University Global Labor Institute, September 2011, http://www.ilr.cornell.edu/globallaborinstitute/research/upload/GLI _KeystoneXL_012312_FIN.pdf.

22. Reinhold Niebuhr, *Moral Man and Immoral Society* (Louisville, KY: Westminster John Knox Press, 2001), 255, 277.

23. Reinhold Niebuhr, "The Twilight of Liberalism" (letter to the editor), *The New Republic,* June 14, 1919.

24. Abraham J. Heschel, *The Prophets* (New York: Harper Perennial Modern Classics, 2001), 19.

25. Ibid., xxix.

26. Vaclav Havel, "The Power of the Powerless," in *The Power of the Powerless: Citizens Against the State in Central-Eastern Europe,* ed. John Keane (Abingdon, Oxon, UK: Routledge, 2010), 10–59.

27. Lyof N. Tolstoy, *The Novels and Other Works of Lyof N. Tolstoy,* vol. 20 (New York: Charles Scribner's Sons, 1902), 469.

28. *The Dialogues of Plato,* vol. 1, trans. R. E. Allen (New Haven, CT: Yale University Press), 311.

29. Ibid.

30. Martin Luther King, address at the Penn Community Center, Frogmore, South Carolina, May 22, 1967.

31. David J. Garrow, *Bearing the Cross: Martin Luther King Jr. and the Southern Christian Leadership Conference* (New York: HarperCollins, 2004), 524.

32. W. H. Auden, *Selected Poems* (Boston: Faber and Faber, 1979), 89. Copyright © 1939 by W. H. Auden, renewed. Reprinted by permission of Curtis Brown, Ltd.

33. Lucy Burns, "White Rose: The Germans Who Tried to Topple Hitler," BBC World Service, February 21, 2013, http://www.bbc.com/news/magazine-21521060.

34. Center for White Rose Studies, "Their Story," http://www.white-rose-studies.org/Their_Story.html.

35. Vaclav Havel, *Disturbing the Peace: A Conversation with Karel Hvizdala,* trans. Paul Wilson (New York: Vintage, 1990), 110.

36. Garrow, *Bearing the Cross,* 469.

37. John Milton, *Paradise Lost,* ed. David Scott Kastan (Indianapolis, IN: Hackett Publishing Co., 2005), 81.

38. Harold C. Goddard, *The Meaning of Shakespeare,* vol. 2 (Chicago: University of Chicago Press, 1960), 10.

39. Percy Bysshe Shelley, "A Defence of Poetry," reprinted in *English Essays: Sidney to Macaulay,* vol. 27, The Harvard Classics (New York: P. F. Collier & Son, 1909–1914).

40. Goddard, *The Meaning of Shakespeare,* 11.

41. John G. Neihardt, *Black Elk Speaks* (Albany: State University of New York Press, 2008), 37.

42. Ralph Ellison, "The Blues," *New York Review of Books,* February 6, 1964.

43. William Faulkner, *The Sound and the Fury* (New York: Vintage, 1990), 343.

44. James H. Cone, *The Cross and the Lynching Tree* (Maryknoll, NY: Orbis Books, 2011), 2.

45. Primo Levi, *Survival in Auschwitz* (New York: Simon & Schuster, 1996), 113.

46. Ibid., 114–115.

47. Used with permission. Calderwood Ltd., dba Haka Taka Music.

48. William Shakespeare, *King Lear* (New York: Modern Library, 2009), act IV, scene ii, lines 50–51.

49. George Bernard Shaw, *Pygmalion and Major Barbara* (New York: Random House, 2008), 162.

50. James Baldwin, *James Baldwin: Collected Essays* (New York: Library of America, 1998), 669.

51. Ibid., 460.

52. Goddard, *The Meaning of Shakespeare*, vii.

53. Neihardt, *Black Elk Speaks*, 106–107.

54. "You don't fight fascism because you're going to win. You fight fascism because it is fascist"; Jean-Paul Sartre, *The Age of Reason* (New York: Vintage, 1992).

55. This is a point made to me repeatedly by Father Daniel Berrigan, who baptized my youngest daughter.

BIBLIOGRAPHY

Abu-Jamal, Mumia. *All Things Censored.* New York: Seven Stories Press, 2001.

———. *Faith of Our Fathers: An Examination of the Spiritual Life of African and African-American People.* Trenton, NJ: Africa World Press, 2004.

Alexander, Michelle. *The New Jim Crow: Mass Incarceration in the Age of Colorblindness.* New York: New Press, 2010.

Allen, R. E., trans. *The Dialogues of Plato, vol. 1.* New Haven, CT: Yale University Press, 1984.

Anderson, Sean K., and Steven Sloan. *Historical Dictionary of Terrorism.* Lanham, MD: Scarecrow Press, 2009.

Arendt, Hannah. *The Origins of Totalitarianism.* New York: Houghton Mifflin, 1994.

———. *Eichmann in Jerusalem: A Report on the Banality of Evil.* New York: Penguin Books, 2006.

Aristotle. *Politics of Aristotle,* ed. Justin D. Kaplan. New York: Simon & Schuster, 1983.

Assange, Julian, with Jacob Appelbaum, Andy Müller-Maguhn, and Jérémie Zimmermann. *Cypherpunks: Freedom and the Future of the Internet.* New York: OR Books, 2012.

Atwood, Margaret. *Oryx and Crake.* New York: Anchor Books, 2003.

Auden, W. H. *Selected Poems.* Boston: Faber and Faber, 1979.

Avrich, Paul. *Anarchist Portraits.* Princeton, NJ: Princeton University Press, 1988.

Baldwin, James. *James Baldwin: Collected Essays.* New York: Library of America, 1998.

Begler, Elsie. *Thomas Paine: Common Sense for the Modern Era.* San Diego: San Diego State University Press, 2007.

Benjamin, Walter. *Walter Benjamin: Selected Writings, vol. 1, 1913–1926,* ed. Marcus Bullock and Michael W. Jennings, reprint ed., Cambridge, MA: Belknap Press of Harvard University Press, 2004.

———. *Walter Benjamin: Selected Writings, vol. 2, 1927–1934*, ed. Michael W. Jennings, Howard Eiland, and Gary Smith, reprint ed., Cambridge, MA: Belknap Press of Harvard University Press, 2005.

Berman, Morris. *Why America Failed: The Roots of Imperial Decline.* New York: John Wiley & Sons, 2011.

Boorstin, Daniel J. *The Image: A Guide to Pseudo-Events in America.* New York: Vintage, 1987.

Bosworth, Mary, ed. *Encyclopedia of Prisons and Correctional Facilities.* London: Sage Publications, 2004.

Brinton, Crane. *The Anatomy of Revolution.* New York: Vintage, 1965.

Bulgakov, Mikhail. *The Master and Margarita.* New York: Vintage, 1985.

Camus, Albert. *The Rebel.* New York: Vintage, 1984.

Carlyle, Thomas. *The French Revolution: A History, vol. 3* [1837]. Reprint, London, 1888.

Carroll, Lewis. *Lewis Carroll: Complete Illustrated Works*, ed. Edward Guiliano. Avenel, NJ: Crown, 1982.

Carter, William C. *Conversations with Shelby Foote.* Jackson: University Press of Mississippi, 1989.

Céline, Louis-Ferdinand. *Castle to Castle.* New York: Dell Publishing, 1968.

Chomsky, Noam. *The Essential Chomsky*, ed. Anthony Arnove. New York: New Press, 2008.

Cohn, Norman. *The Pursuit of the Millennium: Revolutionary Messianism in Medieval and Reformation Europe and Its Bearing on Modern Totalitarian Movements.* New York: Harper & Row, 1961.

Cone, James H. *The Cross and the Lynching Tree.* Maryknoll, NY: Orbis Books, 2011.

Conway, Moncure Daniel. *The Life of Thomas Paine [1892], vol. 2.* New York: G. P. Putnam's, 1908.

Davidson, Eddy W., and Daniel Foxx. *Nathan Bedford Forrest: In Search of an Enigma.* Gretna, LA: Pelican Publishing Co., 2007.

Davies, James C., ed. *When Men Revolt and Why.* New Brunswick, NJ: Transaction Publishers, 1997.

Delbanco, Andre. *Melville: His World and Work.* New York: Vintage, 2006.

Duster, Alfreda M., ed. *Crusade for Justice: The Autobiography of Ida B. Wells.* Chicago: University of Chicago Press, 1972.

Ellul, Jacques. *Violence: Reflections from a Christian Perspective.* New York: Seabury Press, 1969.

———. *The Presence of the Kingdom.* Philadelphia: Wesminster Press, 1951.

———. *What I Believe*. Grand Rapids, MI: Zondervan, 1989.

Everitt, Anthony. *Cicero: The Life and Times of Rome's Greatest Politician*. New York: Random House, 2001.

Faulkner, William, *The Sound and the Fury*. New York: Vintage, 1990.

Fitzgerald, F. Scott. *The Short Stories of F. Scott Fitzgerald*. New York: Scribner, 1989.

———. *The Great Gatsby*. Ware, Hertfordshire, UK: Wordsworth Editions, 1993.

Foner, Eric. *Tom Paine and Revolutionary America*. New York: Oxford University Press, 1976.

Foote, Shelby. *The Civil War: A Narrative, vol. 3, Red River to Appomattox*. New York: Vintage Books, 1986.

Garrow, David J. *Bearing the Cross: Martin Luther King Jr. and the Southern Christian Leadership Conference*. New York: Harper Perennial Modern Classics, 2004.

Goddard, Harold C. *The Meaning of Shakespeare, 2 vols*. Chicago: University of Chicago Press, 1951.

Goldman, Emma. "Minorities Versus Majorities." In *Anarchism and Other Essays*. New York: Dover Publications, 1969.

Gottschalk, Marie. *Caught: The Prison State and the Lockdown of American Politics*. Princeton, NJ: Princeton University Press, 2015.

Gramsci, Antonio. *Prison Notebooks, vol. 2*. New York: Columbia University Press, 1996.

Grandin, Greg. *The Empire of Necessity: Slavery, Freedom, and Deception in the New World*. New York: Henry Holt/Metropolitan Books, 2014.

Guicciardini, Francesco. *Maxims and Reflections of a Renaissance Statesman (Ricordi)* [1528], trans. Mario Domandi. Philadelphia: University of Pennsylvania Press, 1965.

Hamilton, Clive. *Requiem for a Species: Why We Resist the Truth About Climate Change*. London: Earthscan, 2010.

Havel, Vaclav. *Disturbing the Peace: A Conversation with Karel Hvizdala*, trans. Paul Wilson. New York: Vintage, 1990.

———. "The Power of the Powerless." In *The Power of the Powerless: Citizens Against the State in Central-Eastern Europe*, ed. John Keane. Abingdon, Oxon, UK: Routledge, 2010.

Herzen, Alexander. *From the Other Shore: The Russian People and Socialism*. Westport, CT: Hyperion Press, 1981.

Heschel, Abraham J. *The Prophets*. New York: Harper Perennial Modern Classics, 2001.

Hofstadter, Richard, and Michael Wallace. *American Violence: A Documentary History.* New York: Alfred A. Knopf, 1970.

Horne, Gerald. *The Counter-Revolution of 1776.* New York: New York University Press, 2014.

James, C.L.R. *Mariners, Renegades, and Castaways: The Story of Herman Melville and the World We Live In.* Hanover, NH: University Press of New England, 2001.

Kasrils, Ronnie. *Armed and Dangerous: My Undercover Struggle Against Apartheid.* Oxford: Heinemann Educational Publishers, 1993.

Kafka, Franz. *Franz Kafka: The Complete Short Stories.* New York: Schocken Books, 1995.

Keane, John. *Tom Paine: A Political Life.* New York: Grove Press, 1995.

Koehler, John O. *Stasi: The Untold Story of the East German Secret Police.* Boulder, CO: Westview Press, 1999.

Krall, Hanna. *Shielding the Flame: An Intimate Conversation with Dr. Marek Edelman, the Last Surviving Leader of the Warsaw Ghetto Uprising.* New York: Henry Holt, 1986.

Kropotkin, Peter. *Anarchism: A Collection of Revolutionary Writings.* Mineola, NY: Courier/Dover Publications, 2012.

Lawrence, D. H. *Studies in Classic American Literature, vol. 2.* New York: Penguin, 1990.

Lenin, Vladimir. *"Left-Wing" Communism: An Infantile Disorder.* Chippendale, Australia: Resistance Books, 1999.

Levi, Primo. *Survival in Auschwitz.* New York: Simon & Schuster, 1996.

Lewis, Sinclair. *It Can't Happen Here.* New York: New American Library, 2005.

Loewen, James W. *Lies Across America: What Our Historic Sites Get Wrong.* New York: Simon & Schuster, 2007.

Lynd, Staughton. *Lucasville: The Untold Story of a Prison Uprising.* Oakland, CA: PM Press, 2004.

Mandela, Nelson. *Conversations with Myself.* Toronto: Random House, 2011.

Marcuse, Herbert. "Repressive Tolerance." In *A Critique of Pure Tolerance* by Robert Paul Wolff, Barrington Moore Jr., and Herbert Marcuse, 95–137. Boston: Beacon Press, 1965.

Martelle, Scott. *Blood Passion: The Ludlow Massacre and Class War in the American West.* New Brunswick, NJ: Rutgers University Press, 2008.

Marx, Karl. *The Manifesto of the Communist Party* [1848]. Authorized English translation, edited and annotated by Friedrich Engels. New York: International Publishers, 1968.

———. "The German Ideology." In *Karl Marx: A Reader,* ed. John Elster. Cambridge: Cambridge University Press, 1986.

———. *The Civil War in France* [1871]. In *The First International and After: Political Writings, vol. 3,* 226–228. New York: Verso Books, 2010.

———. *The Revolutions of 1848: Political Writings, vol. 1,* ed. David Frenbach. London: Verso, 2010.

McCoy, Alfred. *A Question of Torture: CIA Interrogation, from the Cold War to the War on Terror.* New York: Macmillan, 2007.

Melville, Herman. *Moby-Dick.* New York: W. W. Norton & Co., 1976.

Milton, John. *Paradise Lost,* ed. David Scott Kastan. Indianapolis, IN: Hackett Publishing Co., 2005.

Montaigne, Michel de. *The Complete Essays of Michel de Montaigne.* New York: Digireads, 2004.

Neihardt, John G. *Black Elk Speaks.* Albany: State University of New York Press, 2008.

Niebuhr, Reinhold. *Beyond Tragedy: Essays on the Christian Interpretation of History.* New York: Scribner's, 1965.

———. *Moral Man and Immoral Society: A Study in Ethics and Politics.* Louisville, KY: Westminster John Knox Press, 2001.

Nikiforuk, Andrew. *Saboteurs: Wiebo Ludwig's War Against Big Oil.* Toronto: Macfarlane, Walter & Ross, 2002.

Offer, Avner. *The Challenge of Affluence: Self-control and Well-being in the United States and Britain Since 1950.* Oxford: Oxford University Press, 2006.

Ong, Walter J. *Rhetoric, Romance, and Technology.* Ithaca, NY: Cornell University Press, 1971.

Orwell, George. *1984.* New York: New American Library, 1983.

Paine, Thomas. *Rights of Man and Common Sense.* New York: Everyman's Library, 1994.

———. *The Age of Reason.* Toronto: Carol Publishing Group/Citadel Press, 1998.

Parker, Peter, and Joyce Mokhesi-Parker. *In the Shadow of Sharpeville: Apartheid and Criminal Justice.* New York: New York University Press, 1998.

Philbrick, Nathaniel. *In the Heart of the Sea: The Tragedy of the Whaleship Essex.* New York: Penguin Books, 2000.

———. *Why Read Moby-Dick?* New York: Penguin Books, 2013.

Piketty, Thomas. *Capital in the Twenty-First Century.* Cambridge, MA: Belknap Press of Harvard University Press, 2014.

Pocock, J.G.A. *Politics, Language, and Time*. New York: Atheneum, 1971.

Redman, Charles L. *Human Impact on Ancient Environments*. Tucson: University of Arizona Press, 1999.

Rorty, Richard. *Achieving Our Country: Leftist Thought in Twentieth-Century America*. Cambridge, MA: Harvard University Press, 1998.

Roth, Joseph. *Hotel Savoy*. New York: Overlook Press, 1986.

Sartre, Jean-Paul. *The Age of Reason*. New York: Vintage, 1992.

Saul, John Raulston. *Voltaire's Bastards: The Dictatorship of Reason in the West*. New York: Vintage Books, 1992.

Savage, Lon. *Thunder in the Mountains: The West Virginia Mine War 1920–21*. Pittsburgh: University of Pittsburgh Press, 1990.

Schelling, Thomas C. "Some Questions on Civilian Defense." In *Civilian Resistance as a National Defence: Nonviolent Action Against Aggression*, ed. Adam Roberts, 351–352. Harrisburg, PA: Stackpole, 1967.

Schlögel, Karl. *Moscow, 1937*. Malden, MA: Polity Press, 2013.

Sennett, Richard. *The Fall of Public Man*. New York: W. W. Norton & Co., 1974.

Shakespeare, William. *The Tempest*. In *The Riverside Shakespeare*. New York: Houghton Mifflin, 1997.

———. *King Lear*. New York: Modern Library, 2009.

Shaw, George Bernard. *Pygmalion and Major Barbara*. New York: Random House, 2008.

Shelley, Percy Bysshe. "A Defence of Poetry." In *English Essays: Sidney to Macaulay*, vol. 27, The Harvard Classics. New York: P. F. Collier & Son, 1909–1914.

Shogan, Robert. *The Battle of Blair Mountain: The Story of America's Largest Labor Uprising*. New York: Basic Books, 2006.

Sluka, Jeffrey A., ed. *Death Squad: The Anthropology of State Terror*. Philadelphia: University of Pennsylvania Press, 1999.

Smith, Jennifer B. *An International History of the Black Panther Party*. New York: Routledge, 1999.

Slotkin, Richard. *Regeneration Through Violence: The Mythology of the American Frontier, 1600–1860*. Norman: University of Oklahoma Press, 1973.

Stephan, Maria J., and Erica Chenoweth. "Why Civil Resistance Works: The Strategic Logic of Nonviolent Conflict." *International Security* 33, no. 1 (Summer 2008): 7–44.

Stokes, Melvyn. *D. W. Griffith's* The Birth of a Nation: *A History of the Most Controversial Motion Picture of All Time*. Oxford: Oxford University Press, 2008.

Tainter, Joseph A. *The Collapse of Complex Societies.* Cambridge: Cambridge University Press, 1988.

Thoreau, Henry David. *Thoreau: Political Writings,* ed. Nancy L. Rosenblum. Cambridge: Cambridge University Press, 1996.

———. *Walden: A Fully Annotated Edition.* New Haven, CT: Yale University Press, 2004.

Tolstoy, Lyof N. *The Novels and Other Works of Lyof N. Tolstoy,* vol. 20. New York: Charles Scribner's Sons, 1902.

Trotsky, Leon. *History of the Russian Revolution.* Chicago: Haymarket Books, 2008.

Ulam, Adam B. *Ideologies and Illusions: Revolutionary Thought from Herzen to Solzhenitsyn.* Cambridge, MA: Harvard University Press, 1976.

———. *The Bolsheviks: The Intellectual and Political History of the Triumph of Communism in Russia.* Cambridge, MA: Harvard University Press, 1998.

Van Doren, Carl. *The American Novel.* New York: Macmillan, 1921.

Weber, Max. *The Vocation Lectures.* Indianapolis: Hackett, 2004.

West, Cornel. *The Cornel West Reader.* New York: Basic Civitas Books, 1999.

Wills, Brian Steel. *A Battle from the Start: The Life of Nathan Bedford Forrest.* New York: HarperCollins, 1992.

Wolin, Sheldon S. *Democracy Incorporated: Managed Democracy and the Specter of Inverted Totalitarianism.* Princeton, NJ: Princeton University Press, 2010.

Wright, Richard. *Black Boy.* New York: HarperCollins, 2005.

Wright, Richard. Journals of Richard Wright, 1945–1947. Richard Wright Papers, Beinecke Rare Book and Manuscript Library, Yale University.

Wright, Ronald. *A Short History of Progress.* New York: Carroll & Graf, 2005.

Zinn, Howard. *The Politics of History.* Boston: Beacon Press, 1970.

Zweig, Stefan. *Chess Story.* New York: New York Review Book Classics, 2006.

Index

Chris Hedges is a Pulitzer Prize–winning journalist. He spent
nearly two decades as a correspondent in Central America,
the Middle East, Africa, and the Balkans, with fifteen years at
the *New York Times*. He is the author of numerous bestselling
books, including *Empire of Illusion; Death of the Liberal Class;
War is a Force That Gives Us Meaning;* and *Days of Destruction,
Days of Revolt* which he co-wrote with Joe Sacco. He writes a
weekly column for the online magazine Truthdig. He lives in
Princeton, New Jersey.

The Nation Institute
The Nation.

NATION BOOKS

Founded in 2000, **Nation Books** has become a leading voice in American independent publishing. The inspiration for the imprint came from the *Nation* magazine, the oldest independent and continuously published weekly magazine of politics and culture in the United States.

The imprint's mission is to produce authoritative books that break new ground and shed light on current social and political issues. We publish established authors who are leaders in their area of expertise, and endeavor to cultivate a new generation of emerging and talented writers. With each of our books we aim to positively affect cultural and political discourse.

Nation Books is a project of The Nation Institute, a nonprofit media center established to extend the reach of democratic ideals and strengthen the independent press. The Nation Institute is home to a dynamic range of programs: our award-winning Investigative Fund, which supports ground-breaking investigative journalism; the widely read and syndicated website TomDispatch; our internship program in conjunction with the *Nation* magazine; and Journalism Fellowships that fund up to 20 high-profile reporters every year.

For more information on Nation Books, the *Nation* magazine, and The Nation Institute, please visit:

www.nationbooks.org
www.nationinstitute.org
www.thenation.com
www.facebook.com/nationbooks.ny
Twitter: @nationbooks

DATE			